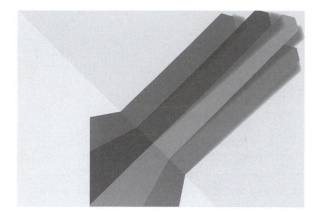

A Stata® Companion to Political Analysis

Third Edition

CQ Press, an imprint of SAGE, is the leading publisher of books, periodicals, and electronic products on American government and international affairs. CQ Press consistently ranks among the top commercial publishers in terms of quality, as evidenced by the numerous awards its products have won over the years. CQ Press owes its existence to Nelson Poynter, former publisher of the *St. Petersburg Times,* and his wife Henrietta, with whom he founded Congressional Quarterly in 1945. Poynter established CQ with the mission of promoting democracy through education and in 1975 founded the Modern Media Institute, renamed The Poynter Institute for Media Studies after his death. The Poynter Institute (www.poynter.org) is a nonprofit organization dedicated to training journalists and media leaders.

In 2008, CQ Press was acquired by SAGE, a leading international publisher of journals, books, and electronic media for academic, educational, and professional markets. Since 1965, SAGE has helped inform and educate a global community of scholars, practitioners, researchers, and students spanning a wide range of subject areas, including business, humanities, social sciences, and science, technology, and medicine. A privately owned corporation, SAGE has offices in Los Angeles, London, New Delhi, and Singapore, in addition to the Washington DC office of CQ Press.

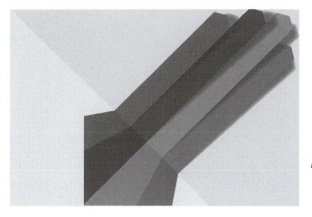

A Stata® Companion
to Political Analysis

Third Edition

Philip H. Pollock III
University of Central Florida

Los Angeles | London | New Delhi
Singapore | Washington DC | Boston

Los Angeles | London | New Delhi
Singapore | Washington DC | Boston

For information:

CQ Press

An Imprint of SAGE Publications, Inc.

2455 Teller Road

Thousand Oaks, California 91320

E-mail: order@sagepub.com

SAGE Publications Ltd.

1 Oliver's Yard

55 City Road

London, EC1Y 1SP

United Kingdom

SAGE Publications India Pvt. Ltd.

B 1/I 1 Mohan Cooperative Industrial Area

Mathura Road, New Delhi 110 044

India

SAGE Publications Asia-Pacific Pte. Ltd.

3 Church Street

#10-04 Samsung Hub

Singapore 049483

Printed in the United States of America

Cataloging-in-publication data is available for this title from the Library of Congress.

ISBN: 978-1-4522-4042-8

This book is printed on acid-free paper.

Acquisitions Editor: Sarah Calabi

Editorial Assistant: Raquel Christie

Associate Digital Content Editor: Allison Hughes

Production Editor: Kelly DeRosa

Copy Editor: Cate Huisman

Typesetter: C&M Digitals (P) Ltd.

Proofreader: Theresa Kay

Cover Designer: Anupama Krishnan

Marketing Manager: Amy Whitaker

16 17 18 10 9 8 7 6 5 4 3 2

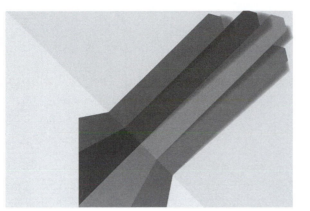

Contents

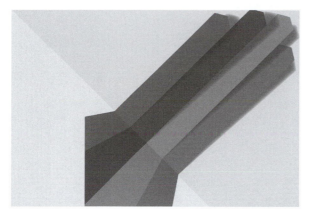

Figures

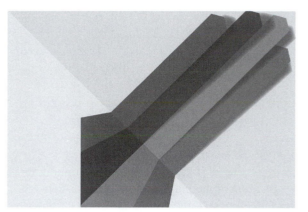

Preface

If this edition had a subtitle, it would be "Back to Stata® Basics." To be sure, like the book that preceded it, this edition of *A Stata® Companion to Political Analysis* provides a guided tour of Stata's two most powerful attractions, command-line data analysis and graphics. But, whereas the previous edition took an eclectic approach to these features—it covered the command line, drop-down dialogs, and the new (at the time) Graph Editor—this edition takes a unified approach: Do it all in Do-files. Stata's syntactical conventions are straightforward and consistent. Plus, students' keyboarding skills range from competent to expert—and, in more than a few instances, to downright scary. For every Stata command and skill set, students are typing, running, and saving Do-files.

A continued hope for this edition is to guide students in creating attractive, presentation-quality graphs. Nicely optioned Stata graphics require a fair amount of TLC, but with an appropriate set of font, text, and color options recorded in a Do-file, students can recycle those options, or tailor them to meet immediate graphics goals. Additionally, this book describes several graphic forms not covered in earlier editions: box plots and strip charts (Chapter 4), bubble plots (Chapter 8), and linear predication overlays (Chapter 9).

Apart from the Do-file focus and the expanded treatment of graphs, what else is new? This book makes a clearer distinction between the analysis of weighted and unweighted data. For example, a discussion of the mean command and the lincom command (Chapter 6) replaces the previous edition's coverage of the ttest command, which does not permit probability weights. Also in Chapter 6, I drop the discussion of one-tailed tests of statistical significance. The 95 percent confidence interval is almost universally applied in political research—for example, all of Stata's regression commands return two-tailed P-values—so this book follows convention. Chapter 7 covers two commands from Stata's survey suite, svyset and svy: tabulate, again to accommodate probability weights. Finally, Chapter 10 describes margins and marginsplot, two postestimation commands introduced in recent releases of Stata. (According to Stata help, the adjust command "has been superseded by margins." Count me among those who will miss it.)

CHAPTER ORGANIZATION AND DATASETS

Improvements and fine-tuning aside, the structure and organization of *A Stata® Companion to Political Analysis* follows the template of previous editions. This volume guides students in constructing meaningful descriptions of variables and performing substantive analysis of political relationships. The chapters cover all major topics in data analysis: descriptive statistics (Chapter 2), transforming variables (Chapter 3), cross-tabulations and mean comparisons (Chapter 4), controlled comparisons (Chapter 5), statistical inference (Chapter 6), chi-square and measures of association (Chapter 7), correlation and linear regression (Chapter 8), dummy variables and interactions effects (Chapter 9), and logistic regression (Chapter 10). A final chapter (Chapter 11) describes several manageable research projects, illustrates how to import data into Stata, and lays out a framework for a well-organized research paper.

All of the examples and exercises in this book use research-quality data. Students analyze variables from two survey datasets, the 2012 American National Election Study (the dataset named "nes2012" in this book), and the 2012 General Social Survey ("gss2012"). Additionally, two aggregate-level datasets are used: one containing information on the fifty states ("states"), and one containing data on countries of the world ("world"). I wrote each chapter as a tutorial, taking students through a series of guided examples, which they then use to perform the analysis. The figures and annotated command-line screen shots—most of which flow directly with the text—allow students to check their work along the way. This book also contains end-of-chapter exercises, all of which are based on the datasets, and all of which give students opportunities to apply their new skills, discover the meaning of their findings, and learn to interpret them. After completing this book, students not only are confident Stata users, they will have learned a fair amount about substantive political science, too. Adopters can obtain a complete set of the Do-files that I used to construct the guided examples and the exercises. Instructors may find these files useful for re-creating the graphics, performing the exercises, or for troubleshooting students' difficulties with the examples or exercises.

DIFFERENT RELEASES OF STATA

I wrote this book using Stata 13. However, I saved the accompanying datasets in Stata 12 format. Because Stata 11 can also read Stata 12 datasets—and because later releases can always read datasets from earlier releases—the book is compatible with Stata 11 and later. (The only exception of which I am aware: Chapter 10's marginsplot command, introduced in release 12.) Suppose you inadvertently save one of the data files in Stata 13 format (on a lab computer, for example), and you later realize that your laptop's installation of Stata 11 or 12 is unable to read it. Download and install Sergiy Radyakin's command, use13. In the command window, type: "ssc install use13." The use13 command will import the Stata 13 dataset. In fact, use13 also permits Stata 10 users to read Stata 13 data files.[1]

ACCOMPANYING CORE TEXT

Instructors will find that this book makes an effective supplement to any of a variety of methods textbooks. However, it is a particularly suitable companion to my own core text, *The Essentials of Political Analysis*. The textbook's substantive chapters cover basic and intermediate methodological issues and ideas: measurement, explanations and hypotheses, univariate statistics and bivariate analysis, controlled relationships, sampling and inference, statistical significance, correlation and linear regression, and logistic regression. Each chapter also includes end-of-chapter exercises. Students can read the textbook chapters, do the exercises, and then work through the guided examples and exercises in *A Stata® Companion to Political Analysis*. The idea is to get students to experience political research firsthand, early in the academic term. An instructor's solutions manual, free to adopters, provides solutions for all the textbook and workbook exercises.

ACKNOWLEDGMENTS

I gratefully acknowledge the encouragement I have received from my colleagues at the University of Central Florida over the years, as well as the suggestions of the many reviewers of this project:

Ryan Black, *Michigan State University*
Parina Patel, *Georgetown University*
Scott Desposato, *UC-San Diego*
Philip Klinkner, *Hamilton College*
Dino Christenson, *Boston University*
Alana Querze, *West Virginia University*
Matthew Wright, *American University*
Saul Sandoval Perea, *Colby College*

Special thanks to John Transue of the University of Illinois, Springfield for advising me in the proper use of analytic weights and probability weights. I am grateful to everyone at CQ Press/SAGE, the best publisher any author could hope for. I thank Sarah Calabi, Cate Huisman, Allison Hughes, and Kelly DeRosa. I also thank Catherine Forrest and Theresa Kay for getting this book to the finish line. Finally, a special thanks to Charisse Kiino, without whom this project would never have left the starting line.

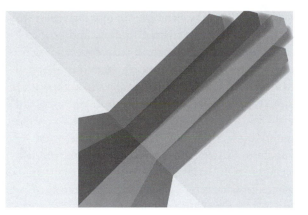

Introduction: Getting Started

For this introduction you will need

- Access to a Microsoft Windows-based computer
- A USB flash drive or other portable medium

As you have learned about political research and explored techniques of political analysis, you have studied many examples of other people's work. You may have read textbook chapters that present frequency distributions, or you may have pondered research articles that use cross-tabulation, correlation, or regression analysis to investigate interesting relationships between variables. As valuable as these learning experiences are, they can be greatly enhanced by performing political analysis firsthand—handling and modifying social science datasets, learning to use data analysis computer software, obtaining your own descriptive statistics for variables, setting up the appropriate analysis for interesting relationships, and running the analysis and interpreting your results.

This book is designed to guide you as you learn these valuable practical skills. By reading this volume, you will gain a working knowledge of Stata, powerful data analysis and graphics software widely used in academic institutions. Stata will perform a great variety of statistical analysis procedures, from basic descriptive statistics to multivariate modeling, and it will construct a wide array of graphic images, from simple bar charts and histograms to sophisticated graphic overlays. In this book, you will learn to use Stata's command language for virtually all the data analyses that you perform and the graphs you create. Although this book assumes that you have practical knowledge of the Windows operating system and that you know how to perform elemental file-handling tasks, it also assumes that you have never heard of Stata and that you have never used a computer to analyze data of any kind. By the time you complete the guided examples and the exercises in this book, you will be well on your way to becoming a Stata aficionado. The skills you learn will be durable, and they will serve you well as you continue your educational career or enter the business world.

This book's chapters are written in tutorial fashion. Each chapter contains several guided examples, and each includes exercises at the end. You will read each chapter while sitting in front of a computer, doing the analysis described in the guided examples, analyzing the datasets that accompany this text. Each data analysis procedure is described in step-by-step fashion, and the book has many figures that show you what your computer screen should look like as you perform the procedures. Thus, the guided examples allow you to develop your skills and to become comfortable with Stata. The end-of-chapter exercises allow you to apply your new skills to different substantive problems.

In Chapter 1 you will learn how to navigate in Stata—how to obtain information about a dataset, how to write Stata syntax, how to keep track of your work by using a log file, how to print output, and how to use Stata's extensive help system. Chapter 2 demonstrates how to obtain and interpret frequency distributions and how to create bar charts and histograms. Chapter 3 covers data transformations in Stata— recoding variables and generating new variables that you will want to add to your data files. In Chapter 4 you will explore and apply cross-tabulation analysis and mean comparison analysis—again learning to add graphic support to the relationships you analyze. In Chapter 5 you will learn to make controlled comparisons, producing and interpreting the tabular and graphic output for the relationship between a dependent variable and an independent variable, controlling for a third variable. In Chapter 6 you will use Stata to obtain the information you need in order to establish the boundaries of random sampling error and to assess the statistical significance of an empirical relationship. In Chapter 7 you will learn how tests of significance and measures of association add statistical support to your cross-tabulation analyses. In Chapter 8 you will learn correlation and linear regression, and Chapter 9 shows how to use linear regression to model and estimate complex relationships. Chapter 10 describes how to perform logistic regression, a technique that has gained widespread use in political research. Finally, in Chapter 11 we will consider some of the challenges you might face in finding your own data, and we will offer some suggestions on how best to organize and present your original research.

DATASETS

Before proceeding, open a browser and follow this link:

http://college.cqpress.com/sites/pollock-data/

Download the datasets to a USB drive or other portable medium. (Or download the datasets to the default location, and then copy them to a USB drive.) There are four datasets.

1. **gss2012.** This dataset has selected variables from the 2012 General Social Survey, a random sample of 1,974 adults aged 18 years or older, conducted by the National Opinion Research Center and made available through the Inter-university Consortium for Political and Social Research (ICPSR) at the University of Michigan.[2] Some of the scales in gss2012 were constructed by the author. All other variables retain their original names. To find information on coding and question wording, visit the following link at the University of California–Berkeley's Social Data Archive and search the alphabetical variable list: http://sda.berkeley.edu/D3/GSS12/Doc/gs12.htm.

2. **nes2012.** This dataset includes selected variables from the 2012 American National Election Study, a random sample of 5,916 citizens of voting age, conducted by the University of Michigan's Institute for Social Research (ISR) and made available through ICPSR.[3] With the exception of scales constructed by the author, all variables in nes2012 retain the variable names assigned to them by ISR. For specific coding and question wording, go to the following link and search on variable name: http://www.electionstudies .org/studypages/anes_timeseries_2012/anes_timeseries_2012_userguidecodebook.pdf.

3. **states.** This dataset includes variables on each of the fifty states. These variables were compiled by the author from various sources, including the following:

   Americans United for Life (AUL), http://aul.org/featured-images/AUL-1301_DL13%20Book_FINAL.pdf

   Brady Campaign, http://www.bradycampaign.org

   Bureau of Alcohol, Tobacco, Firearms, and Explosives, https://www.atf.gov

   Gallup, http://www.gallup.com (Gallup-Healthways Well-Being Index; Gallup State of States)

   Guttmacher Institute, http://www.guttmacher.org

   Marijuana Policy Project, http://www.mpp.org

   National Conference of State Legislatures, http://www.ncsl.org/legislatures-elections/elections/statevote-charts.aspx; http://www.ncsl.org/legislatures-elections/wln/women-in-state-legislatures-2011.aspx

   National Journal, http://www.nationaljournal.com/2011voteratings

Survey USA, surveyusa.com

US Census Bureau, census.gov

Williams Institute, http://williamsinstitute.law.ucla.edu

4. **world.** This dataset includes variables on 191 countries. Many of these variables are based on data compiled by Pippa Norris, John F. Kennedy School of Government, Harvard University, and made available to the scholarly community through her Internet site.[4] Other variables were compiled by the author from various sources, including the following:

Association of Religious Data Archives (ARDA), http://www.thearda.com

Center for Systemic Peace, http://www.systemicpeace.org/polity/polity4.htm

CIA World Factbook, https://www.cia.gov/library/publications/the-world-factbook

Freedom House, http://www.freedomhouse.org

Heritage Foundation, http://www.heritage.org/index

Inter-Parliamentary Union, http://www.ipu.org

United Nations, http://data.un.org

World Bank, http://data.worldbank.org

When you begin each chapter's guided examples, or when you do the exercises, you will want to insert the personal media containing the datasets into the appropriate computer drive. Stata will read the data from the drive. If you make any changes to a dataset, you can save the newly modified dataset directly to your drive. If you have modified a dataset during a data analysis session, it is important that you copy the dataset to your personal drive and take the datasets with you.

NOTES

1. For more information, see this Statalist post: http://www.stata.com/statalist/archive/2013–07/msg00633.html. See also Radyakin's information page: http://radyakin.org/transfer/use13/use13.htm. Chapter 10's margins command was introduced in Stata 11, so Stata 10 users will not be able to run the postestimation commands, margins and marginsplot, covered in Chapter 10.

2. Gss2012 was created from the General Social Survey 1972–2012 Cumulative Data File. Tom W. Smith, Michael Hout, and Peter V. Marsden, General Social Survey, 1972–2012 Cumulative File [Data file], ICPSR34802-v1. (Storrs, Conn: Roper Center for Public Opinion Research, University of Connecticut /Ann Arbor, Mich: Inter-university Consortium for Political and Social Research [distributors], 2013-09-11).

3. The American National Election Studies (ANES; http://www.electionstudies.org). The ANES 2012 time series study [Dataset] (Stanford, Cal.: Stanford University /Ann Arbor, Mich., University of Michigan [producers]). These materials are based on work supported by the National Science Foundation under grants SES-0937727 and SES-0937715, Stanford University and the University of Michigan. Any opinions, findings, and conclusions or recommendations expressed in these materials are those of the author(s) and do not necessarily reflect the views of the funding organizations.

4. http://www.pippanorris.com

SAGE | 50 YEARS

SAGE was founded in 1965 by Sara Miller McCune to support the dissemination of usable knowledge by publishing innovative and high-quality research and teaching content. Today, we publish more than 750 journals, including those of more than 300 learned societies, more than 800 new books per year, and a growing range of library products including archives, data, case studies, reports, conference highlights, and video. SAGE remains majority-owned by our founder, and after Sara's lifetime will become owned by a charitable trust that secures our continued independence.

Los Angeles | London | Washington DC | New Delhi | Singapore | Boston

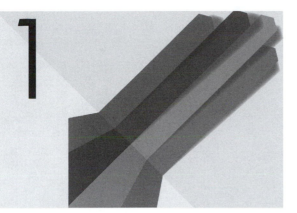

1

Introduction to Stata

In this chapter you will learn these Stata basics:

- How to obtain information about a dataset
- How to obtain information about variables
- How to write and save a Do-file (a file that contains Stata syntax)
- How to create a log file (a file that saves your commands and results)
- How to print output and how to copy/paste output into Word
- How to use Stata's help system

Let's open one of the datasets, gss2012, and see what the Stata interface looks like. Start Stata as you would start any program. Once Stata loads, click the Open File icon, locate gss2012 on your computer, and open the dataset. Consider Stata's opening window—or windows, to be more precise (Figure 1-1). There are four windows: Command, Results, Review, and Variables. When running Stata interactively on the fly, the user types a command in the Command window, presses the Enter key, and views the output in the Results window. The Review window keeps a record of each command that has been entered. Clicking on a previous command in the Review window returns the command to the Command window, where the command can be rerun or edited. (Pressing the Page Up key returns the most recently entered command to the Command window.) The Variables window displays the names of all the variables in the current dataset. These variables, of course, are the objects we want to analyze by typing and entering commands in the Command window.

So that you can become comfortable with Stata, we will run a few basic commands by typing and entering them from the Command window. However, it is vastly more efficient to write, run, and save commands in a separate script file—a *Do-file,* in Stata parlance. With your commands safely preserved in a Do-file, you can mark and run a series of commands. In this chapter, you will learn to open, write, run, and save a Do-file.

Figure 1-1 Stata's Opening Interface

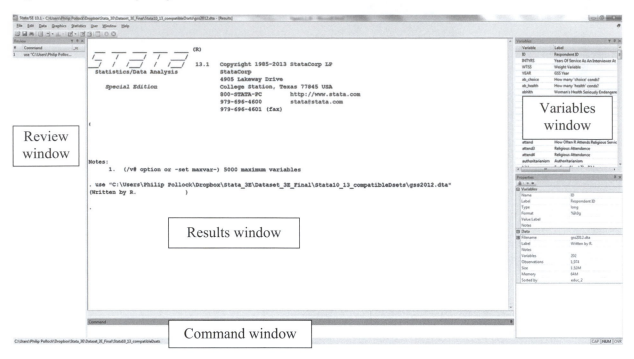

INFORMATION ABOUT A DATASET

The describe command provides descriptive information about a dataset. Click in the Command window and type "describe" (without the quotes):

<code>describe</code>

Stata tells us that gss2012 has 1,974 observations and 202 variables (Figure 1-2). It fills the screen with basic information about the dataset's variables, including each variable's name and label. The "more" message at the bottom of the screen informs us that the command produced additional results, which Stata will display when prompted to do so. To scroll through long output line by line, press the Enter key. To see the next screen, click the Go button on the menu bar (see Figure 1-2) or press any key except the Enter key. To end the command without seeing more results, click the red Break button on the menu bar.

By default, Stata will pause long output and display the "more" message. Perhaps you like this default. Perhaps you don't. To switch off the default—that is, to instruct Stata to scroll through all the output without pausing—type "set more off." To reinstate the default, type "set more on":

<code>set more off</code>

<code>set more on</code>

When running the "set more" commands, make sure to type them in the Command window, not in a Do-file. If the commands appear in a Do-file, Stata ignores them. (Do-files are discussed below.)

INFORMATION ABOUT VARIABLES

The codebook command provides information about the variables in a dataset. The general syntax of the codebook command is as follows:

codebook *varname*

For example, suppose we want Stata to display specific coding and labeling information for the variable, attend. Click in the Command window and type "codebook attend":

<code>codebook attend</code>

Figure 1-2 Results from the describe Command

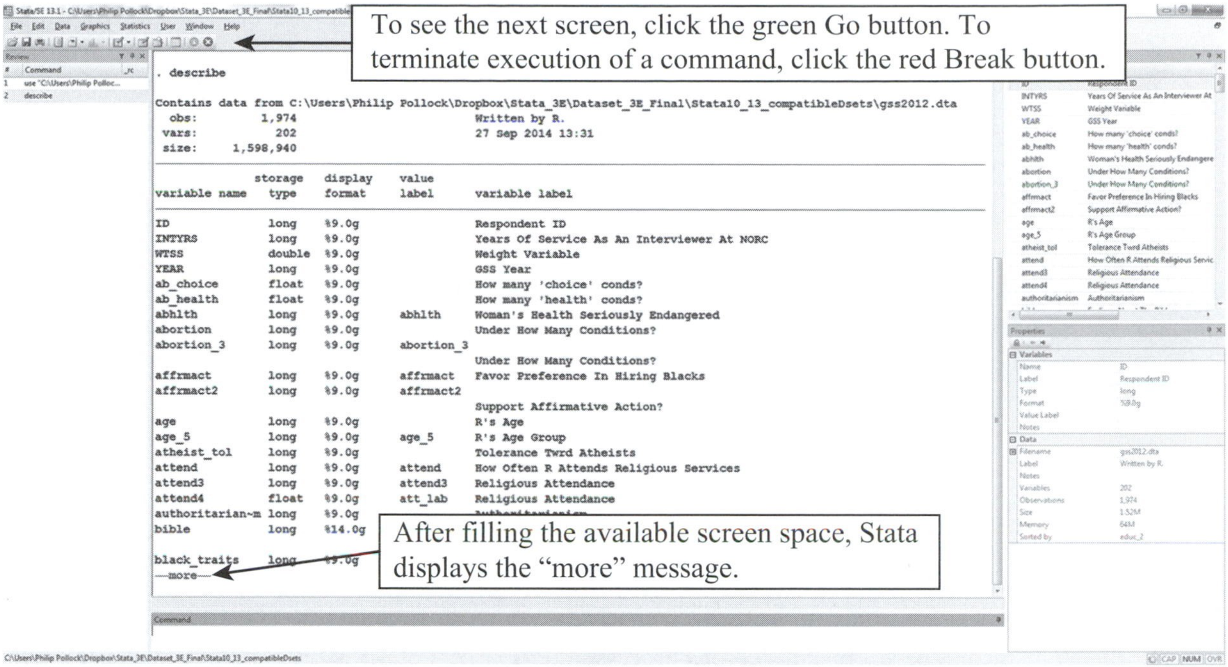

To see the next screen, click the green Go button. To terminate execution of a command, click the red Break button.

After filling the available screen space, Stata displays the "more" message.

Consider the output (Figure 1-3). Along the top line of results, Stata displays the variable's name, "attend," and its label, "How Often R Attends Religious Services." (In the idiom of survey research, "R" means "respondent.") Below, codebook offers a fair amount of detail, including (under "Freq.") the number of respondents falling into each category of the variable.

Take special note of the entries beneath "Numeric" and "Label." In storing information and running analyses, Stata relies on numbers, not words. So when Stata looks at the attend variable, it sees that some respondents are coded 1, some are coded 2, some are coded 3, and so on. When a case does not have a valid

Figure 1-3 Results from the codebook Command

```
. codebook attend
```

code on a variable, it has the missing-value designator ".", which tells Stata to exclude the case from any analyses. As long as a variable has numeric codes, Stata will analyze it.[1]

To understand a variable in human language, therefore, we need a set of value labels—descriptive words that tell us what each numeric code means. Thus, all respondents coded 1 on attend "Never" attend religious services, while those coded 9 attend "More than once a week." In Chapter 3 you will learn how to supply value labels for any new variables you create.

DO-FILES

When you are after quick information about a dataset or variables, or when you are running preliminary analyses of interesting variables, the Command line will serve you well. However, when you become immersed in a line of analysis—or (especially) when you are building command-intensive presentation-quality graphs—you will want to create Do-files. Open the Do-file editor by clicking the icon on the menu bar:

The Stata Do-file editor is a primitive word processor, reminiscent of MS Word's Notepad (Figure 1-4). The user types a command, marks the line(s), and clicks the Execute Selection button. (Refer to Figure 1-4.)

By default, Stata expects a command to occupy only one line. The default is the carriage return (cr) delimiter. For simple commands, this default works fine. For longer commands, such as regression commands with many variables or graphing commands with many options, you will want to override the cr default with the semicolon (;) delimiter. Once the semicolon delimiter is in place, Stata will run the script until it encounters a semicolon. To declare the semicolon delimiter, type

#delimit ;

in the Do-file editor. Figure 1-5 illustrates. If you execute a semicolon-delimited command, or a series of semicolon delimited commands, Stata will expect the semicolon delimiter for all commands. When you return to the Do-file and run a carriage return command, Stata will run that command, too, because it resets to the default between runs. However, if you run semicolon-delimited and carriage return–delimited commands in the same group of commands, then you must reset the carriage-return default within the group, as shown in Figure 1-5.

#delimit cr

Insert short comments by starting the comment line with an asterisk (*). Insert longer, multiline comments by enclosing them between "/*" at the beginning and "*/" at the end, as shown in Figure 1-6.

One last point on Do-files: Save them. Click on the Save File icon, select a location (such as your USB device), and save the Do-file, giving it a mundane but descriptive name ("Chapter01"). At the beginning of each chapter in this book, open the Do-file editor, write the syntax as described in the chapter, and save the file.

LOG FILES

Unlike most data analysis packages, Stata does not automatically save results to an output file. This is not a huge disadvantage, because Do-files will permit you to replicate your work. Also, Stata permits the user to select desired output and print it directly from the Results window. (This procedure is discussed below.) Even so, you may want to keep a log file. To begin a log file, click File→Log→Begin, as shown in Figure 1-7. Find a suitable location, name the file, and click Save. Stata will now record everything, including commands that are typed in the Command window and Do-file syntax that sends output to the Results window. From within Stata, you can

Figure 1-4 The Do-file Editor

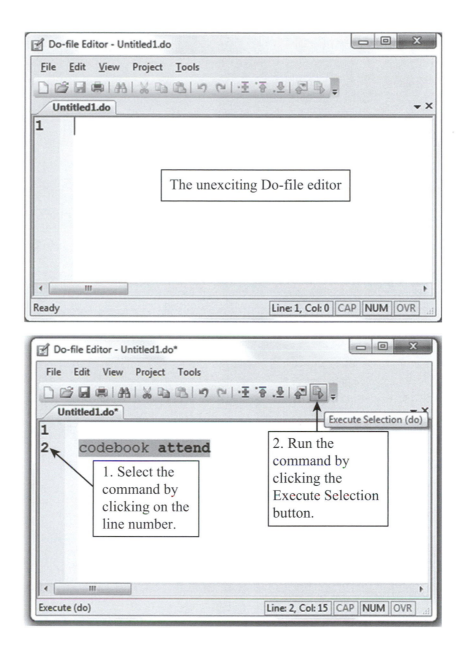

open and view log files, including the current log, by clicking File→Log→View. Ordinarily, Stata correctly assumes that you want to view the active log file. If Stata is remiss, you can browse to the current log's location. Of course, using the File→Log menu, log files can be suspended, resumed, and closed.

PRINTING RESULTS AND COPYING OUTPUT

Any tabular or text output can be selected and printed directly from the screen or from a log file. (In the next chapter, we will describe how to print graphs.) To illustrate, we will use the tabulate command to obtain a frequency distribution of the variable, bible, which measures respondents' feelings toward the Bible. (The tabulate command is covered in Chapter 2.) Type and run the command "tabulate bible [aw=gssw]" as shown in Figure 1-8. (What does the bracketed term "[aw=gssw]" mean? The statement weights the data to correct for sampling bias. See "A Closer Look.") Stata produces tabular output displaying the desired frequency distribution. To print the table, select it, right-click on the selection, and then click Print. In the Print window, click the Selection radio

Figure 1-5 The Semicolon Delimiter

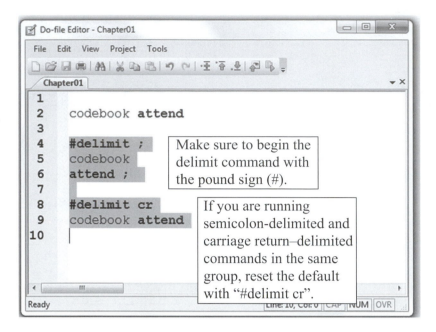

Figure 1-6 Making Comments in a Do-file

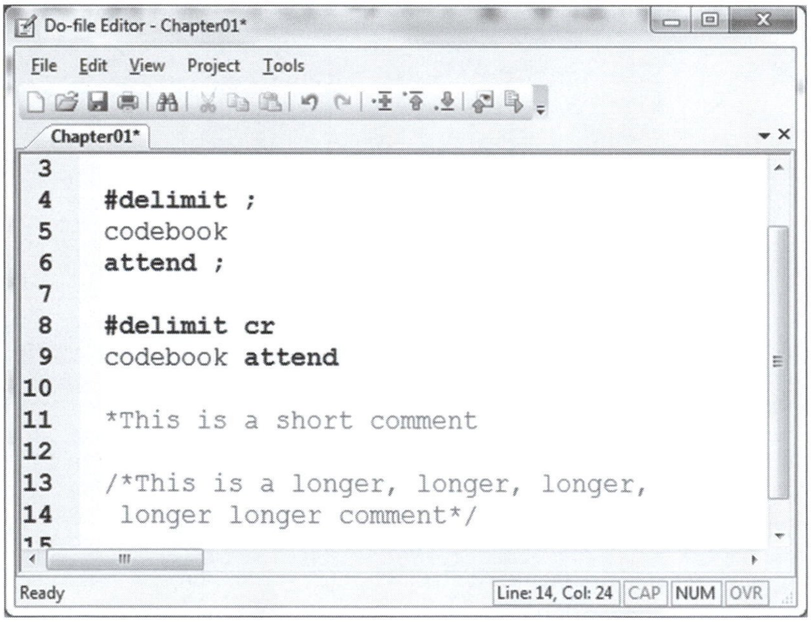

button. (The All button is Stata's default assumption, but you rarely want to print all the output you have produced during a session.) When the Output Settings window appears, uncheck all the boxes along the top of the window. (Refer to Figure 1-8.)

You can copy/paste output into a word processor, too, but (truth be told) this is one of Stata's less satisfactory features. To obtain the most workable result, select the tabular output, right-click, and choose Copy Table as HTML, as shown in Figure 1-9. When pasted into a Word document, the table is editable but not of presentation quality. A bit of editing, however, produces a presentable result.

Figure 1-7   Beginning a Log File

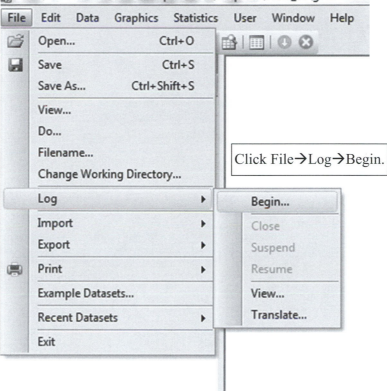

A Closer Look   **Weighting the gss2012 and nes2012 Datasets**

Many of this book's guided examples and exercises use the two survey datasets: gss2012 and nes2012. Before proceeding, you need to learn about a feature of these datasets that will require special treatment throughout the book. In raw form, these datasets are not completely representative of all groups in the population. This lack of representativeness may be intentional (e.g., the American National Election Study purposely oversampled Latino respondents so that researchers could gain insights into the attitudes of this group) or unintentional (e.g., some income groups are more likely to respond to surveys than are other groups). For some Stata commands, including recode and generate, this lack of representativeness does not matter. For most Stata commands, however, the raw data produce incorrect results. Fortunately, survey designers included the necessary corrective in gss2012 and nes2012: a weight variable. A *weight variable* adjusts for the distorting effect of sampling bias and calculates results that accurately reflect the makeup of the population. Therefore, to obtain correct results *you must specify the weight variable whenever you analyze gss2012 or nes2012*. In analyzing gss2012, you will specify the weight variable, *gssw*. For nes2012, the weight variable is *nesw*. In Chapters 2-5, you will use the weight variables as *analytic weights*. In chapters 6-11, you will use them as *probability weights*.

Figure 1-8 Sending Results to the Printer

```
.  tabulate bible [aw=gssw]
```

Feelings About The Bible	Freq.	Percent	Cum.
Word of God	619.762868	32.57	32.57
Inspired word	862.477204	45.32	77.89
Book of fables	420.759929	22.11	100.00
Total	1,903	100.00	

1. Select the table, right-click, and then select Print.

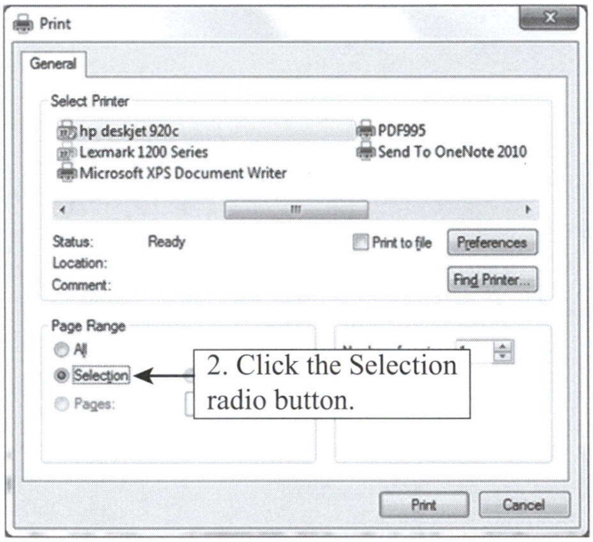

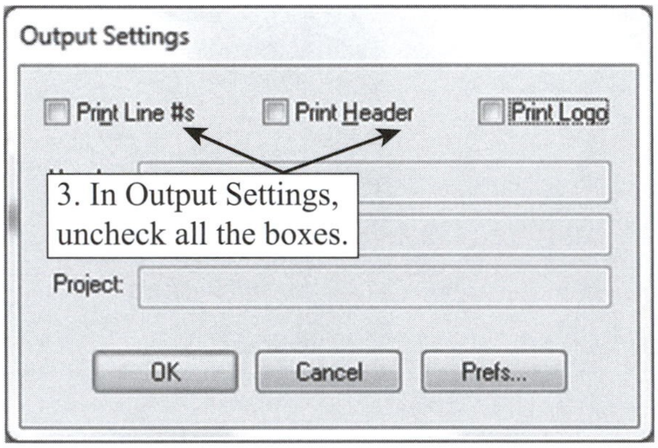

3. In Output Settings, uncheck all the boxes.

2. Click the Selection radio button.

GETTING HELP

Two commands will retrieve potentially useful information. Use the search command if you don't know or can't remember the name of a Stata command—or if you want to delve through Stata's resources on a particular topic. Use the help command to view Stata command syntax.

The syntax of the search command is as follows:

search *keyword*

Suppose we are interested in doing probit analysis, a specialized modeling technique, and we want access to Stata's information on the topic. Typing the command "search probit" returns many pages of output, including hyperlinks to descriptions of every probit-related Stata command, links to frequently asked questions (FAQs), examples of probit analysis, and references to technical reports and bulletins.[2]

search probit

The syntax of the help command is as follows:

help *command_name*

The command "help probit" retrieves specific syntax information—that is, how to type the probit command and what options can be used.

Figure 1-9   Copying and Pasting Results into Word

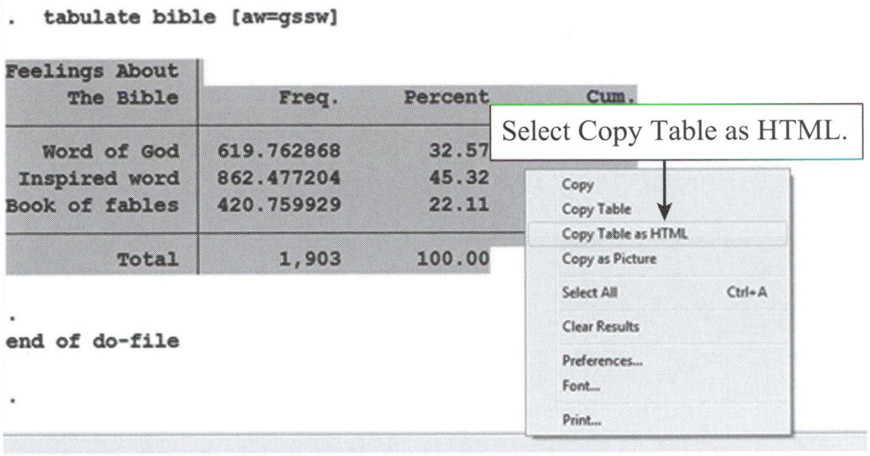

```
. tabulate bible [aw=gssw]
```

Feelings About The Bible	Freq.	Percent	Cum.
Word of God	619.762868	32.57	
Inspired word	862.477204	45.32	
Book of fables	420.759929	22.11	
Total	1,903	100.00	

Select Copy Table as HTML.

Copy
Copy Table
Copy Table as HTML
Copy as Picture
Select All   Ctrl+A
Clear Results
Preferences...
Font...
Print...

```
.
end of do-file

.
```

Feelings About The Bible	Freq.	Percent	Cum.
Word of God	619.762868	32.57	32.57
Inspired word	862.477204	45.32	77.89
Book of fables	420.759929	22.11	100.00
Total	1,903	100.00	

When you paste the table into Word, it looks like this.

Feelings About the Bible			
	Frequency	Percent	Cumulative percent
Word of God	619.762868	32.57	32.57
Inspired word	862.477204	45.32	77.89
Book of fables	420.759929	22.11	100.00
Total	1,903	100.00	

After editing in Word, the table looks like this.

```
help probit
```

The help command also will show you permissible abbreviations for Stata commands. Consider the describe command, which has a longish name. Can this command be abbreviated? Run "help describe."

```
help describe
```

Stata displays the requested information in a separate window, the Viewer (Figure 1-10). In addition to a raft of information on options and useful links to command elements, Stata communicates—by way of underlined letters—the minimum acceptable command abbreviation. As Figure 1-10 shows, instead of typing "describe," we can simply type "d", and Stata will know that we mean "describe." Because "d" is the shortest acceptable abbreviation for "describe," each of the following is also acceptable: d, de, des, desc, descr, descri, describ, and (of course) describe. If none of the letters in the command syntax is underlined, then the command may not be abbreviated.

Figure 1-10 The help Command

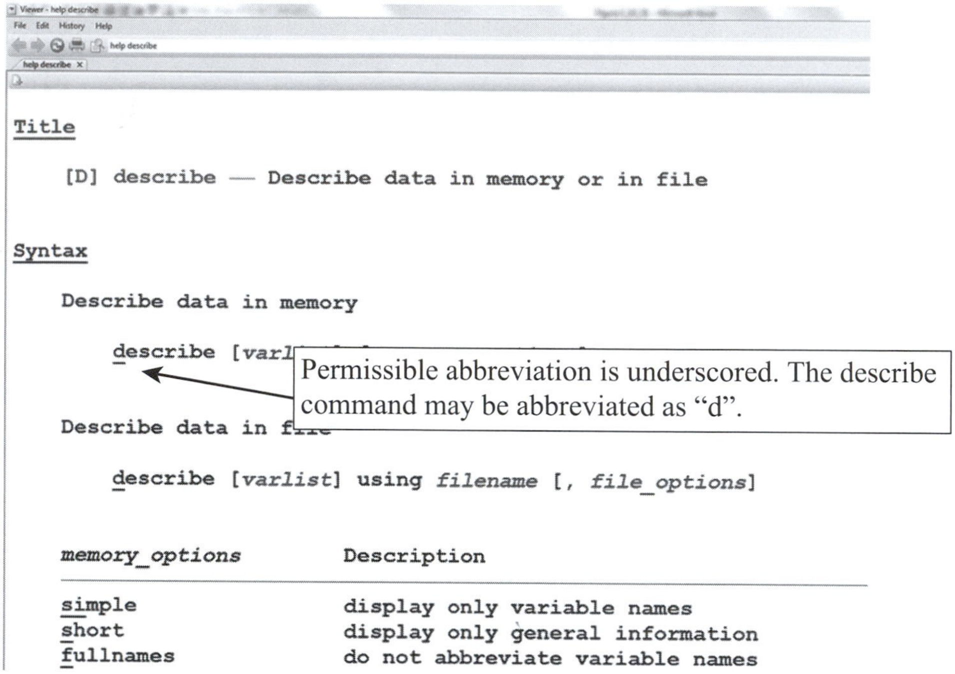

Stata follows three rules in determining abbreviations. First, the more commonly used commands, such as the describe command, generally have shorter acceptable abbreviations. Second, commands that are destructive of data may not be abbreviated. The recode command, discussed in Chapter 3, is an example of a destructive command. Third, commands that are implemented as ado-files (external program files that Stata must access) do not have abbreviations. For example, the codebook command is implemented as an ado-file, and so may not be abbreviated.

EXERCISES

For the following exercises, you will use dataset nes2012. Click File→Open, locate nes2012 on your computer, select it, and click Open.

1. Run the describe command. According to the results, nes2012 has (fill in the blanks) _____ observations and _____ variables.

2. Dataset nes2012 contains the variable discrim_gays, which asks respondents how much discrimination exists toward homosexuals. Run "codebook discrim_gays."

    A. What is the variable label for discrim_gays? _____

    B. Respondents who think there is "a lot" of discrimination have what numeric code on discrim_gays? (circle one)

    1   2   3   4   5

    C. According to the codebook results, how many respondents have missing values on discrim_gays?

    _____

3. Obtain tabular output for discrim_gays. Run "tabulate discrim_gays [aw=nesw]."

   A. Print the table.

   B. Copy/paste the table into a blank Word document. Edit the table for appearance and readability. Print the Word document.

4. In Chapter 2, you will learn how to interpret output from the summarize command. Which of the following are acceptable abbreviations for the summarize command? (Circle all that apply.)

su   sum   summ   summa   summar   summari   summariz

NOTES

1. Some variables do not have numeric codes but, rather, are recorded as words. Thus, a dataset might contain the variable friends, which takes on the values "Aileen," "Bruce," "Charisse," and "Doug." Variables that are recorded as words are called string variables. Although Stata will analyze string variables, strings are not covered in this book.
2. Another help-related command, findit, casts an even wider net than the search command. The findit command is equivalent to running search with the all option.

2

Descriptive Statistics

Analyzing descriptive statistics is the most basic—and sometimes the most informative—form of analysis you will do. Descriptive statistics reveal two attributes of a variable: its typical value (central tendency) and its spread (degree of dispersion or variation). The precision with which we can describe central tendency for any given variable depends on the variable's level of measurement. For nominal-level variables, we can identify the *mode,* the most common value of the variable. For ordinal-level variables, those whose categories can be ranked, we can find the mode and the *median*—the value of the variable that divides the cases into two equal-size groups. For interval-level variables, we can obtain the mode, median, and arithmetic *mean,* the sum of all values divided by the number of cases.

Finding a variable's central tendency is ordinarily a straightforward exercise. Simply read the computer results, and report the numbers. Describing a variable's degree of dispersion or variation, however, often requires informed judgment.[1] Here is a general rule that applies to any variable at any level of measurement: A variable has no dispersion if all the cases—states, countries, people, or whatever—fall into the same value of the variable. Using ordinary language, we might describe such a variable as "homogeneous." A variable has maximum dispersion if the cases are spread evenly across all values of the variable. The number of cases in one category equals the number of cases in every other category. In this circumstance, we would describe the variable as "heterogeneous."

INTERPRETING MEASURES OF CENTRAL TENDENCY AND VARIATION

Central tendency and variation work together in providing a complete description of any variable. Some variables have an easily identified typical value and show little dispersion. For example, suppose you were to ask a large number of US citizens what sort of economic system they believe to be the best: capitalism, communism, or socialism. What would be the modal response, the economic system preferred by most people? Capitalism. Would there be a great deal of dispersion, with large numbers of people choosing the alternatives, communism or socialism? Probably not. In other instances, however, you may find that one value of a variable has a more tenuous grasp on the label "typical." And the variable may exhibit more dispersion, with the cases more evenly spread out across the variable's other values. For example, suppose a large sample of voting-age adults were asked, in the weeks preceding a presidential election, how interested they are in the campaign: very interested, somewhat interested, or not very interested. Among your own acquaintances you probably know a number of people who fit into each category. So even if one category, such as "somewhat interested," is the median, there are likely to be many people at either extreme: "very interested" and "not very interested." This would be an instance in which the amount of dispersion in a variable—its degree of spread—is essential to understanding and describing it.

These and other points are best understood by working through some guided examples using gss2012. In the examples that follow, you will learn Stata's basic data description commands—codebook, tabulate, summarize, sort, and list. Tabulate (abbreviated "tab") and summarize ("sum") are especially important and versatile. Tabulate produces frequency distributions for nominal, ordinal, or interval variables. The summarize command returns descriptive statistics for interval-level variables. You will also learn to use histogram ("hist"), a command that creates graphic displays. By default, histogram produces descriptive graphs for interval variables. However, when supplied with the necessary options, histogram generates attractive bar charts for nominal and ordinal variables.

For basic data descriptions (codebook, tabulate, and summarize), you may wish to type and run the commands from the Command window instead of using the Do-file editor. However, nicely optioned bar charts and histograms, created with the histogram command, require a fair amount of typing. You will want to type and run these commands from a Do-file. (Do-files were covered in Chapter 1.) Open gss2012, and let's get started.

DESCRIBING NOMINAL VARIABLES

In this section you will obtain a frequency distribution for a nominal-level variable, zodiac, which records respondents' astrological signs. But first we will review the codebook command, introduced in Chapter 1. In the Command window (or from the Do-file editor), type and run "codebook zodiac."

Stata responds:

```
codebook zodiac

──────────────────────────────────────────────────────────────────────
zodiac
──────────────────────────────────────────────────────────────────────

                type:   numeric (long)
               label:   z_lab

               range:   [1,12]                  units:  1
       unique values:   12                   missing .:  61/1974

            examples:   3       Gemini
                        5       Leo
                        8       Scorpio
                        10      Capricorn
```

Zodiac has 12 unique numeric codes, each of which has a nonnumeric value label. Respondents who are coded 3 on zodiac, for example, are labeled "Gemini," those coded 5 are labeled "Leo," and so on.

Now we will ask Stata to produce a frequency distribution of zodiac. Type and run "tab zodiac [aw=gssw]." The Results window displays a frequency distribution of respondents' astrological signs (Figure 2-1). The value labels for each astrological code appear in the left-most column, with Aries occupying the top row of numbers and Pisces the bottom row.[2] There are three columns of numbers: labeled "Freq." (frequency), "Percent," and "Cum." (cumulative percent). What does each column mean? The frequency column shows raw frequencies, the number of respondents having each zodiac sign, weighted by gssw. Percentage is the percentage of respondents in each category of the variable. So, for example, 146.329214 ≈ 146 of the 1,913 respondents, or 7.65 percent, have Aries as their astrological sign. Finally, cumulative percent reports the percentage of cases that fall in *or below* each value of the variable. For ordinal variables, as we will see, the cumulative percent column can provide valuable clues about how a variable is distributed. But for nominal variables, which cannot be ranked, the cumulative percentage column provides no information of value.

Figure 2-1 Frequency Distribution (nominal variable)

```
. tab zodiac [aw=gssw]
```

R's Astrological Sign	Raw frequencies (weighted) Freq.	Percentages in each value of zodiac Percent	Cumulative percentages Cum.
Aries	146.329214	7.65	7.65
Taurus	172.228583	9.00	16.65
Gemini	162.004553	8.47	25.12
Cancer	148.281074	7.75	32.87
Leo	191.061969	9.99	42.86
Virgo	159.175852	8.32	51.18
Libra	184.057627	9.62	60.80
Scorpio	145.6597	7.61	68.42
Sagittarius	145.90119	7.63	76.04
Capricorn	140.819986	7.36	83.40
Aquarius	174.166276	9.10	92.51
Pisces	143.313978	7.49	100.00
Total	1,913	100.00	

Consider the percent column more closely. What is the mode, the most common astrological sign? For nominal variables, the answer to this question is (almost) always an easy call: Simply find the value with the highest percentage of responses. Leo is the mode. Does this variable have little dispersion or a lot of dispersion? Again study the percent column. Apply the rule: A variable has no dispersion if the cases are concentrated in one value of the variable; a variable has maximum dispersion if the cases are spread evenly across all values of the variable. Are most of the cases concentrated in Leo, or are there many cases in each value of zodiac? Since respondents show great heterogeneity in astrological signs, we would conclude that zodiac has a high level of dispersion.

DESCRIBING ORDINAL VARIABLES

Next, you will analyze and describe two ordinal-level variables, one of which has little variation and the other of which is more spread out. Scroll through the variables list until you find these variables: helppoor and helpsick. Each of these is a 5-point ordinal scale. Helppoor asks respondents to place themselves on a scale between 1 ("the government should take action to help poor people") and 5 ("people should help themselves"). Helpsick, using a similar 5-point scale, asks respondents about government responsibility or individual responsibility for medical care.

Type and run two tab commands, one for helppoor ("tab helppoor [aw=gssw]") and one for helpsick ("tab helpsick [aw=gssw]"). Stata returns two frequency distributions, one for each variable (Figure 2-2). First let's focus on the frequency distribution for helppoor. How would you describe its central tendency and dispersion? Because helppoor is an ordinal variable, we can report both its mode and its median. Its mode, clearly enough, is the response "Agree with both," the option chosen by 44.59 percent of the sample. What about the median? This is where the cumulative percent column ("Cum.") of the frequency distribution comes into play. *The median for any ordinal (or interval) variable is the category below which 50 percent of the cases lie.* Is the first category, "Govt," the median? No, this code contains fewer than half the cases. How about code 2, the next higher category? No, again. According to the cumulative percent column, only 26.80 percent of the cases fall in or below this response category. It is not until we notch up in rank, to "Agree with both," that the cumulative percentage exceeds the magic number of 50 percent. Because more than 50 percent of the cases fall in or below "Agree with both" (the cumulative percentage is equal to 71.39 percent), "Agree with both" is the median.

Figure 2-2 Frequency Distributions (ordinal variables)

```
. tab helppoor [aw=gssw]
```

Govt imprv stndrd living?	Freq.	Percent	Cum.
Govt	192.933206	14.91	14.91
2	153.8775532	11.89	26.80
Agree w/both	576.956907	44.59	71.39
4	192.525579	14.88	86.27
Help selves	177.706755	13.73	100.00
Total	1,294	100.00	

```
. tab helpsick [aw=gssw]
```

Govt pay medical care?	Freq.	Percent	Cum.
Govt	368.100382	28.38	28.38
2	235.23296	18.14	46.52
Agree w/both	407.136425	31.39	77.91
4	160.571405	12.38	90.29
Help selves	125.958829	9.71	100.00
Total	1,297	100.00	

Does helppoor have a high or low degree of dispersion? If helppoor had a high level of variation, then the percentages of respondents in each response category would be roughly equal, as they were for the zodiac variable that you analyzed earlier. So, roughly one-fifth of the cases would fall into each of the five response categories: 20 percent in "Govt," 20 percent in response category "2," 20 percent in "Agree with both," 20 percent in response category "4," and 20 percent in "Help selves." If helppoor had no dispersion, then all the cases would fall into one value. That is, one value would have 100 percent of the cases, and each of the other categories would have 0 percent. Which of these two scenarios comes closer to describing the actual distribution of respondents across the values of helppoor? The equal-percentages-in-each-category, high-variation scenario? Or the 100-percent-in-one-category, low-variation scenario? It seems clear that helppoor is a variable with a relatively low degree of dispersion. "Agree with both," with 44.59 percent of the cases, contains nearly three times as many cases as its nearest rival ("Govt"), and more than three times as many cases as any of the other response categories.

Now contrast helppoor's distribution with the distribution of helpsick. Interestingly, helpsick has the same mode as helppoor ("Agree with both," with 31.39 percent of the cases), and the same median (again, "Agree with both," where the cumulative percentage exceeds 50.0). Yet, with helppoor it seemed reasonable to say that "Agree with both" was the typical response. Would it be reasonable to say that "Agree with both" is helpsick's *typical* response? No, it would not. Notice that, unlike respondents' values on helppoor, values on helpsick are more spread out, with sizable numbers of cases falling in the first value ("Govt," with 28.38 percent), making it a close rival to "Agree with both" for the distinction of being the modal opinion on this issue. Clearly, the public is more divided—more widely dispersed—on the question of medical assistance than on the question of assistance to the poor.

DESCRIBING INTERVAL VARIABLES

We now turn to the descriptive analysis of interval-level variables. An interval-level variable represents the most precise level of measurement. Unlike nominal variables, whose values stand for categories, and ordinal variables, whose values can be ranked, the values of an interval variable *tell us the exact quantity of the characteristic being measured.* For example, age qualifies as an interval-level variable, since its values impart each respondent's age in years.

Because interval variables have the most precision, they can be described more completely than can nominal or ordinal variables. For any interval-level variable, we can report its mode, median, and arithmetic average, or *mean.* In addition to these measures of central tendency, we can make more sophisticated judgments about variation. Specifically, one can determine if an interval-level distribution is *skewed.* What is skewness, and how do you know it when you see it?

Skewness refers to how symmetrical a distribution is. If a distribution is not skewed, the cases tend to cluster symmetrically around the mean of the distribution, and they taper off evenly for values above and below the mean. If a distribution is skewed, by contrast, one tail of the distribution is longer and skinnier than the other tail. Distributions in which a small number of cases occupy extremely high values of an interval variable—distributions with a skinnier right-hand tail—have a *positive skew.* By the same token, if the distribution has a few cases at the extreme lower end—the distribution has a skinnier left-hand tail—then the distribution has a *negative skew.* Skewness has a predictable effect on the mean. A positive skew tends to "pull" the mean upward; a negative skew pulls it downward. However, skewness has less effect on the median. Since the median reports the middle-most value of a distribution, it is not tugged upward or downward by extreme values. For badly skewed distributions, it is a good practice to use the median instead of the mean in describing central tendency. A step-by-step analysis of a gss2012 variable, age, will clarify these points.

In obtaining descriptive information for a nominal or an ordinal variable, tab is the command of choice. The tab command also is useful for describing an interval-level variable, providing that the variable has, say, thirty or fewer values. For an interval variable with many unique values, such as age, tab is somewhat less informative. Running "tab age [aw=gssw]" elicits a rather lengthy response from Stata. See Page 18.

The cumulative percent column leads us directly to the median age: 45 (cumulative percentage, 50.84). But locating the modal age is a chore.[3]

Although tab may (or may not) be a valuable descriptive tool for interval-level variables, summarize will always fill the bill. Go ahead; type and run "sum age [aw=gssw]":

age	Freq.	Percent	Cum.
18	18.1052705	0.92	0.92
19	27.7253147	1.41	2.33
20	27.1527242	1.38	3.71
21	40.9504904	2.08	5.79
22	44.8351	2.28	8.06
23	38.7811936	1.97	10.03
24	31.9930128	1.62	11.66
25	34.602659	1.76	13.42
26	30.8581949	1.57	14.98
27	33.4392105	1.70	16.68
28	39.40395367	2.00	18.68
29	29.0608107	1.48	20.16
30	51.3732467	2.61	22.77
31	33.890736	1.72	24.49
32	48.8631265	2.48	26.97
33	40.889958	2.08	29.05
34	35.7884593	1.82	30.86
35	35.7486527	1.82	32.68
36	27.4744673	1.40	34.07
37	37.6260663	1.91	35.99
38	37.033979	1.88	37.87
39	38.6306854	1.96	39.83
40	31.1090424	1.58	41.41
41	38.3193054	1.95	43.35
42	43.4606108	2.21	45.56
43	35.6379506	1.81	47.37
44	31.3702529	1.59	48.97
45	36.8731077	1.87	50.84
46	28.5487527	1.45	52.29
47	40.779256	2.07	54.36
48	44.1273375	2.24	56.60
49	38.5303463	1.96	58.56
50	29.4725295	1.50	60.05
51	47.9791558	2.44	62.49
52	38.6203224	1.96	64.45
53	32.8512838	1.67	66.12
54	34.8750453	1.77	67.89
55	53.5321805	2.72	70.61
56	31.0190664	1.58	72.19
57	26.1389714	1.33	73.51
58	30.3357738	1.54	75.05
59	27.5644434	1.40	76.45
60	24.0198443	1.22	77.67
61	35.2407552	1.79	79.46
62	30.0849265	1.53	80.99
63	24.5924347	1.25	82.24
64	26.2289476	1.33	83.57
65	33.3285086	1.69	85.26
66	16.8199442	0.85	86.12
67	17.9045926	0.91	87.03
68	22.3729686	1.14	88.16
69	15.02256	0.76	88.93
70	15.6851265	0.80	89.72
71	29.0608106	1.48	91.20
72	12.1405274	0.62	91.82
73	18.46682	0.94	92.75
74	10.4434821	0.53	93.29
75	13.5261927	0.69	93.97
76	18.1554401	0.92	94.89
77	13.6265317	0.69	95.59
78	12.3412054	0.63	96.21
79	7.92299893	0.40	96.62
80	8.02333794	0.41	97.02
81	8.28454836	0.42	97.44
82	5.86440421	0.30	97.74
83	4.11718943	0.21	97.95
84	10.6201159	0.54	98.49
85	3.29375154	0.17	98.66
86	5.35234626	0.27	98.93
87	8.07350745	0.41	99.34
88	4.57907788	0.23	99.57
89	8.43505689	0.43	100.00
Total	1,969	100.00	

```
. sum age [aw=gssw]
```

Variable	Obs	Weight	Mean	Std. Dev.	Min	Max
age	1969	1969.85697	46.10235	17.27753	18	89

Stata tells us the number of respondents or observations in the data ("Obs"), the mean age, the standard deviation of the distribution ("Std. Dev."), and the minimum and maximum observed values. By running summarize on its defaults, you can get a quick and concise profile of any interval variable in the dataset. But because we are currently after a more detailed description, we will need to append an option to the summarize command. Edit "sum age [aw=gssw]" to read "sum age [aw=gssw], detail." (Hint: If you are working from the Command window, press the Page Up key, which returns "sum age [aw=gssw]" to the command line, where it can be easily modified.) The detail option, not surprisingly, instructs Stata to provide a fuller description of the variable. Consider the output:

```
. sum age [aw=gssw], detail
```

age

	Percentiles	Smallest		
1%	19	18		
5%	21	18		
10%	23	18	Obs	1969
25%	32	18	Sum of Wgt.	1969.85697
50%	45		Mean	46.10235
		Largest	Std. Dev.	17.27753
75%	58	89		
90%	71	89	Variance	298.5129
95%	77	89	Skewness	.3375539
99%	87	89	Kurtosis	2.274741

The mean age, 46.10235 (or 46.1), is again on display. Now notice the two left-hand columns of numbers, under the heading "Percentiles." Percentiles are synonymous with cumulative percentages. So, the left-most column displays cumulative percentages in ascending order ("1%, 5%, 10% . . . 99%"). The next column lists corresponding values of the age variable. Thus the pairing "25% 32" can be read, "25 percent of respondents are age 32 or younger." The pairing "50% 45" means, "50 percent of respondents are age 45 or younger." The median is the same as the 50th percentile. To find the median of an interval-level variable, run summarize with the detail option, and look for the value of the variable that is associated with "50%" in the percentiles column.

Summarize with the detail option is so meticulous in providing percentiles, the numbers permit us to determine the *interquartile range,* the values of a variable that bracket the "middle half" of a distribution, between the top of the lowest quartile ("25%") and bottom of the highest quartile ("75%"). For age, we can see that the middle half falls between 32 and 58 years of age. Now, the interquartile range has limited analytic value for describing a single variable. However, it is quite useful when comparing two or more distributions. (This is illustrated in Chapter 4.)

We have discovered that the mean age, at 46.1, is higher than the median age of 45. What does this comparison tell us about the skewness of the distribution? When a distribution is perfectly symmetrical—no skew—its mean will be equal to its median, and it will have a skewness of zero. If the mean is lower than the median—that is, if a few extremely low values pull the mean down, away from the center of the distribution—the distribution has a negative skew. If the mean is higher than the median, as is the case with our current analysis, the distribution has a positive skew. Thus, it comes as no shock that Stata has reported a positive value for the skewness statistic: .3375539, or about .34. Even so, the mean (46.1) and the median (45) are only about 1 year apart. In this case, it would not be a distortion of reality to use the mean instead of the median to describe the central tendency of the distribution.

However, sometimes the mean paints a less accurate view of a variable's typical value. To illustrate this point, we will obtain descriptive statistics for income06, which measures total family income on a scale that ranges from 1 (under $1,000) to 25 ($150,000 or more). Because this variable has fewer than thirty unique values, the tabulate command provides useful information. In fact, we will run tab twice—once to see income06's value labels, and again (using the nolabel option) to see income06's underlying numeric codes:[4]

```
. tab income06 [aw=gssw]
```

Total Family Income	Freq.	Percent	Cum.
UNDER $1 000	21.05014818	1.20	1.20
$1 000 TO 2 999	22.6546167	1.29	2.49
$3 000 TO 3 999	14.8438306	0.84	3.33
$4 000 TO 4 999	7.18647994	0.41	3.74
$5 000 TO 5 999	5.87615807	0.33	4.07
$6 000 TO 6 999	16.5227329	0.94	5.01
$7 000 TO 7 999	14.6903952	0.84	5.85
$8 000 TO 9 999	23.3917776	1.33	7.18
$10000 TO 12499	56.4778241	3.21	10.39
$12500 TO 14999	48.2984576	2.75	13.14
$15000 TO 17499	56.047534	3.19	16.33
$17500 TO 19999	41.9755461	2.39	18.72
$20000 TO 22499	60.51108	3.44	22.16
$22500 TO 24999	53.2223098	3.03	25.18
$25000 TO 29999	91.4473532	5.20	30.39
$30000 TO 34999	80.2787628	4.57	34.95
$35000 TO 39999	102.564799	5.83	40.79
$40000 TO 49999	148.831843	8.47	49.25
$50000 TO 59999	130.081558	7.40	56.65
$60000 TO 74999	153.4327553	8.73	65.38
$75000 TO $89999	164.232765	9.34	74.72
$90000 TO $109999	129.706654	7.38	82.10
$110000 TO $129999	73.8294437	4.20	86.30
$130000 TO $149999	53.89776104	3.07	89.37
$150000 OR OVER	186.947414	10.63	100.00
Total	1,758	100.00	

```
tab income06 [aw=gssw], nolabel
```

The nolabel option tells Stata to show a variable's numeric codes.

Total Family Income	Freq.	Percent	Cum.
1	21.05014818	1.20	1.20
2	22.6546167	1.29	2.49
3	14.8438306	0.84	3.33
4	7.18647994	0.41	3.74
5	5.87615807	0.33	4.07
6	16.5227329	0.94	5.01
7	14.6903952	0.84	5.85
8	23.3917776	1.33	7.18
9	56.4778241	3.21	10.39
10	48.2984576	2.75	13.14
11	56.047534	3.19	16.33
12	41.9755461	2.39	18.72
13	60.51108	3.44	22.16
14	53.2223098	3.03	25.18
15	91.4473532	5.20	30.39
16	80.2787628	4.57	34.95
17	102.564799	5.83	40.79
18	148.831843	8.47	49.25
19	130.081558	7.40	56.65
20	153.4327553	8.73	65.38
21	164.232765	9.34	74.72
22	129.706654	7.38	82.10
23	73.8294437	4.20	86.30
24	53.89776104	3.07	89.37
25	186.947414	10.63	100.00
Total	1,758	100.00	

The cumulative frequency column leads us quickly to the median: $50,000 to $59,999 (first tabulate analysis), which corresponds to numeric code 19 (second tabulate analysis). However, notice that the cumulative percentages build slowly, from sparsely populated lower values to more heavily populated higher values. This pattern—skinnier in the lower range—is the field mark of a negative skew. A summary analysis illustrates this:

```
. sum income06 [aw=gssw], d
```
⟵ The detail option can be abbreviated as "d."

```
                         Total Family Income

              Percentiles      Smallest
     1%              1             1
     5%              6             1
    10%              9             1         Obs                    1758
    25%             14             1         Sum of Wgt.    1725.21515

    50%             19                       Mean            17.51313
                              Largest        Std. Dev.       5.669809
    75%             22            25
    90%             25            25         Variance        32.14674
    95%             25            25         Skewness       -.8652981
    99%             25            25         Kurtosis        3.329206
```

Find the median, numeric code 19, at the 50th percentile. Now note the way the negative skew (−.8652981) pulls the mean downward, off the median, to 17.5. According to our first tab run, 17.5 corresponds to a mean income of about $40,000, not the $50,000 to $59,999 conveyed by the median. You have to exercise judgment, but in this case the median would seem to be a more faithful measure of central tendency.[5]

OBTAINING BAR CHARTS AND HISTOGRAMS

Thus far you have learned to wring a fair amount of information out of a dry handful of numbers: the mode, median, mean, and skewness. Visual displays can add richness and nuance to these numerical descriptions of central tendency and variation. Two related types of graphs provide appropriate support for descriptive statistics. For nominal and ordinal variables, a *bar chart* is used. A bar chart displays each value of a variable and shows you the percentage of cases that fall into each category. Bar charts can also be used for interval variables that have a manageable number of values—generally thirty or fewer. For an interval variable with many values, a *histogram* is generally a better choice. A histogram is similar to a bar chart, but instead of displaying each discrete value, it collapses categories into ranges (called *bins*), resulting in a compact display.

Stata's histogram command (abbreviated "hist") with the discrete option ("d") and the percent option ("percent" must be typed in full) produces bar charts of nominal or ordinal variables:

hist *varname* [fw=*weightvar*], d percent

For a histogram of an interval variable with many unique values, omit the discrete option:

hist *varname* [fw=*weightvar*], percent

One item to note: Stata does not permit analytic weights ("aw") in the histogram command. However, it does permit frequency weights ("fw"). In gss2012, the frequency weight is named gssw_rnd. (In nes2012, nesw_rnd is the frequency weight.)

For quick, unadorned visual displays, these pithy commands work fine. Type and run "hist zodiac [fw=gssw_rnd], d percent." Stata delivers a bare bones bar chart (Figure 2-3). The axis titles ("R's Astrological Sign" and "Percent") are acceptable, and the y-axis tick marks are nicely scaled and legible. And, of course, the twelve bars represent the percentages of respondents falling into each category of zodiac. However, much important information is missing. In particular, the horizontal axis is completely devoid of labels. Consider Figure 2-4, a noticeable improvement.

Figure 2-3 Bar Chart (nominal variable)

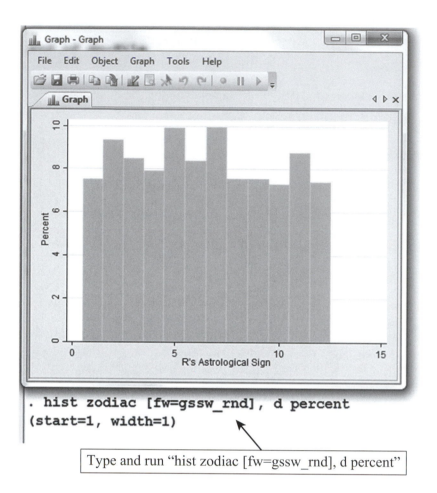

```
. hist zodiac [fw=gssw_rnd], d percent
(start=1, width=1)
```

Type and run "hist zodiac [fw=gssw_rnd], d percent"

Figure 2-4 has several features worth noting. As in our earlier effort, the y-axis records the percentage of respondents falling into each category of zodiac. The use of percentages makes the chart directly analogous to zodiac's frequency distribution, which you analyzed earlier. There are twelve tick marks along the x-axis, one for each category of zodiac. The ticks are labeled using zodiac's value labels, from "Aries" (numeric code 1 on zodiac) to "Pisces" (code 12). Because each tick is labeled—and because some of the label names, such as "Sagittarius" and "Capricorn," are pretty long—the value labels appear in smallish font, and they are angled at 45 degrees. These adjustments help to make the labels readable. Plus, they don't run into each other, as they would if they were to be displayed horizontally along the axis. Each of these x-axis features—the labeling of each value, the use of word labels, the 45-degree angle, the small label font size—requires a special suboption within histogram's xlabel option. Indeed, presentation-quality Stata graphs almost always require a fair number of (sometimes esoteric) options, and they are best created and preserved in a Do-file. If you have not done so already, open the Do-file editor, and let's obtain a bar chart of zodiac. (As you progress through the chapter, adding commands to the Do-file, make sure to save it frequently.)

Take a few minutes to study Figure 2-5, which shows the annotated syntax for creating Figure 2-4's bar chart. (For readability, Figure 2-5 uses the semicolon delimiter and adds extra spaces.) The first line of the graphing syntax re-creates the basic chart: "histogram zodiac [fw=gssw_rnd], discrete percent." The xlabel option contains the refinements. The first suboption, "1(1)12," sometimes called the *range-delta* suboption, means this: label the x-axis values between 1 and 12, in increments of 1 unit. So, the first number, "1," sets the starting value, the last number, "12," sets the ending value, and the parenthesized value, "(1)," sets the increment. Unless instructed otherwise, Stata will use numeric codes to label the x-axis. The suboption, "valuelabel," overrides the default and requests word labels instead. The suboption, "angle(forty_five),"

Figure 2-4   Bar Chart with Value Labels (nominal variable)

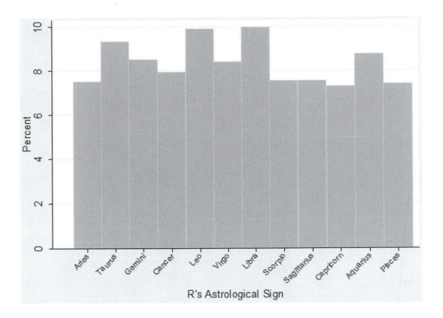

logically enough, gives us the nicely positioned value labels. For a complete list of acceptable angle options, type "help anglestyle." Finally, "labsize(small)" downsizes the large type that Stata would otherwise use for value labels. For Stata's lengthy list of permissible label font sizes, type "help textsizestyle." Figure 2-5's arrows remind you to enclose xlabel's suboptions in parentheses. Go ahead; type and run the syntax. Make sure that your finished product looks like the bar chart in Figure 2-4.

Figure 2-5   Creating a Bar Chart (Do-file editor)

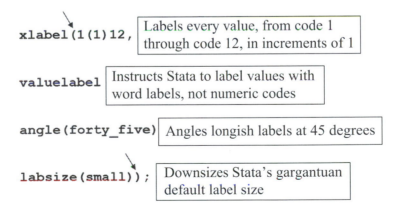

Now let's create a histogram of age—first a bare bones result, then a well-optioned graphic. In the Do-file, type and run "hist age [fw=gssw_rnd], percent." (See Figure 2-6.) Notice that the histogram's graphic signature—combining adjacent values of a variable—results in a compact, readable display. One can easily locate the center of the distribution (45–46 years of age). And the skinny right-hand tail reaffirms the presence of the positive skew we found in our numerical analysis. For the product of a terse command running on Stata defaults, this graph is quite presentable as is. A curmudgeon, however, might find two aspects to grumble about: The x-axis labels (this is a common source of complaint) and the bland bar color. Currently, the x-axis ranges from "20" to "100" in 20-year increments. Suppose we prefer that it range from "20" to "90" in 10-year increments. Suppose further that we plan to print in color, and so prefer a bolder fill color for the bars. Consider how the syntax in Figure 2-7 will make the desired changes.

Figure 2-6 Histogram (interval variable)

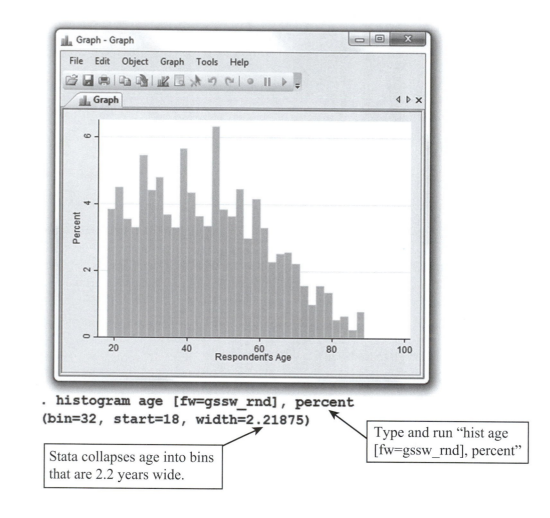

```
. histogram age [fw=gssw_rnd], percent
(bin=32, start=18, width=2.21875)
```

Type and run "hist age [fw=gssw_rnd], percent"

Stata collapses age into bins that are 2.2 years wide.

Figure 2-7 Creating a Histogram (Do-file editor)

```
#delimit ;
histogram age [fw=gssw_rnd], percent

fcolor(blue)

xlabel(20(10)90,

valuelabel

labsize(medsmall)) ;
```

Asks for blue fill color for the bars

x-axis will range from 20 through 90, in increments of 10

With one exception, the fcolor option, this command is similar to the bar chart syntax we just ran. However, review the range-delta suboption: "20(10)90." This statement sets 20 as the lowest displayed value, 90 as the highest displayed value, and 10 as the increment. The x-axis will read: "20 30 40 50 60 70 80 90." Type and run the syntax. A nicely tweaked histogram appears in the Graph Window (Figure 2-8).

Figure 2-8   Histogram with X-Axis Labels and Fill Color (interval variable)

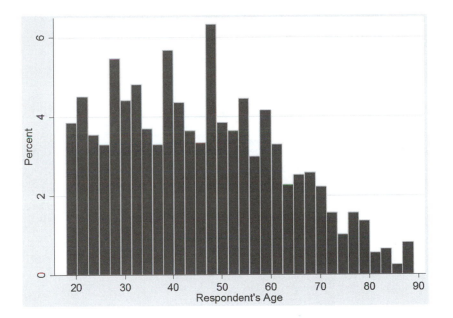

Before moving on, a word about Stata colors. In the graphic we just created, the author arbitrarily requested blue as the fill color. This may or may not be to your liking. To retrieve the names of all built-in colors, type "help colorstyle." If you want to see a palette of Stata's colors, install this user-contributed program: palette_all. Type "ssc install palette_all":[6]

```
.  ssc install palette_all
checking palette_all consistency and verifying not already installed...
installing into c:\ado\plus\...
installation complete.
```

After installation, type "palette_all" to see the colors.[7]

OBTAINING CASE-LEVEL INFORMATION WITH sort AND list

When we analyze a large survey dataset, as we have just done, we generally are not interested in how respondent x or respondent y answered a particular question. Rather, we want to know how the entire sample of respondents distributed themselves across the response categories of a variable. Sometimes, however, we gather data on particular cases because the cases are themselves inherently important. The states dataset (50 cases) and world dataset (191 cases) are good examples. With these datasets, we may want to push the descriptions beyond the relative anonymity of a tabulate analysis or a summary command and find out where particular cases "are" on an interesting variable. Stata's sort and list commands are ready-made for such elemental insights. Before beginning this guided example, close gss2012, and open states.

Suppose that we are interested in studying state laws that regulate abortions. The states dataset contains the variable abortlaw10, which records the number of restrictions imposed by each state, from no restrictions (a value of 0 on abortlaw10) to 10 restrictions (abortlaw10 value of 10). If we were to run "tab abortlaw10," we would find that one state has 0 restrictions, three states have 10, and a fair amount of variation exists among states. But exactly which states are the least restrictive? Which are the most restrictive? Where does your state fall on the list? By enlisting the sort command, we can sort states on the basis of abortlaw10, from lower values to higher values.[8] The list command will then display the sorted values of abortlaw10 along with, at our request, the name of each state. (The states dataset contains the variable state, which records the states' names.)

With the states dataset open, type and run this command:

```
sort abortlaw10
```

Stata silently sorts the states from low numbers of abortion restrictions to high numbers of abortion restrictions. Now type and run this command:

```
list abortlaw10 state
```

Stata responds by giving us a table reporting which states go with which values of abortlaw10:

	abort~10	state
1.	0	Vermont
2.	1	Oregon
3.	1	NewHampshire
4.	2	Hawaii
5.	2	Washington
6.	3	NewYork
7.	3	Maryland
8.	3	NewMexico
9.	4	WestVirginia
10.	4	Colorado
11.	4	Maine
12.	4	Connecticut
13.	4	California
14.	5	Alaska
15.	5	Wyoming

[Note: Some output omitted.]

	abort~10	state
35.	8	Ohio
36.	8	Pennsylvania
37.	8	Nebraska
38.	9	Wisconsin
39.	9	Arkansas
40.	9	Louisiana
41.	9	NorthDakota
42.	9	SouthDakota
43.	9	Virginia
44.	9	Missouri
45.	9	Georgia
46.	9	Idaho
47.	9	Utah
48.	10	Indiana
49.	10	Oklahoma
50.	10	SouthCarolina

Vermont has no restrictions; Oregon and New Hampshire each have one restriction. At the other end of the scale, a large contingent of ten states have nine restrictions each, and three (Indiana, Oklahoma, and South Carolina) have ten.

EXERCISES

1. (Dataset: gss2012. Variables: femrole, [aw=gssw], [fw=gssw_rnd].) Two pundits are arguing about how the general public views the role of women in the home and in politics.

   Pundit 1: "Our society has a minority of traditionally minded individuals who think that the proper 'place' for women is taking care of the home and caring for children. This small but vocal group of traditionalists aside, the typical adult supports the idea that women belong in work and in politics."

   Pundit 2: "Poppycock! It's just the opposite. The extremist feminist crowd has distorted the overall picture. The typical view among most citizens is that women should be in the home, not in work and politics."

   A. Dataset gss2012 contains femrole, an interval-level variable that measures respondents' attitudes toward women in society and politics. Scores can range from 0 (women belong in the home) to 9 (women belong in work and politics).

   If Pundit 1 is correct, femrole will have (circle one)

   a negative skew.   no skew.   a positive skew.

   If Pundit 2 is correct, femrole will have (circle one)

   a negative skew.   no skew.   a positive skew.

   If Pundit 1 is correct, femrole's mean will be (circle one)

   lower than its median.   the same as its median.   higher than its median.

   If Pundit 2 is correct, femrole's mean will be (circle one)

   lower than its median.   the same as its median.   higher than its median.

B. Run "tab femrole [aw=gssw]." Run "sum femrole [aw=gssw], detail." Fill in the table that follows.

Statistics for femrole	
Mean	?
Median	?
Mode	?
Skewness	?

C. Obtain a bar chart of femrole by running histogram with the "d percent" options. (Even though we are treating femrole as an interval variable, the "d" option works nicely for interval variables having fewer than thirty values.) Don't forget to specify "[fw=gssw_rnd]." Make the x-axis range from 0 to 9 in increments of 1. Request "valuelabel." Ask for a font size of "small" or "medsmall." Override the default bar fill color with a color of your choice. Print the bar chart.

D. Consider the evidence you obtained in parts B and C. Based on your analysis, whose assessment is more accurate? (circle one)

Pundit 1's   Pundit 2's

Citing *specific evidence* obtained in parts B and C, explain your reasoning._____

_____

_____

_____

_____

_____

_____

2. (Dataset: gss2012. Variables: attend, [aw=gssw], [fw=gssw_rnd].) The General Social Survey provides a rich array of variables that permit scholars to study religiosity in the adult population. Dataset gss2012 contains attend, a 9-point ordinal scale that measures how often respondents attend religious services. Values can range from 1 ("Never attend") to 9 ("Attend more than once a week").

A. The shell of a bar chart is given below. The categories of attend appear along the horizontal axis. What would a bar chart of attend look like if this variable had maximum dispersion? Sketch inside the axes a bar chart that would depict maximum dispersion.

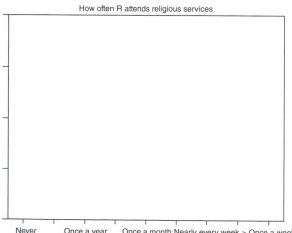

How often R attends religious services

Never   Once a year   Once a month Nearly every week > Once a week
   < Once/year   Several times/year 2–3 times/month   Every week

B. What would a bar chart of attend look like if this variable had no dispersion? Sketch inside the axes a bar chart that would depict no dispersion.

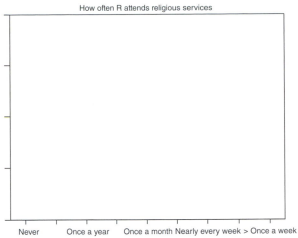

How often R attends religious services

Never   Once a year   Once a month Nearly every week > Once a week
  < Once/year   Several times/year 2–3 times/month   Every week

C. Perform a tabulate analysis of attend. Complete the following table.

Services	Freq.*	Percent	Cum.
Never	496.97	?	?
<Once/yr	97.77	?	?
Once/yr	255.93	?	?
Sev times/yr	212.61	?	?
Once/mo	133.36	?	?
2-3 times/mo	174.08	?	?
Nrly evry wk	79.34	?	?
Every wk	388.04	?	?
>Once/wk	127.90	?	100.00
Total	1,966	100.00	

*Weighted frequencies rounded to two decimal places

D. Obtain and print a bar chart of attend. (Remember that attend is a discrete variable.) Be sure to specify "[fw=gssw_rnd]." Make the x-axis range from 1 to 9 in increments of 1. Request "valuelabel." Ask for a font size of "small" and an angle of 45 degrees. Override the default bar fill color.

E. Based on your examination of the frequency distribution,

the mode of attend is _____.

the median of attend is _____.

F. Based on your examination of the frequency distribution and bar chart, you would conclude that attend has (circle one)

low dispersion.   high dispersion.

3. (Data set: gss2012. Variables: science_quiz, [aw=gssw], [fw=gssw_rnd].) The late Carl Sagan once lamented, "We live in a society exquisitely dependent on science and technology, in which hardly anyone knows anything about science and technology." This is a rather pessimistic assessment of the scientific acumen of ordinary Americans. Sagan seemed to be suggesting that the average level of scientific knowledge is quite low and that most people would fail even the simplest test of scientific facts.

Dataset gss2012 contains science_quiz, which was created from 10 true-false questions testing respondents' knowledge of basic scientific facts. Values on science_quiz range from 0 (the respondent did not answer any of the questions correctly) to 10 (the respondent correctly answered all 10).[9]

A. Obtain a frequency distribution of science_quiz. Fill in the table that follows.

science_quiz	Freq.*	Percent	Cum.
0	6.86	?	?
1	13.15	?	?
2	18.01	?	?
3	37.28	?	?
4	69.69	?	?
5	67.05	?	?
6	65.81	?	?
7	91.97	?	?
8	53.98	?	?
9	56.03	?	?
10	28.17	?	100.0
Total	508	100.0	

*Weighted frequencies rounded to two decimal places.

B. Run summary with the detail option.

C. Use histogram to create a bar chart for science_quiz. Specify appropriate parameters for graphing options fcolor and xlabel. Print the bar chart.

D. Examine the frequency distribution, the summary statistics, and the bar chart. Based on your analysis, science_quiz has a mean equal to _____, a median equal to _____, and a skewness equal to _____.

E. Exercise your judgment. What would be the more accurate measure of science_quiz's central tendency: the mean or the median? (circle one)

mean   median

F. Briefly explain your choice in E.

_____

_____

_____

G. According to conventional academic standards, any science_quiz score of 5 or lower would be an F, a failing grade. A score of 6 would be a grade of D, a 7 would be a C, an 8 a B, and scores of 9 or 10 would be an A. Based on these standards, about what percentage of people got passing grades on science_quiz? (circle one)

About 30 percent   About 40 percent   About 50 percent   About 60 percent

What percentage got a B or better? (circle one)

About 30 percent   About 40 percent   About 50 percent   About 60 percent

4. (Dataset: world. Variables: women13, country.) (Note: This exercise introduces a new skill not covered in the chapter.) What percentage of members of the U.S. House of Representatives are women? In 2013 the number was 17.8 percent, according to the Inter-Parliamentary Union, an international organization of parliaments.[10] How does the United States compare to other democratic countries? Is 17.8 percent comparatively low, comparatively high, or average for a typical national legislature?

A. World contains women13, the percentage of women in the lower house of the legislature in each of 109 democracies. Perform a summary analysis (with detail) on women13. Fill in the table that follows.

Statistics for women13	
Mean	?
Median	?
Skewness	?

B. Examine the results of the summary analysis. Recall that 17.8 percent of US House members are women. Now, consider the following statement: "The percentage of women in the US House is about average for a democratic country." Is this statement accurate? Answer yes or no, and explain your reasoning.

_____

_____

_____

C. Suppose a women's advocacy organization vows to support female congressional candidates so that the US House might someday "be ranked among the top one-fourth of democracies in the percentage of female members." According to the percentiles column of the summary analysis, to meet this goal women would need to constitute about what percentage of the House? (circle one)

About 25 percent   About 40 percent   About 45 percent

D. Create a histogram of women13. Because women13 is an interval-level (continuous) variable, specify only the percent option. In xlabel, request that the x-axis range from 0 to 50 in increments of 10. Request a preferred color in fcolor. Print the histogram.

E. Run "sort women13." To obtain a ranked list of countries, from low values of women13 to high values of women13, run the following command, just as you see it here:

list country women13 if women13!=.

This command is very similar to this chapter's guided example, except it adds the logical operator, "if women13!=.," which translates, "if women13 is not equal to missing." (Logical operators like this are discussed in Chapter 5.) Because many countries have missing values on women13, we do not want Stata to include them in the sorted list. The five countries with the lowest percentages of women legislators are

_____

_____

_____

_____

_____

The five countries with the highest percentages of women legislators are

_____

_____

_____

_____

_____

5. (Dataset: states. Variables: defexpen, state.) Here is the conventional political wisdom: Well-positioned members of Congress from a handful of states are successful in getting the federal government to spend revenue in their states—defense-related expenditures, for example. The typical state, by contrast, receives far fewer defense budget dollars.

   A. Suppose you had a variable that measured the amount of defense-related expenditures in each state. The conventional wisdom says that, when you look at how all 50 states are distributed on this variable, a few states would have a high amount of defense spending. Most states, however, would have lower values on this variable.

      If the conventional wisdom is correct, the distribution of defense-related expenditures will have (circle one)

      a negative skew.   no skew.   a positive skew.

      If the conventional wisdom is correct, the mean of defense-related expenditures will be (circle one)

      lower than its median.   the same as its median.   higher than its median.

   B. Dataset states contains the variable defexpen, defense expenditures per capita for each of the 50 states. Perform a summary analysis of defexpen (with detail). Fill in the table that follows.

Statistics for defexpen	
Mean	?
Median	?
Skewness	?

   C. Which is the better measure of central tendency? (circle one)

      mean   median

      Briefly explain your answer._____

      _____

   D. Obtain a histogram of defexpen. Because defexpen is an interval-level (continuous) variable, specify only the percent option. Request x-axis labels that range from 0 to 4500 in increments of 500. Print the histogram.

   E. Based on your analysis, would you say that the conventional wisdom is accurate or inaccurate? (check one)

      ❑ The conventional wisdom is accurate.

      ❑ The conventional wisdom is inaccurate.

F. Use the sort command and the list command to obtain a ranked list of states, from lowest per capita defense spending to highest per capita defense spending. The state with the lowest per capita defense spending is _____, with $_____ per capita. The state with the highest per capita defense spending is _____, with $_____ per capita.

6. (Dataset: states. Variables: blkpct10 hispanic10.) Two demographers are arguing over how best to describe the racial and ethnic composition of the "typical" state.

Demographer 1: "The typical state is 8.25 percent black and 8.20 percent Hispanic."

Demographer 2: "The typical state is 11.26 percent black and 10.61 percent Hispanic."

A. Run summary (with detail) for blkpct10 (the percentage of each state's population that is African American) and hispanic10 (the percentage of each state's population that is Hispanic). (Hint: Stata will permit you to name more than one variable after the sum command: "sum blkpct10 hispanic10, detail.") Record the appropriate statistics for each variable in the table that follows.

	blkpct10	hispanic10
Mean	?	?
Median	?	?
Skewness	?	?

B. Based on your analysis, which demographer is more accurate? (circle one)

Demographer 1   Demographer 2

Write a few sentences explaining your reasoning. _____

_____

_____

_____

C. Run sort and list to obtain information on the percentage of Hispanics.

Which five states have the lowest percentages of Hispanics?

_____

_____

Which five states have the highest percentages of Hispanics?

_____

_____

_____

7. (Dataset: nes2012. Variables: budget_deficit_x, inspre_self, presapp_scale, [aw=nesw], [fw=nesw_rnd].) We frequently describe public opinion by referring to how citizens distribute themselves on a political issue. *Consensus* is a situation in which a large majority, 60–70 percent of the public, holds the same position, or very similar positions, on an issue. *Dissensus* is a situation in which opinion is spread out evenly across all positions on an issue. *Polarization* refers to a configuration of opinion in which people are split between two extreme poles of an issue, with only a few individuals populating the more moderate, middle-of-the-road positions.

In this exercise you will decide whether consensus, dissensus, or polarization best describes public opinion, as measured by three nes2012 variables: Opinions about reducing the federal budget deficit (budget_deficit_x), opinions on whether medical insurance should be provided by the government or by the private sector (inspre_self), and opinions about how well the president is performing his job (presapp_scale). The deficit reduction question is measured on a 7-point scale, from "Favor strongly" (point 1) to "Oppose strongly" (point 7). The medical insurance question also uses a 7-point scale, from "Favor government plan" (point 1) to "Favor private plan" (point 7). Presidential approval is measured on a 6-point scale, from "Disapprove" (point 0) to "Approve" (point 5).

A. Perform a tabulate analysis on budget_deficit_x, inspre_self, presapp_scale. Remember to weight the analyses using nesw. In the tables that follow, write the appropriate percentage next to each question mark.

Favor reducing federal budget deficit	Percentage	Medical insurance scale, self-placement	Percentage
FavStrng	?	GovtPlan	?
FavWeak	?	2	?
FavLean	?	3	?
Neither	?	4	?
OppLean	?	5	?
OppWeak	?	6	?
OppStrng	?	PrvtPlan	?
	100.0		100.0

Presidential approval scale	Percentage
Disappr	?
1	?
2	?
3	?
4	?
Apprv	?
	100.0

B. Examine the percentages you entered in the table above. Of the three issues, which one *most closely approximates* consensus? (circle one)

Favor reducing federal budget deficit   Medical insurance scale, self-placement   Presidential approval scale

Briefly explain your reasoning.

_____

_____

C. Of the three issues, which one *most closely approximates* dissensus? (circle one)

Favor reducing federal budget deficit   Medical insurance scale, self-placement   Presidential approval scale

Briefly explain your reasoning.

_____

_____

D. Of the three issues, which one *most closely approximates* polarization? (circle one)

Favor reducing federal budget deficit	Medical insurance scale, self-placement	Presidential approval scale

Briefly explain your reasoning.

_____

_____

E. Use histogram to create a bar chart of the variable you chose in part D. Remember to use the frequency weight, "[fw=nesw_rnd]." Request appropriate options for fcolor and xlabel. Print the bar chart.

8. (Dataset: nes2012. Variables: congapp_job_x, hseinc_approval_x, [aw=nesw], [fw=nesw_rnd].) Pedantic pontificator claims he has discovered how voters evaluate the performance of House incumbents: "I call it my 'guilt by association' theory. When voters disapprove of the way Congress has been handling its job, they transfer that negative evaluation to their House incumbent. My theory is eminently plausible and surely correct. The distribution of opinions about House incumbents will be very similar to the distribution of opinions about Congress as a whole."

nes2012 contains congapp_job_x, which gauges respondent approval or disapproval of "the way the US Congress has been handling its job." The dataset also has hseinc_approval_x, which measures approval or disapproval of the way each respondent's House incumbent "has been handling his or her job."

A. To test pedantic pontificator's theory, perform a frequencies analysis of congapp_job_x and hseinc_approval_x. Refer to the percent column of the frequency distributions. In the table that follows, write the appropriate percentage next to each question mark.

	Approve/disapprove Congress handling job	Approve/disapprove House incumbent
	percentage	percentage
AppStrng	?	?
AppWeak	?	?
DisappWk	?	?
DisappStr	?	?
Total	100.0	100.0

B. Consider the evidence. Does pedantic pontificator's theory appear to be correct or incorrect? (circle one)

correct   incorrect

Explain your reasoning.

_____

_____

_____

_____

_____

That concludes the exercises for this chapter.

NOTES

1. In this chapter, we will use the terms *dispersion, variation,* and *spread* interchangeably.

2. Unless instructed otherwise, Stata will use a variable's value labels (not its numeric codes) when it displays results. If we wanted Stata to use zodiac's numeric codes, we would enter this command: "tab zodiac [aw=gssw], nolabel." The nolabel option suppresses value labels and instead displays the numeric codes.

3. The mode of age is 55, with 2.72 percent of the cases. Many interval-level variables have multiple modes. That is, several values may "tie" for the distinction of being the most common. Thus, the description of an interval-level variable usually centers on its median and mean, which generally provide more useful information than its mode.

4. Technically, income06 is measured at the ordinal level. However, because this variable has many values, we can treat it as an interval-level variable for illustrative purposes.

5. Many demographic variables are skewed, so their median values rather than their means are often used to give a clearer picture of central tendency. One hears or reads reports, for example, of median family income or the median price of homes in an area.

6. The Statistical Software Components (SSC) archive, which is maintained by Boston College, is provided by http://www .repec.org. According to Stata, the SSC "has become the premier Stata download site for user-written software on the web." For more information, type "help ssc."

7. Palette_all was written by Adrian Mander, version 1.01, September 27, 2006. In Stata, you can use RGB triplet coding to request custom colors. For example, the statement "fcolor ("0 0 255")" produces the same color as "fcolor (blue)." The statement "fcolor("93 97 255")" produces the particularly stunning blue offered in the SPSS color palette. For more information on Stata colors, see Vince Wiggins's Stata Listserv post: http://www.stata.com/statalist/archive/2003–02/ msg00587.html.

8. A related Stata command, gsort, permits the user to sort in ascending or descending order.

9. Science_quiz was created by summing the number of correct responses to the following questions (all are in true-false format, except for earthsun): The center of the Earth is very hot (General Social Survey variable, hotcore); it is the father's gene that decides whether the baby is a boy or a girl (boyorgrl); electrons are smaller than atoms (electron); the universe began with a huge explosion (bigbang); the continents on which we live have been moving their locations for millions of years and will continue to move in the future (condrift); human beings, as we know them today, developed from earlier species of animals (evolved); does the Earth go around the sun, or does the sun go around the Earth (earthsun); all radioactivity is manmade (radioact); lasers work by focusing sound waves (lasers); antibiotics kill viruses as well as bacteria (viruses).

10. See Inter-Parliamentary Union web site (http://www.ipu.org/english/home.htm).

3

Transforming Variables

Commands Covered

recode, generate ( )	Creates a new variable by translating or combining codes of an existing variable
generate, recode( )	Creates a new variable by combining codes of an existing variable
xtile, nquantiles ( )	Creates a new variable by collapsing an existing variable into categories containing approximately equal numbers of cases
generate	Creates a new variable from the codes of one or more existing variables
tabulate, generate ( )	Creates a set of indicator variables from the codes of an existing variable
label variable	Labels a variable
label define	Creates and names a label that connects a set of numeric codes to a set of value labels
label values	Labels the values of a variable using a previously defined label
drop	Deletes variables from a dataset
aorder	Changes the order in which variables appear in a dataset

Political researchers sometimes must modify the variables they wish to analyze. Generally speaking, there are three situations in which variable transformations become desirable or necessary. In the first situation, a researcher may want to collapse a variable, combining its values or codes into a smaller number of useful categories. For categorical variables, those measured by a handful of nominal or ordinal values, the recode command accomplishes this. Although the recode command may also be used to collapse interval-level variables, you might prefer the simplicity of another procedure—the generate command with the recode function. Another command, xtile, is a quick and efficient way to collapse an interval-level variable into a set of ordinal categories containing equal numbers of cases. In a second situation, a dataset may contain several variables that provide similar measures of the same concept. The researcher may wish to combine the codes of different variables, creating a new and more precise measure. Stata's generate command is designed for this task. In a third set of (more specialized) circumstances, the researcher may wish to transform a nominal or ordinal variable into a set of new indicator variables. In order to graph relationships between categorical variables (covered in Chapter 4), indicator variables are required. Stata's omnicompetent tabulate command, with the right option, will create indicator variables.

With this arsenal of Stata commands at your disposal, you can modify any variable at any level of measurement—nominal, ordinal, or interval. But you should exercise vigilance and care. Here are three rules.

1. Before transforming a variable, obtain a frequency distribution.

2. After transforming a variable, check your work.

3. Properly label any new variables that you create.

We will follow these rules as we work through several examples. The variables you modify or create in this chapter (and in this chapter's exercises) will become permanent variables in the datasets. After you complete each guided example and each exercise, be sure to save the dataset. Open a new Do-file, and let's create some new variables.

TRANSFORMING CATEGORICAL VARIABLES

Dataset nes2012 contains dem_marital, a demographic variable (hence, the "dem" prefix) that measures marital status in six categories: married: spouse present (code 1), married: spouse absent (code 2), widowed (code 3), divorced (code 4), separated (code 5), and never married (code 6). This is a perfectly fine variable, and we do not want to alter or destroy it. But suppose we wish to use dem_marital to create a new variable that collapses respondents into two categories: married (codes 1 and 2) or not married (codes 3 through 6). The recode command will accomplish this goal. Following the first rule of data transformations, we will run tabulate on dem_marital, which will tell us what the new, collapsed variable should look like. When obtaining statistics for variables in nes2012 (and gss2012), make sure to include the weight variable. (However, certain data transformation commands, including recode and generate, do not require weights.)

```
. tab dem_marital [aw=nesw]

          PRE: Marital status |      Freq.      Percent        Cum.
  --------------------------------+----------------------------------------
       1. Married: spouse present |   3,043.5926       51.53       51.53
  2. Married: spouse absent {VOL} |    319.946103        5.42       56.95
                      3. Widowed  |    628.722498       10.65       67.60
                      4. Divorced |   347.4509175        5.88       73.48
                     5. Separated |   1,042.55418       17.65       91.13
                 6. Never married |    523.7337199        8.87      100.00
  --------------------------------+----------------------------------------
                           Total  |      5,906         100.00
```

According to the frequency distribution, 51.53 + 5.42, or 56.95 percent, of the sample is married. This means that the rest of the sample, 43.05 percent, must fall into the other four values of dem_marital. The two numbers, 56.95 and 43.05, will help us verify that we performed the recode correctly.

Now let's use dem_marital to create a new variable, named "married." Respondents who are married will be coded 1 and labeled "Yes" on married. Unmarried respondents will be coded 0 and labeled "No." Any respondents who have missing values on dem_marital will have a missing value on married. Consider this recoding protocol:

Marital status	Existing numeric code (dem_marital)	New numeric code (married)
Married: spouse present	1	1
Married: spouse absent	2	1
Widowed	3	0
Divorced	4	0
Separated	5	0
Never married	6	0
(missing)	.	.

We know the name of the existing variable (dem_marital) and the name of the new variable (married), and we know the rule for transforming the existing numeric codes into the new numeric codes: existing codes 1 and 2 = new code 1; existing codes 3 through 6 = new code 0. And note that any respondent who has a missing value on dem_marital (which appears as a "." in the dataset) will be assigned a missing value on married. The general syntax for the recode command is as follows:

recode *old_var* (*old_code(s)* = *new_code* "*value label*"), gen(*new_var*)

Applying this syntax to the marital-into-married recode gives the following:

```
recode dem_marital (1/2=1 "Yes") (3/6=0 "No") (.=.), gen(married)
```

The first part of the syntax tells Stata how to translate or combine the original codes. For example, the statement, (1/2=1 "Yes"), says that each respondent coded 1 or 2 on dem_marital is to be coded 1 on the new variable, and that the new numeric code is to be labeled "Yes." The "gen" part of the syntax tells Stata the name of the new variable. The statement, "gen(married)," instructs Stata to create or generate a new variable, named married, and to add this new variable to the dataset. By specifying this option, we ensure that the original variable, dem_marital, remains unchanged.

Here are five noteworthy facts about the recode command. First, Stata's syntax for combining codes is a bit eccentric. In combining codes, be sure to use a slash (as in "3/6") and not a dash ("3–6"). Second, it is a good practice always to use quotation marks to enclose the new variable's value labels. Quotation marks will always work and will never annoy Stata.[1] Third, whenever you run recode, *always generate a new variable.* This is important. Stata will not second-guess you. If you run recode without generating a new variable, Stata will replace the existing variable, destroying its codes. Fourth, make sure to recode missing values on the original variable into missing values on the new variable. That is, the recode syntax should always include the argument, "(.=.)." The fifth fact was mentioned earlier: For recode (and for generate), do not use the weight variable.

Back to the recode at hand. Type and run the recode command (as shown above). Stata reports an error-free run:

```
.    recode dem_marital (1/2=1 "Yes") (3/6=0 "No") (.=.), gen(married)
(3073 differences between dem_marital and married)
```

But did the recode work correctly? This is where the second rule of data transformations—the check-your-work rule—takes effect. Always run tab on the newly created variable to ensure that you did things right. Run the command "tab married [aw=nesw]":

```
.    tab married [aw=nesw]
```

RECODE of dem_marital (PRE: Marital status)	Freq.	Percent	Cum.
No	2,542.4613	43.05	43.05
Yes	3,363.5387	56.95	100.00
Total	5,906	100.00	

Yes, our new variable classifies 56.95 percent as married and 43.05 percent as unmarried. So the new variable, married, checks out.

However, notice the clunky default variable label that Stata has used: "RECODE of dem_marital (PRE: Marital status)." Let's follow the third rule of data transformations and give married a better label, such as "Is R married?" The general syntax for labeling a variable is this:

label var *varname* "*variable label*"

Relabel married by typing and running the following command:

```
label var married "Is R Married?"
```

Stata says nothing, which generally is a good sign. Just to make sure, run tab on married one last time:

```
.  tab married [aw=nesw]
```

Is R Married?	Freq.	Percent	Cum.
No	2,542.4613	43.05	43.05
Yes	3,363.5387	56.95	100.00
Total	5,906	100.00	

All is well. Before going to the next guided example, save nes2012.

TRANSFORMING INTERVAL VARIABLES

Once you become familiar with the recode command, you will probably find yourself using it to collapse any variable at any level of measurement. That's fine. The existing variable may be nominal level, such as marital. Or it may be ordinal level. For example, it might make sense to collapse four response categories such as "strongly agree/agree/disagree/strongly disagree" into two, "agree/disagree." At other times the original variable is interval-level, such as age or income. Recode will always work. With Stata, however, there is usually more than one way to accomplish a desired goal. When working with interval-level variables, the generate command with the recode function is a powerful and parsimonious alternative to recode. In this section, we demonstrate the generate command with the recode function. (Another command, xtile, can be used to collapse a variable into categories containing approximately equal numbers of cases. See "A Closer Look" for a discussion of the xtile command.)

Dataset nes2012 contains the variable ftgr_fedgov, which measures respondents' attitudes toward "the federal government in Washington." Ftgr_fedgov is one of the many "feeling thermometer" scales used by the American National Election Studies to record respondents' ratings of groups, political personalities, and other political objects. Scale scores can range from 0 (cold or negative feelings) to 100 (warm or positive feelings). Run "tab ftgr_fedgov [aw=nesw]" to find out how people distributed themselves along this scale:

```
tab ftgr_fedgov [aw=nesw]
```

POST: Feeling thermometer: FEDERAL GOVERNMENT IN WASHINGTON	Freq.	Percent	Cum.
0	511.808345	9.39	9.39
1	9.99229394	0.18	9.57
2	11.43303583	0.21	9.78
3	4.713244244	0.09	9.87
4	8.60530972	0.16	10.03
5	33.3130525	0.61	10.64
6	.526563547	0.01	10.65
7	.93560128	0.02	10.67
9	.149760276	0.00	10.67
10	89.7097092	1.65	12.32
12	.407636254	0.01	12.32
15	448.9385628	8.24	20.56
16	.26638508	0.00	20.57
20	55.9955274	1.03	21.59
22	1.66067734	0.03	21.62
23	1.844574147	0.03	21.66
25	50.2064319	0.92	22.58
27	2.77286766	0.05	22.63
30	608.18349	11.16	33.79 ←———
32	.786741983	0.01	33.80
33	3.38282033	0.06	33.86
34	1.20238679	0.02	33.89
35	59.3723414	1.09	34.98
38	1.562071769	0.03	35.00
39	.452884685	0.01	35.01
40	979.92764	17.98	52.99
42	.9322977478	0.02	53.01
43	6.00762944	0.11	53.12
44	1.91364796	0.04	53.16
45	84.1072135	1.54	54.70
47	5.67987883	0.10	54.80
48	1.85918977	0.03	54.84
49	3.38582353	0.06	54.90
50	832.4816407	15.27	70.17 ←———
51	2.73652869	0.05	70.22
52	1.54395241	0.03	70.25
53	2.33539939	0.04	70.30
55	51.062748	0.94	71.23
58	1.04531866	0.02	71.25
59	2.55673623	0.05	71.30
60	660.382554	12.12	83.42
61	1.52663381	0.03	83.44
62	.358483653	0.01	83.45
65	52.76406892	0.97	84.42
67	1.10318064	0.02	84.44
68	2.18904268	0.04	84.48
69	2.011652967	0.04	84.52
70	410.9456028	7.54	92.06
73	.229745874	0.00	92.06
75	66.9353353	1.23	93.29
77	.61696027	0.01	93.30
78	.87293421	0.02	93.32
80	54.2479573	1.00	94.31
84	2.75675024	0.05	94.36
85	214.443502	3.93	98.30
87	.372798963	0.01	98.30
88	.081987745	0.00	98.31
89	.6004425961	0.01	98.32
90	11.4021027	0.21	98.53
95	1.17996282	0.02	98.55
97	.502237488	0.01	98.56
100	78.6781028	1.44	100.00

A Closer Look   The xtile Command[1]

If you want to quickly collapse an interval-level variable into a few manageable categories containing roughly equal numbers of cases, then the xtile command (with the nquantiles option) is the best way to go. The syntax for the xtile command is as follows:

xtile *new_var* = *old_var*, nquantiles (#)

Stata will create a new variable by collapsing an existing variable into # categories, in which "#" is a user-specified number. Here, for example, is the frequency distribution of nes2012 variable, incgroup_prepost, a measure of respondents' incomes:

```
tab    incgroup_prepost [aw=nesw]
```

CASI/WEB: PREPOST SUMMARY- Family income	Freq.	Percent	Cum.
01. Under $5,000	546.851074	9.57	9.57
02. $5,000-$9,999	157.811151	2.76	12.33
03. $10,000-$12,499	170.128727	2.98	15.30
04. $12,500-$14,999	69.9629767	1.22	16.53
05. $15,000-$17,499	154.170095	2.70	19.22
06. $17,500-$19,999	95.0206837	1.66	20.88
07. $20,000-$22,499	191.985582	3.36	24.24
08. $22,500-$24,999	100.307337	1.75	26.00
09. $25,000-$27,499	221.9156101	3.88	29.88
10. $27,500-$29,999	81.3587323	1.42	31.30
11. $30,000-$34,999	333.626124	5.84	37.14
12. $35,000-$39,999	270.411697	4.73	41.87
13. $40,000-$44,999	273.026646	4.78	46.64
14. $45,000-$49,999	173.913173	3.04	49.68
15. $50,000-$54,999	320.4841944	5.61	55.29
16. $55,000-$59,999	145.462289	2.54	57.84
17. $60,000-$64,999	253.487026	4.43	62.27
18. $65,000-$69,999	174.244378	3.05	65.32
19. $70,000-$74,999	190.063327	3.32	68.64
20. $75,000-$79,999	202.248641	3.54	72.18
21. $80,000-$89,999	297.438588	5.20	77.38
22. $90,000-$99,999	203.704221	3.56	80.94
23. $100,000-$109,999	262.490842	4.59	85.54
24. $110,000-$124,999	188.234528	3.29	88.83
25. $125,000-$149,999	217.230201	3.80	92.63
26. $150,000-$174,999	145.74045	2.55	95.18
27. $175,000-$249,999	171.631134	3.00	98.18
28. $250,000 or more	104.050571	1.82	100.00
Total	5,717	100.00	

The following command will create a new variable, income3, by collapsing incgroup_prepost into three ordinal categories:

```
xtile income3 = incgroup_prepost [aw=nesw], nquantiles(3)
```

(continued)

Suppose we want to use ftgr_fedgov to create a new variable, ftgr_fedgov3, by classifying respondents into three ordinal categories—those who rated the federal government at 30 degrees or lower, those giving

A Closer Look   The xtile Command   *(continued)*

After running "tab income3 [aw=nesw]," we get the following:

```
.  tab  income3 [aw=nesw]

3 quantiles
         of
incgroup_pr
     epost           Freq.        Percent           Cum.

         1      2,123.1381          37.14          37.14
         2      1,801.0927          31.50          68.64
         3      1,792.7692          31.36         100.00

     Total          5,717         100.00
```

Similarly, the following command would create a four-category variable from incgroup_prepost:

```
xtile income4 = incgroup_prepost [aw=nesw], nquantiles(4)

.  xtile income4 = incgroup_prepost [aw=nesw], nquantiles(4)

.  tab  income4 [aw=nesw]

4 quantiles
         of
incgroup_pr
     epost           Freq.        Percent           Cum.

         1      1,486.2376          26.00          26.00
         2      1,674.7362          29.29          55.29
         3      1,262.9442          22.09          77.38
         4      1,293.0819          22.62         100.00

     Total          5,717         100.00
```

Stata provides descriptive variable labels (for example, "4 quantiles of incgroup_prepost"), but of course you will probably wish to supply value labels for the numeric codes that Stata has assigned to each category of the new variable.

```
label define income3_label 1 "Low" 2 "Mid" 3 "High"
label define income4_label 1 "Low" 2 "MidLow" 3 "MidHi" 4 "High"
label values income3 income3_label
label values income4 income4_label
```

---

[1] The xtile command is a special application of the pctile command. Type "help pctile" for more information.

ratings of 31 through 50, and those who rated the government at 51 or higher. The two cumulative percentage markers (indicated with arrows) will help us verify that we performed the variable transformation correctly: 33.79 percent of the cases will fall into the first category, and 70.17 percent will fall into the first *and* second categories of the transformed variable.

Now consider the general syntax of the generate command with the recode function:

generate *new_var* = recode(*old_var, max_1, max_2, . . . max_n*)

One types the generate command, followed by a name for the new, collapsed variable and an equals sign. One then types "recode" followed immediately by a left parenthesis. *Do not leave a space between the word "recode" and the left parenthesis.* The name of the original variable is the first entry inside the parentheses, followed by a comma. The values of the original variable that define the *upper boundaries* of the collapsed categories come next, separated by commas.

Apply these syntactical rules to the ftgr_fedgov transformation. The group giving the government the coldest ratings has a maximum value of 30 on the scale, so the first upper boundary is 30. The middle group is bracketed by 31 at the low end and 50 at the high end, so the second upper boundary is 50. Finally, the group giving the warmest ratings has a maximum value of 100, making 100 the third upper boundary. Therefore, the command is: "gen ftgr_fedgov3=recode(ftgr_fedgov, 30, 50, 100)." Type and run the command, and let's see if Stata likes it:

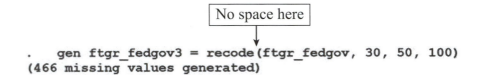

```
.    gen ftgr_fedgov3 = recode(ftgr_fedgov, 30, 50, 100)
(466 missing values generated)
```

Seems fine. Check your work of running "tab ftgr_fedgov3 [aw=nesw]":

```
. tab ftgr_fedgov3 [aw=nesw]
```

ftgr_fedgov 3	Freq.	Percent	Cum.
30	1,841.4631	33.79	33.79
50	1,983.0542	36.39	70.17
100	1,625.4827	29.83	100.00
Total	5,450	100.00	

The cumulative percent markers, 33.79 percent and 70.17 percent, are just where they are supposed to be. Using the label variable command, give ftgr_fedgov3 the name, "Feeling thermo: Federal Govt":

```
label var ftgr_fedgov3 "Feeling thermo: Federal Govt"
```

Now, notice that Stata has adopted the boundary maximums ("30," "50," and "100") as default numeric codes for the categories of the new variable. These are not terribly informative codes. Before proceeding to the next example, we will use ftgr_fedgov3 to acquire a new skill—defining and assigning labels to the values of a newly created variable.

THE LABEL DEFINE AND LABEL VALUES COMMANDS

Suppose we want to use the label "Low" for numeric code 30, "Medium" for numeric code 50, and "High" for code 100. What command will instruct Stata to apply these labels to ftgr_fedgov3's numeric codes? Actually, two commands are required. The first command, label define, creates and names a label that connects a set of numeric codes to a set of value labels. The second command, label values, tells Stata to label the values of a variable using a previously defined label. Confused? Welcome to Stata's oddly inefficient way of dealing with labels.[2]

First, run label define. The syntax of the label define command is as follows:

label define *label_name code_1* "*label 1*" *code_2* "*label 2*" . . . *code_n* "*label n*"

Accordingly, the following command defines a label, which we will name "ftgr_fedgov3_label," that connects the numeric codes with the desired value labels:

```
label define ftgr_fedgov3_label 30 "Low" 50 "Medium" 100 "High"
```

Now run label values. The label values command conforms to this syntax:

label values *varname label_name*

The following command tells Stata to label the numeric codes of ftgr_fedgov3 using ftgr_fedgov3_label:

```
label values ftgr_fedgov3 ftgr_fedgov3_label
```

Did all of our typing pay off? Run "tab ftgr_fedgov3 [aw=nesw]":

```
.  tab ftgr_fedgov3 [aw=nesw]
```

Feeling thermo: Federal Govt	Freq.	Percent	Cum.
Low	1,841.4631	33.79	33.79
Medium	1,983.0542	36.39	70.17
High	1,625.4827	29.83	100.00
Total	5,450	100.00	

A flawless set of Stata labels is a thing of uncommon beauty. Save the dataset, and let's move to the next example.

CREATING AN ADDITIVE INDEX

We just demonstrated one of the several ways in which the generate command can create new variables. Let's now consider another (and perhaps more typical) use of generate—to create a simple *additive index* from similarly coded variables. Consider a simple illustration. Suppose you have three variables, each of which measures whether or not a respondent engaged in each of the following activities during an election campaign: tried to convince somebody how to vote, put a campaign bumper sticker on his or her car, or gave money to one of the candidates or parties. Each variable is identically coded: 0 if the respondent did not engage in the activity and 1 if he or she did. Now, each of these variables is interesting in its own right, but you might want to add them together, creating an overall measure of campaigning: People who did not engage in any of these activities would end up with a value of 0 on the new variable; those who engaged in one activity, a code of 1; two activities, a code of 2; and a code of 3 for respondents who engaged in all three activities.

Here are some suggested guidelines to follow in using generate to create a simple additive index. First, before running generate, make sure that each of the variables is identically coded. In the above illustration, if the "bumper sticker" variable were coded 1 for no and 2 for yes, and the other variables were coded 0 and 1, the resulting additive index would be incorrect. Second, make sure that the variables are all coded in the same *direction*. If the "contribute money" variable were coded 0 for yes and 1 for no, and the other variables were coded 0 for no and 1 for yes, the additive index would again be incorrect.[3] Third, after running generate, obtain a frequency distribution of the newly created variable. Upon examining the frequency distribution, you may decide to run recode to collapse the new variable into more useful categories. Suppose, for example, that we add the three campaign acts together and get this frequency distribution for the new variable:

Additive Index: Number of Campaign Acts		
Value label	Value	Percentage of sample
Engaged in none	0	60
Engaged in one	1	25
Engaged in two	2	13
Engaged in three	3	2
Total		100

Clearly, it looks like a recode run may be in order—collapsing respondents coded 2 or 3 into the same category.

These points are best understood firsthand. The 2012 American National Election Study included a number of questions about gay rights. Respondents were asked whether they supported antidiscrimination laws (gay_disc), gays serving in the military (gay_mil), gay adoption (gay_adopt), and gay marriage (gay_marry). For each of these variables, respondents who supported the gay rights position are coded 1; those giving other responses are coded 0. We are going to add these variables together, using the expression "gay_disc + gay_mil + gay_adopt + gay_marry." Think about this expression for a moment. Perhaps a respondent does not support any of the gay rights measures. What would be his or her score on an additive index? It would be $0 + 0 + 0 + 0 = 0$. Another, strong gay rights supporter might favor all the policies. For that respondent, $1 + 1 + 1 + 1 = 4$. Thus, we know from the start that the values of the new variable will range from 0 to 4.

We will ask Stata to generate a new variable, which we will name gay_rights, by summing the codes of gay_disc, gay_mil, gay_adopt, and gay_marry. In the Do-file editor, type and run this expression:

```
generate gay_rights =  gay_disc + gay_mil + gay_adopt + gay_marry
```

Stata runs the command and deposits our new variable, gay_rights, at the bottom of the Variables window. What does the new variable look like? To find out, run "tab gay_rights [aw=nesw]":

```
.  generate gay_rights = gay_disc+ gay_mil+ gay_adopt+ gay_marry
(3098 missing values generated)

.  tab  gay_rights [aw=nesw]

 gay_rights |       Freq.     Percent        Cum.
------------+-----------------------------------
          0 |   585.446541       20.78       20.78
          1 |  450.9709153       16.00       36.78
          2 |   463.784678       16.46       53.24
          3 |    490.59108       17.41       70.65
          4 |  827.206785       29.35      100.00
------------+-----------------------------------
      Total |       2,818      100.00
```

This is an interesting variable. Although the strongest pro–gay rights position (a value of 4) is the mode of the distribution (with 29.35 percent of the cases), a substantial minority of respondents did not support any of the policies (20.78 percent in value 0). Code 2—yes to two of the questions, no to two of the questions—is the median. You may want to analyze this variable later. Give gay_rights a descriptive variable label, such as "Gay Rights Support":

```
label var gay_rights "Gay Rights Support"
```

Before moving on, use gay_rights to exercise a recently acquired skill, defining and labeling the values of a new variable. Using the label define command, create a label that connects numeric code 0 on gay_rights with value label "Low," code 1 with "MedLow," code 2 with "Mid," code 3 with "MedHi," and code 4 with "High":

```
label define gay_lab 0 "Low" 1 "MedLow" 2 "Mid" 3 "MedHi" 4 "High"
```

Now run label values, instructing Stata to apply the new label to numeric codes:

```
label values gay_rights gay_lab
```

Check your work by running "tab gay_rights [aw=nesw]":

```
.  tab  gay_rights [aw=nesw]
```

Gay Rights Support	Freq.	Percent	Cum.
Low	585.446541	20.78	20.78
MedLow	450.9709153	16.00	36.78
Mid	463.784678	16.46	53.24
MedHi	490.59108	17.41	70.65
High	827.206785	29.35	100.00
Total	2,818	100.00	

Well, maybe Stata's two-command system for labeling a variable's values isn't so bad after all.

CREATING INDICATOR VARIABLES

As you are well aware by now, by default the tabulate command will produce a frequency distribution of a variable. In Chapter 4 you will use other applications of tabulate to produce cross-tabulations and perform mean comparison analyses. Frequency distributions, cross-tabulations, and mean comparisons are standard forms of description and analysis that you will use in just about every research question you address. Stata's tabulate, the "command that does it all," also can be used—in specialized situations—to create new variables from existing variables.

Consider penalty_favopp_x, a four-category ordinal variable tapping strength of support for (or opposition to) capital punishment. Respondents can "Approve strongly" (coded 1), "Approve not strongly" (coded 2), "Disapprove not strongly" (coded 4), or "Disapprove strongly" (coded 5). A tabulate run shows how respondents distributed themselves on this issue:

```
. tab penalty_favopp_x [aw=nesw]
```

PRE: SUMMARY- Favor death penalty	Freq.	Percent	Cum.
1. Approve strongly	3,075.8183	53.55	53.55
2. Approve not strongly	1,137.3455	19.80	73.35
4. Disapprove not strongly	709.913831	12.36	85.71
5. Disapprove strongly	820.922305	14.29	100.00
Total	5,744	100.00	

Suppose that we want to use penalty_favopp_x to create a new variable. We would like this new variable to be coded 1 for the 53.55 percent of the sample who "Approve strongly," and coded 0 for individuals who gave any other response—the 46.45 percent who "Approve not strongly," "Disapprove not strongly," or

"Disapprove strongly." Again, we could run recode. But here is a quicker way. Add the generate option to "tab penalty_favopp_x [aw=w]":

```
tab penalty_favopp_x [aw=nesw], gen(deathdum)
```

Running this command produces a (by now familiar) frequency distribution of penalty_favopp_x in the Results window. But scroll to the bottom of the Variables window and see what else Stata has done (Figure 3-1). There you will find four new variables, each named sequentially and according to deathdum, the name "stem" we supplied (as indicated by the arrow in the command line above) in the generate option: deathdum1, deathdum2, deathdum3, and deathdum4. What do these new variables measure? The first variable, deathdum1, takes on a value of 1 for all respondents falling into the lowest numeric code of deathpen, and a value of 0 for all respondents not falling into the lowest code. Because the lowest code of penalty_favopp_x is the value for "Approve strongly," Stata assigned a code of 1 to respondents in this category, and a code of 0 to everybody else. Stata then moved to the next-highest numeric code of penalty_favopp_x (code 2, "Approve not strongly") and created a second variable, deathdum2, which assumes a value of 1 for individuals who gave the "Approve not strongly" response and a value of 0 for all other respondents. Stata generated deathdum3 and deathdum4 in the same way, assigning codes of 1 ("Disapprove not strongly") or 0 (all other responses) for deathdum3, and assigning codes of 1 ("Disapprove strongly") or 0 (all other responses) for deathdum4. Go ahead and run this command: "tab deathdum1 [aw=nesw]":

```
. tab deathdum1 [aw=nesw]
```

penalty_fav opp_x==1. Approve strongly	Freq.	Percent	Cum.
0	2,668.1817	46.45	46.45
1	3,075.8183	53.55	100.00
Total	5,744	100.00	

These results show that the percentage of respondents falling into code 1 of the newly generated deathdum1—the "Approve strongly" respondents—matches the percentage of respondents who fall into the "Approve strongly" category of the original variable, 53.55 percent. And notice that Stata has supplied a useful variable label for deathdum1: "penalty_favopp_x==Approve strongly." Thankfully, we won't need to change the variable label or create value labels.

Stata uses the term *indicator variables* for variables such as these—variables that are coded 1 for cases falling into a specific value and coded 0 for cases not falling into that value. Indicator variables, also called *dummy variables* or *binary variables,* play key roles in graphing and analyzing complex relationships. In the chapters that follow, you will be making frequent use of the tabulate command with the generate option.

The ease with which Stata generates indicator variables has one small disadvantage: Datasets tend to become overpopulated with superfluous variables. Certainly we want deathdum1 to become a permanent variable in the dataset. But we really have no use for deathdum2, deathdum3, and deathdum4. Let's perform two housekeeping chores. First, use the drop command to get rid of the unwanted variables:

```
drop deathdum2 deathdum3 deathdum4
```

Figure 3-1 Creating Indicator Variables

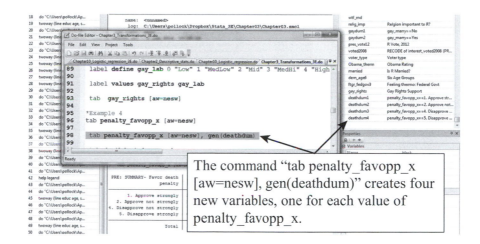

Stata deletes the variables without comment. All right, now we will realphabetize the variable names in the Variable window. In the Command window, type and run the command:

aorder

Stata puts everything neatly in alphabetical order. Before beginning the exercises, be sure to save the dataset.

EXERCISES

For the exercises in this chapter, you will use gss2012.dta.

1. (Dataset: gss2012. Variables: polviews, [aw=gssw].) Dataset gss2012 contains polviews, which measures political ideology—the extent to which individuals "think of themselves as liberal or conservative." Here is how polviews is coded:

Numeric code	Value label
1	ExtrmLib
2	Liberal
3	SlghtLib
4	Moderate
5	SlghtCons
6	Conserv
7	ExtrmCons

A. Run tab on polviews, making sure to use the weight variable, gssw. Eyeball the percent column, and make some rough-and-ready estimates.

The percentage of respondents who are either "extremely liberal," "liberal," or "slightly liberal" is (circle one)

about 17 percent.   about 27 percent.   about 37 percent.

The percentage of respondents who are either "slightly conservative," "conservative," or "extremely conservative" is (circle one)

about 15 percent.   about 25 percent.   about 35 percent.

B. (i) Use recode to create a new variable named polview3. Collapse the three "liberal" codes into one category (coded 1 on polview3), put the "moderates" into their own category (coded 2 on polview3), and collapse the three "conservative" codes into one category (coded 3 on polview3). (Don't forget to recode missing values on polviews into missing values on polview3.) (ii) Using the label var command, give polview3 this label: "Ideology: 3 categories." (iii) Run tab on polview3.

The percentage of respondents who are coded 1 on polview3 is (circle one)

about 17 percent.   about 27 percent.   about 37 percent.

The percentage of respondents who are coded 3 on polview3 is (circle one)

about 15 percent.   about 25 percent.   about 35 percent.

C. (i) Run label define to create a label named "polview3_label." In the label define command, connect the following numeric codes and value labels: 1 "Lib" 2 "Mod" 3 "Cons." (ii) Run label values to label the values of polview3 using polview3_label. (iii) Run tab on polview3. Based on your findings, fill in this table.

Ideology: Three Categories

	Frequency*	Percent	Cumulative Percent
Lib			
Mod			
Cons			100.0
Total		100.0	

*Round weighted frequencies to two decimal places.

2. (Dataset: gss2012. Variables: Variables: mslm_col2, mslm_lib2, mslm_spk2, [aw=gssw].) Dataset gss2012 contains three variables that gauge tolerance toward "anti-American Muslim clergymen"—whether they should be allowed to teach in college (mslm_col2), whether their books should be removed from the library (mslm_lib2), and whether they should be allowed to preach hatred of the United States (mslm_spk2). For each variable, a less-tolerant response is coded 0, and a more-tolerant response is coded 1.

A. Imagine creating an additive index from these three variables. The additive index would have scores that range between a score of _____ and a score of _____.

B. Suppose a respondent takes the more-tolerant position on two questions and the less-tolerant position on the third question. This respondent would have a score of _____.

C. Use generate to create an additive index from mslm_col2, mslm_lib2, and mslm_spk2. Name the new variable muslim_tol. Run tab on muslim_tol. Referring to your output, fill in the table that follows.

muslim_tol		
Score on muslim_tol	Frequency*	Percent
?	?	?
?	?	?
?	?	?
?	?	?
Total	?	100.0

*Round weighted frequencies to two decimal places.

D. In this chapter, you learned to use generate with the recode function. Recall that you run this command by telling Stata, in the recode expression, the upper boundaries of the range of codes you want to combine. (i) Use generate with the recode function to create a new variable, muslim_tol3, from muslim_tol. Keep the least tolerant group in one category (upper boundary, 0), combine the two middle categories (upper boundary, 2), and keep the most tolerant group in one category (upper boundary, 3). (ii) Run tab on muslim_tol3 to make sure that the percentages check out.

E. (i) Label muslim_tol3 with the following label: "Tolerance twrd Muslim clergy." (ii) Run label define to create the label, muslimtol3_label, using this syntax: label define muslimtol3_label 0 "Low" 2 "Mid" 3 "High." (iii) Run label values to label the values of muslim_tol3 using muslimtol3_label. (iv) Run tab on muslim_tol3. Print the frequency table.

3. (Dataset: gss2012. Variables: rincom06, [aw=gssw].) In this chapter you learned to use the xtile command to collapse an nes2012 measure of income into three roughly equal ordinal categories. In this exercise you will use xtile to collapse a similar variable from gss2012, rincom06. You will collapse rincom06 into rincom06_3, a three-category ordinal measure of respondents' incomes.

A. For guidance, refer back to this chapter's "A Closer Look" box on pages 42–43. Run xtile, using rincom06 to create rincom06_3. Run tabulate on rincom06_3. Referring to the Results window, fill in the numbers next to the question marks:

3 quantiles of rincom06	Frequency*	Percent	Cumulative Percent
1	399.15	?	?
2	426.84	?	?
3	316.01	?	100.00
Total	1,142	100.00	

*Weighted frequencies are rounded to two decimal places.

B. (i) Run label define to create a label, rincom6_label. In the label define command, connect the following numeric codes and value labels: 1 "Low" 2 "Mid" 3 "High." (ii) Run label values to label of the values of rincom06_3 using rincom_label.

4. (Dataset: gss2012. Variables: pornlaw2, [aw=gssw].) In this chapter you learned to use tabulate (with the generate option) to create indicator variables. In this exercise, you will create indicator variables from pornlaw2, which measures individuals' opinions about pornography. Respondents thinking pornography should be "Illegal to all" are coded 1, and those saying "Not illegal to all" are coded 2. You will create an indicator variable coded 1 for individuals saying "Illegal to all," and coded 0 for any other response.

A. Run tab on pornlaw2. Make sure to include the weight variable, gssw. The percentage of respondents saying "Illegal to all" is _____.

B. Run tabulate on pornlaw2 with the generate option. In the generate option, use "porn" as the name stem. Run tab on porn1. The percentage of respondents coded 1 on porn1 is _____.

C. Use drop to delete porn2 from the dataset. Run aorder to alphabetize the variables in gss2012.

Before exiting Stata, be sure to save the dataset.

NOTES

1. For single-word value labels, quotation marks are not required. Because we are using the value labels "Yes" and "No," the following syntax also is correct: recode dem_marital (1/2=1 Yes) (3/6=0 No) (.=.), gen(married). For multiple-word value labels, quotation marks are required. Quotation marks always work, so it never hurts to use them.
2. If a dataset contains a number of identically coded variables, then Stata's two-command system makes a certain amount of sense. Suppose, for example, that there are twenty variables, var01 through var20, coded 0 or 1, with 0 denoting "No" and 1 denoting "Yes." In this situation, the researcher would need to define only one label (e.g., label define no_yes_label 0 "No" 1 "Yes"), which could then be applied to each of the twenty identically coded variables (label values var01 no_yes_label; label values var02 no_yes_label; etc.).
3. Survey datasets are notorious for "reverse coding." Survey designers do this so that respondents don't fall into response bias, or automatically giving the same response to a series of questions. Though you may need to be on the lookout for reverse coding in your future research, none of the examples or exercises in this book will require that you "repair" the original coding of any variables.

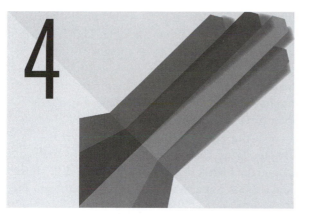

4

Making Comparisons

A ll hypothesis testing in political research follows a common logic of comparison. The researcher separates subjects into categories of the independent variable and then compares these groups on the dependent variable. For example, suppose I think that gender (independent variable) affects opinions about gun control (dependent variable) and that women are less likely than men are to oppose gun control. I would divide subjects into two groups on the basis of gender, women and men, and then compare the percentage of women who oppose gun control with the percentage of men who oppose gun control. Similarly, if I hypothesize that Republicans have higher incomes than do Democrats, I would divide subjects into partisanship groups (independent variable), Republicans and Democrats, and compare the average income (dependent variable) of Republicans with that of Democrats.

Although the logic of comparison is always the same, the appropriate method depends on the level of measurement of the independent and dependent variables. In this chapter, you will learn how to address two common hypothesis-testing situations. First, we will cover situations in which the independent and the dependent variables are both categorical (nominal or ordinal). Then we will consider instances in which the independent variable is categorical and the dependent variable is interval. In this chapter, you also will learn to create box plots, bar charts, and strip charts, all of which can greatly assist you in interpreting relationships.

CROSS-TABULATION ANALYSIS

Cross-tabulations are the workhorse vehicles for testing hypotheses for categorical variables. A cross-tabulation shows how cases defined by categories of the independent variable are distributed across the categories of the dependent variable. When setting up a cross-tabulation, you must observe the following three rules. First, put the independent variable on the columns and the dependent variable on the rows. Second, always obtain percentages of the independent variable, not the dependent variable. Third, interpret the cross-tabulation by comparing the percentages of subjects who fall into the same category of the dependent variable.

Consider this hypothesis: In a comparison of individuals, people who have lower incomes will be more likely to identify with the Democratic Party than those who have higher incomes. The dataset nes2012 contains pid_3, which measures respondents' partisanship in three categories: Democrat ("Dem"), Independent ("Ind"), and Republican ("Rep"). This will serve as the dependent variable. One of the variables that you generated with the xtile command in Chapter 3, income3, is the independent variable. Recall that income3 classifies individuals by terciles of income: the lowest third ("Low"), the middle third ("Mid"), and the highest third ("High"). Open a Do-file, and let's ask Stata to test the party identification–income hypothesis.

Stata's omnipresent tabulate command—the command that produces frequency distributions and generates indicator variables—also cranks out cross-tabulations. Following is the general syntax for a bivariate cross-tabulation that heeds the three rules of cross-tab construction:

tabulate *dep_var indep_var* [aw=*weightvar*], column

This syntax is simple and direct. Type "tabulate" or simply "tab," followed by the name of the dependent variable and the name of the independent variable. To ensure that Stata will report percentages of the independent variable, type a comma and then "col" (an acceptable abbreviation for the column option).[1] Applying the syntax to the analysis at hand, we would run the following command:

```
tab pid_3 income3 [aw=nesw], col
```

Party ID: 3 cats	3 quantiles of incgroup_prepost			
	Low	Mid	High	Total
Dem	830.89059	618.185473	531.4242	1,980.5
	39.32	34.44	29.66	34.75
Ind	849.08481	635.41181	673.11745	2,157.614
	40.18	35.40	37.57	37.85
Rep	433.33679	541.54776	587.0011	1,561.886
	20.51	30.17	32.77	27.40
Total	2,113.3122	1,795.145	1,791.543	5,700
	100.00	100.00	100.00	100.00

The presence of weighted frequencies creates a confusing clutter of digits. Before we rerun the cross-tabulation and request a cleaner display, let's consider the table at hand. The categories of the dependent variable, pid_3, define the rows of the table, and the independent variable, income3, is on the columns. In fact, Stata has given us a set of side-by-side frequency distributions of the dependent variable—one for each category of the independent variable—plus an overall frequency distribution for all analyzed cases. Accordingly, the table has four columns of numbers. The first column shows the distribution for approximately 2,113 respondents in the lowest income category. The middle column shows how the 1,795 individuals in the middle income group are distributed across pid_3, and the next column depicts the 1,792 people in the highest income group. The "Total" column shows the distribution of all 5,700 valid cases across the dependent variable. Each cell reports the column percentage and the weighted frequency of cases in the cell. To get a clearer view of the column percentages, we can rerun the command using the "nofreq" option to suppress frequencies. We'll also include the "nokey" option, which suppresses the space-consuming key box.

```
tab pid_3 income3 [aw=nesw], col nofreq nokey
```

Party ID: 3 cats	3 quantiles of incgroup_prepost			
	Low	Mid	High	Total
Dem	39.32	34.44	29.66	34.75
Ind	40.18	35.40	37.57	37.85
Rep	20.51	30.17	32.77	27.40
Total	100.00	100.00	100.00	100.00

What do you think? Does the cross-tabulation fit the hypothesis? The third rule of cross-tabulation analysis is easily applied. Focusing on the "Dem" value of the dependent variable, we see a pattern in the hypothesized direction. A comparison of respondents in the "Low" column with those in the "Mid" column reveals a decline from 39.32 to 34.44 in the percentage who are Democrats, a drop of about 5 percentage points. Moving from the "Mid" column to the "High" column, we find another decrease, from 34.44 percent to 29.66 percent, about another 5 point drop. Are lower-income people more likely to be Democrats than middle-income and higher-income people? Yes. Across the full range of the independent variable, from "Low" to "High" income, the percentage of Democrats declines by about 10 percentage points.

MEAN COMPARISON ANALYSIS

We now turn to another common hypothesis-testing situation: a categorical independent variable and an interval-level dependent variable. The logic of comparison still applies—divide cases on the independent variable and compare values of the dependent variable—but the method is different. Instead of comparing percentages, we now compare means.

To illustrate, let's say that you are interested in explaining this dependent variable: attitudes toward Barack Obama. Why do some people give him positive ratings while others rate him lower? Here is a plausible (if not self-evident) idea: Partisanship (independent variable) will have a strong effect on attitudes toward Barack Obama (dependent variable). The hypothesis: In a comparison of individuals, those who are Democrats will have more favorable attitudes toward Barack Obama than will those who are Republicans.

Dataset nes2012 contains Obama_therm, a 100-point feeling thermometer. In the survey, each respondent was asked to rate candidate Obama on this scale, from 0 (cold or negative) to 100 (warm or positive). This is the dependent variable. The dataset also has pid_x, which measures partisanship in seven ordinal categories, from Strong Democrat (coded 1) to Strong Republican (coded 7). (The intervening codes capture gradations between these poles: Weak Democrat, Independent-Democrat, Independent, Independent-Republican, and Weak Republican.) This is the independent variable. If the hypothesis is correct, we should find that Strong Democrats have the highest mean scores on Obama_therm, and that mean scores decline systematically across categories of pid_x, hitting bottom among respondents who are Strong Republicans. Is this what happens?

Yet again, tabulate will provide the answer. In using tabulate to perform bivariate mean comparison analyses, the general syntax is as follows:

tabulate *indep_var* [aw=*weightvar*], summarize(*dep_var*)

The syntax to the left of the comma says that you want Stata to divide cases according to the values of the independent variable. In the current example, pid_x is the independent variable, so we would begin the command by typing, "tab pid_x." The summarize option (which can be abbreviated "sum") tells Stata to calculate summary statistics of the dependent variable for each category of the independent variable. So our dependent variable, Obama_therm, would go inside the parentheses. The completed command, including nes2012's weight variable, for the Barack Obama thermometer:

```
tab pid_x [aw=nesw], sum(Obama_therm)
```

Stata responds:

PRE: SUMMARY- Party ID	Summary of Obama Rating			
	Mean	Std. Dev.	Freq.	Obs.
StrDem	90.10	14.43	1078.9432	1384
WkDem	74.19	22.59	832.792	813
IndepDem	75.23	20.52	637.5357	695
Indep	53.26	28.99	749.4443	724
IndepRep	32.81	26.27	672.6726	565
WkRep	36.68	25.90	676.8493	580
StrRep	17.60	21.92	814.3179	713
Total	56.40	34.34	5462.555	5474

By default, the summarize option will display the mean of the dependent variable ("Mean"), its standard deviation ("Std. Dev."), plus frequencies ("Freq."). For weighted data, Stata also displays the unweighted number of cases in each category of the independent variable ("Obs."). Despite this bumper crop of output, the table remains eminently readable. Even so, if you prefer to focus your attention on the mean values of Obama_therm, you may suppress the standard deviation (by adding the "nost" option), the weighted frequencies ("nofreq"), and the number of unweighted cases ("noobs"):

```
tab pid_x [aw=nesw], sum(Obama_therm) nost nofreq noobs
```

A leaner table appears in the Results window:

PRE: SUMMARY- Party ID	Summary of Obama Rating Mean
StrDem	90.10
WkDem	74.19
IndepDem	75.23
Indep	53.26
IndepRep	32.81
WkRep	36.68
StrRep	17.60
Total	56.40

Compared with a cross-tabulation, a mean comparison table is the soul of simplicity. The label of the dependent variable, "Summary of Obama Rating," appears along the top of the table. The label for the independent variable, "PRE: SUMMARY Party ID," defines the left-most column, which shows all seven categories, from the lowest-coded value, Strong Democrat, at the top, to the highest-coded value, Strong Republican, at the bottom. Beside each partisan category, Stata has calculated the mean of Obama_therm, displayed at two-decimal-point precision, as in "90.10" for the Strong Democrat mean. (Sometimes you will need to change the number of decimal points that Stata displays in the Results window or in a graphic. The format command is designed for this purpose. See "A Closer Look" for a discussion of the format command.) The bottom row, "Total," gives the mean for the whole sample.

A Closer Look   The format Command

Reassuringly, Stata always will store numeric data at a high level of precision—up to 16.5 decimal points, depending on a variable's storage type. However, in the interests of clarity or accuracy, you may want to change a variable's display format—that is, the number of decimal points Stata uses when it displays results or creates graphics. Here we will describe how to use a *fixed format* specification, one of the three numeric format types recognized by Stata.

Consider three ways of displaying the mean Barack Obama thermometer rating among Strong Democrats: "90.1042," "90.10," and "90." The first number shows four decimal points, the second rounds to two, and the third rounds to the nearest whole number. Stata's default will give you the second display, "90.10," which works for most purposes. But let's suppose you wanted the more precise rendition, "90.1042." You would type

```
format Obama_therm %9.4f
```

Roughly translated into human language, this command says, "From now on, allow a maximum width of 9 digits for Obama_therm, and display 4 digits to the right of the decimal point."

The general syntax begins with "format *varname*," and is followed by a "%," which signals the beginning of a format specification. You then type a number for the maximum width of the variable ("9" is usually adequate) followed by a period ("."). Finally, type the number of decimals you want displayed, and end the specification with the letter "f."

The command, format Obama_therm %9.2f, would tell Stata to display Obama_therm with two decimal points, "90.10." The command, format Obama_therm %9.0f, would instruct Stata to round to the nearest whole number, "90."

Among Strong Democrats, the mean of Obama_therm is very high—90.10 degrees. Does the mean decline as attachment to the Democratic Party weakens and identification with the Republican Party strengthens? Yes, but take note of some interesting anomalies. To be sure, the mean drops sharply among Weak Democrats (who average 74.19 degrees), but it momentarily stalls among Independent-Democratic leaners (75.23). Obama's ratings then continue to decline predictably, although they bump up slightly between Independent-Republican leaners (32.81) and Weak Republicans (36.68). Strong Republicans, who average 17.60 degrees on the thermometer, have the chilliest response to Obama. On the whole, then, the data support the hypothesis.

Graphing an Interval-Level Dependent Variable

There are two main visual accompaniments for mean comparison analysis: box plots and bar charts. Box plots describe a numeric variable by graphing a five-number summary: minimum, lower quartile, median, upper quartile, and maximum. Box plots also reveal outliers. Bar charts graph the means of a dependent variable across the values of an independent variable. We will consider both kinds of graphs, beginning with box plots. The bare bones syntax:

graph box *dep_var* [aweight = *weightvar*], over (*indep_var*)

For the Obama_therm-pid_x example we would type:

```
graph box Obama_therm [aweight = nesw], over(pid_x)
```

Go ahead and run the basic command. We can add options later.

Consider the box plot shown in the Graph window (Figure 4-1). What is depicted by a box plot? The box itself communicates three values: the lower quartile (the value below which 25 percent of the cases fall),

Figure 4-1 Box Plot

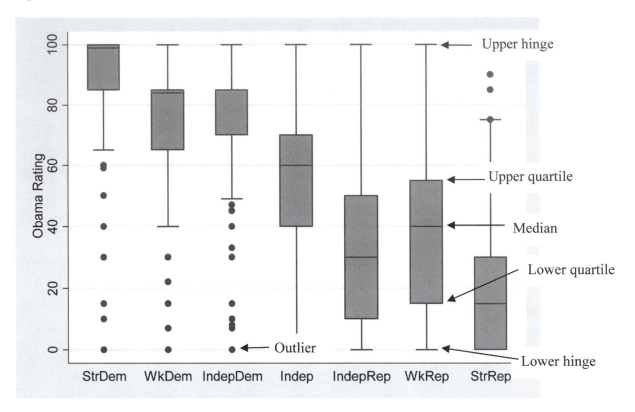

NOTE: Figure annotations based on Robert I. Kabacoff, *R in Action: Data Analysis and Graphics with R* (Shelter Island, NY: Manning Publications, 2011), 133.

the median (the value that splits the cases into two equal-size groups), and the upper quartile (the value below which 75 percent of the cases fall). Thus, the distance between the bottom and top of the box defines the interquartile range, the range of a variable that encompasses the "middle half" of a distribution. For example, notice how spread out Weak Republicans are: Their median rating is 40, but half of them rated Obama in the long interval between approximately 20 (lower quartile) and nearly 60 (upper quartile), an interquartile range of about 40 points. Contrast this to the cohesiveness of all the Democratic groups: High medians and tightly bounded interquartile ranges. The lower and upper hinges connect the minimum and maximum values, as long as those values fall within plus or minus 1.5 times the quartile range for the box. Outliers are defined as cases that fall outside those boundaries.

Before moving on, rerun graph box, adding labeling, color, and other enhancements:

```
#delimit ;
graph box Obama_therm [aweight = nesw], over(pid_x)

bar(1, fcolor(blue))  ← Changes the default bar fill color

graphregion(fcolor(white))  ← Removes color from the graphregion

ytitle("Obama Rating")  ←
ytitle(, size(medsmall))       Y-axis title and font size

title("Obama Ratings, by Party Identification",    Titles the graph
     size(medlarge))
                                Adds a source note
note("Source: 2012 ANES")   ;
```

The finished product appears in the Graph window (Figure 4-2).

Figure 4-2   Box Plot with Options

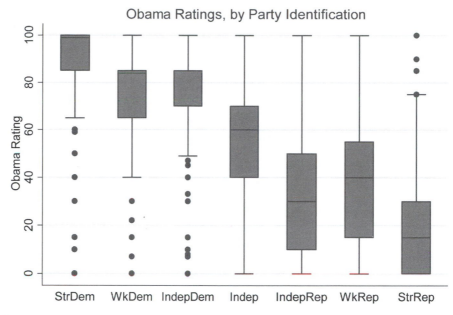

A box plot favors the display of dispersion over central tendency, providing a valuable complement to mean comparison analysis. A bar chart, which plots the mean of a dependent variable across the values of an independent variable, is aimed more squarely at visualizing mean comparisons by reexpressing them in graphic form. The syntax of the basic bar chart command is very similar to the box plot syntax:

graph bar (mean) *dep_var* [aweight = *weightvar*], over (*indep_var*)

You specify "bar" instead of "box," and tell Stata you want to graph the mean values ("mean") of the dependent variable across values of the independent variable. For the current example, we have this:

```
graph bar (mean) Obama_therm [aweight = nesw], over(pid_x)
```

The simplified syntax produced a highly readable chart (Figure 4-3). This graphic is at once simple and informative. The y-axis records mean values of the dependent variable, the Barack Obama feeling thermometer. The bars trace the mean ratings across the values of party identification: approximately 90 degrees for Strong Democrats, 74 degrees for Weak Democrats, and so on, all the way to 17 degrees for Strong Republicans. One can immediately see the negative relationship between the independent and dependent variables—as pid_x increases from low codes to high codes, mean Obama ratings decline—as well as the curious anomalies between the independent leaners and weak partisans of each party. As nice as the graph is, you can always use options to add content and style. With one exception (the bar fill color), these options are identical to those you applied to the box plot of the same relationship:

```
#delimit ;
 graph bar (mean) Obama_therm [aweight = nesw], over(pid_x)
bar(1, fcolor(gs12))
graphregion(fcolor(white))
ytitle("Mean Obama Rating")
ytitle(, size(medsmall))
title("Obama Ratings, by Party Identification",
  size(medlarge))
note("Source: 2012 ANES");
```

Another graphics success appears in the Graph window (Figure 4-4).

Figure 4-3 Bar Chart

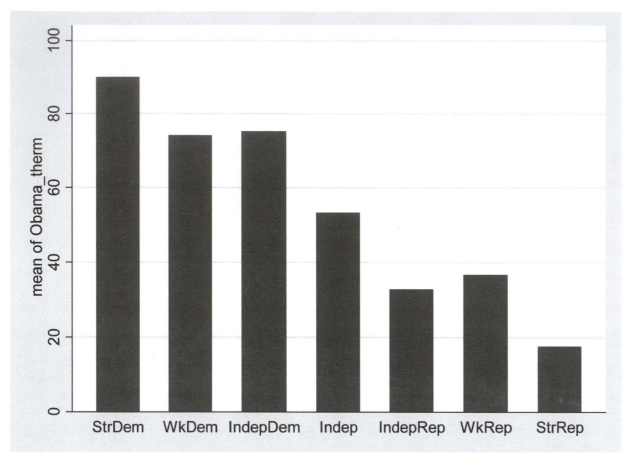

Figure 4-4 Bar Chart with Options

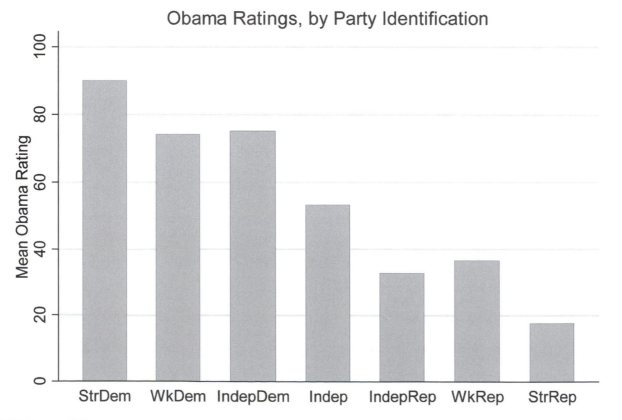

Graphing a Categorical Dependent Variable

As we have just seen, a bar chart will concisely summarize the relationship between an interval-level dependent variable and a categorical independent variable. In fact, for clarifying complex relationships between variables of any level of measurement, bar charts point the researcher toward the correct interpretation. (This use of bar charts is covered in Chapter 5.) Sometimes, however, you may wish to create a bar chart to depict the relationship between two categorical variables, such as the relationship between income (income3) and party identification (pid_3). Let's run the pid_3-income3 analysis again and figure out what a bar chart of the relationship should look like:

```
. tab pid_3 income3 [aw=nesw], col nofreq nokey
```

| Party ID: | 3 quantiles of incgroup_prepost | | | |
3 cats	Low	Mid	High	Total
Dem	39.32	34.44	29.66	34.75
Ind	40.18	35.40	37.57	37.85
Rep	20.51	30.17	32.77	27.40
Total	100.00	100.00	100.00	100.00

Suppose we would like the bar chart's y-axis to display the percentage of respondents who are Democrats. The categories of income3—"Low," "Mid," and "High"—will appear along the horizontal axis. Based on the cross-tabulation analysis, we can anticipate what the bar chart will look like. The bar for the lowest income group will stand at 39.32 percent, the middle group at 34.44 percent, and the highest at 29.66 percent. We can easily state our graphic goal in human language: "I want to graph the percentage of Democrats across different values of income3." As is sometimes the case with Stata, however, this human language cannot be directly translated directly into a single Stata command.

The simple truth is that Stata does not like to graph categorical dependent variables—not in their naturally coded state, anyway. But Stata does like to graph indicator variables, transformations of categorical variables. In Chapter 3 you learned how to run tabulate (with the generate option) to compute a set of indicator variables from a categorical variable. For any categorical variable having K categories, Stata will generate K indicator variables, named sequentially based on the name stem that you supply in the generate option. Each indicator variable will be coded 1 for cases falling into that category of the original variable and coded 0 for cases not falling into that category. The first step in graphing a categorical dependent variable is to generate a set of indicator variables.

Let's get to the example at hand. In Do-file editor, type the following:

```
tab pid_3 [aw=nesw], gen(piddum)
```

Stata produces a frequency distribution in the Results window. Stata also creates three indicator variables—piddum1, piddum2, and piddum3—and lists them at the bottom of the Variables window:

piddum1	pid_3==Dem
piddum2	pid_3==Ind
piddum3	pid_3==Rep

Focus your attention on piddum1. Because "Dem" is the lowest-coded value of pid_3 (code 1), the first indicator variable that Stata generates is coded 1 for respondents who are Democrats and coded 0 for respondents who are Independents or Republicans. Now let's demonstrate why Stata likes to work with indicator variables. The following command will return the mean of piddum1 (dependent variable) for each value of income3 (independent variable):

```
tab income3 [aw=nesw]  , sum(piddum1) nost nofreq noobs
```

3 quantiles of incgroup_pr epost	Summary of pid_3==Dem Mean
Low	.39316983
Mid	.34436519
High	.29662937
Total	.34745619

What is the mean of piddum1 for "Low" income respondents? For this group, the mean of piddum1 is .3932 (that is, .39316983 rounded to four decimal points). Refer back to the cross-tabulation analysis. What percentage of this income group are Democrats? 39.32 percent. You can see that the means of our newly created indicator variable, piddum1, are identical to the proportions of respondents in each income group who fall into the "Dem" category of the original variable, pid_3. A proportion is just a percentage that's been divided by 100. In the cross-tab we found that 34.44 percent of the middle income group are Democrats, which appears as a proportion equal to .3444 on piddum1. For the highest income group, the numbers are the same, as well: 29.66 percent and .2966. *More generally, the mean of an indicator variable is equal to the proportion of cases coded 1 on the indicator variable.* Because a code of 1 on piddum1 denotes "Dem," then the means .3932, .3444, and .2966 report the proportions of respondents in each value of the independent variable, income3, who are Democrats.

Graphically, percentages are more attractive than proportions. Using Stata's replace command, we can convert piddum1 into percentages:

```
replace piddum1=piddum1*100
```

Why use replace instead of generate? (See "A Closer Look" for a discussion of the replace command.)

With the appropriate indicator variable in hand, we can now say, "I want to graph the mean of such-and-such indicator variable across different values of such-and-such independent variable." Applied to our

A Closer Look   The replace Command

Stata's replace command, a special instance of the generate command, can be used to change or replace the values of a variable that already exists. Unlike Stata's devil-may-care attitude toward the recode command–if the user doesn't consciously specify the generate option, the recode command will destroy and replace the original variable–Stata will not permit the generate command to overwrite an existing variable. Suppose you sought to convert piddum1 from a proportion to a percentage; that is, you wanted to multiply piddum1 times 100. If you entered, "generate piddum1 = piddum1 * 100", Stata would refuse, saying "piddum1 already defined":

```
.  gen piddum1=piddum1*100
piddum1 already defined
r(110);
```

However, if you typed, "replace piddum1 = piddum1 * 100", Stata would perform as requested:

```
.  replace piddum1=piddum1*100
(2358 real changes made)
```

Figure 4-5 Bar Chart of Indicator Variable

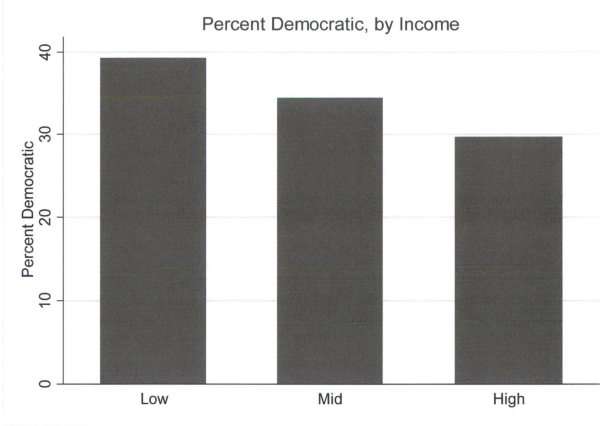

SOURCE: 2012 ANES

example: "I want to graph the mean of piddum1 across different value of income3." Stata will happily graph the mean values of anything all day long.

```
#delimit ;
 graph bar (mean) piddum1 [aweight = nesw], over(income3)
   bar(1, fcolor(blue))
   graphregion(fcolor(white))
   ytitle("Percent Democratic")
   ytitle(, size(medsmall))
   title("Percent Democratic, by Income",
      size(medlarge))
   note("Source: 2012 ANES");
```

A bar chart of the piddum1-income3 relationship appears in the Graph window (Figure 4-5).

Strip Charts: Graphs for Small-n Datasets

The graphic types discussed thus far—box plots and bar charts—excel at displaying summary statistics for large datasets. Strip charts display case-level information, making them particularly appropriate for smaller datasets, such as states or world. Like box plots, strip charts show how the cases are distributed within each value of an independent variable. Thus, the analyst might create a strip chart to complement a mean comparison analysis. Save nes2012. Open states and let's run through an example.

Suppose we are interested in comparing levels of unionization in difference regions of the United States. We would run tabulate with the summary option, obtaining the mean of union10 (percentage of the workforce belonging to a union) by region (of the country):

```
tab region, sum(union10)
```

Census region	Summary of Percent workforce unionized (2010)		
	Mean	Std. Dev.	Freq.
Northeast	16.233333	4.4849749	9
Midwest	11.633333	4.4707806	12
South	6.95625	3.4418926	16
West	13.146154	6.5712271	13
Total	11.358	5.7906712	50

The Northeast has the highest average level of unionization (16.23 percent), followed by the West (13.14 percent), the Midwest (11.63 percent), and the South (6.96 percent). But examine the corresponding standard deviations, which measure variation. Notice that the standard deviation for the West (6.57) is comparatively large, nearly twice that for the South (3.44). This suggests that the thirteen western states are widely dispersed, with some having high levels of unionization and others having lower levels. A strip chart, produced with the scatter command, can provide valuable insights on questions of dispersion and skewness. The basic syntax is as about as straightforward as it gets in Stata:

scatter *dep_var indep_var*

Applied to the union10-region example:

```
scatter union10 region
```

The strip chart created by this terse, three-word command is austere but interpretable (Figure 4-6). We can see why the mean comparison analysis returned interregional differences in the level of unionization. And notice the differences between southern states (code 3 on region) and western states (code 4). A group of western states have low levels of unionization, much like states in the South.

Following is a command for a well-optioned strip chart, adapted to the example at hand, and shown with familiar options in place (unfamiliar options are annotated):

```
#delimit ;
scatter union10 region,
 xlabel(, valuelabel)
 graphregion(fcolor(white))
 title("Unionization, by Region",
       size(medlarge))
 note(Source: "States Dataset")

 jitter(7)    ←  Adds a small amount of random noise to data points so that
                  they do not overlap

 msize(medlarge)
 msymbol(circle)  ←  Marker size and symbol type

 mfcolor(black)   ←  Marker fill color and outline color
 mlcolor(black);
```

The resulting graph is quite presentable (Figure 4-7).

Figure 4-6 Strip Chart

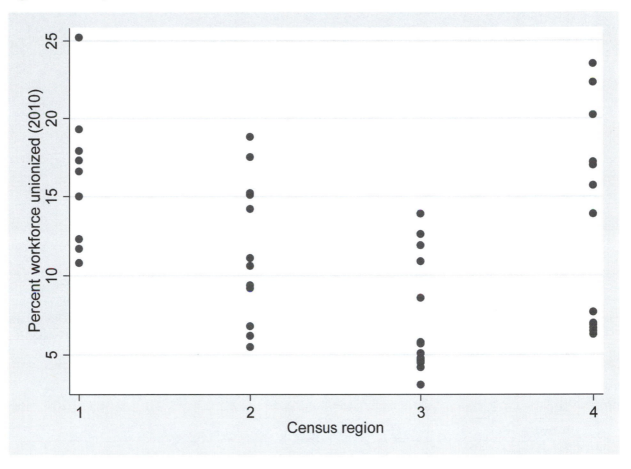

Figure 4-7 Strip Chart with Options

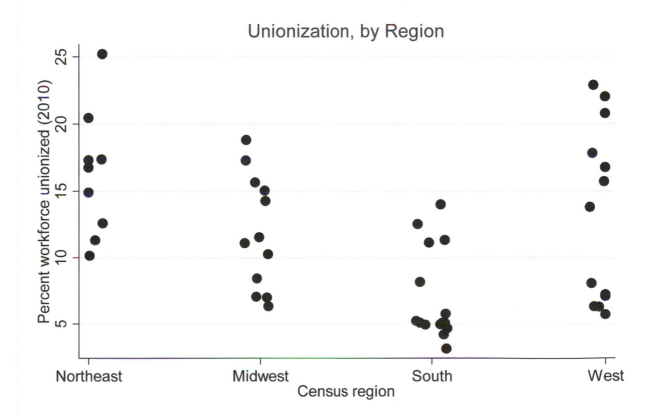

EXERCISES

1. (Dataset: nes2012. Variables: inspre_self, pid_x, [aw=nesw].) Here is a widely remarked difference between Democrats and Republicans: Democrats favor government-funded medical insurance, and Republicans prefer private insurance plans. Is this difference borne out by the data? Dataset nes2012 contains the variable inspre_self, a 7-point scale that measures respondents' opinions on this issue. Respondents indicate their opinions by choosing any position on this scale, from 1 (government plan) at one end to 7 (private plan) at the other end. This is the dependent variable. Use the 7-point party identification scale (pid_x) as the independent variable.

   A. If Democrats are more likely than Republicans to favor government-funded medical insurance, then Democrats will have (check one)

   ❑ a higher mean than do Republicans on inspre_self.

   ❑ about the same mean as do Republicans on inspre_self.

   ❑ a lower mean than do Republicans on inspre_self.

   B. Run tabulate with the summarize option to obtain a mean comparison that shows the mean score on the dependent variable, inspre_self, for each category of the independent variable, pid_x. (Make sure to weight the data with nesw. You might also wish to specify these options: nost, nofreq, noobs.) Write the results in the table that follows.

Summary of Medical Insurance Scale: Self-Placement	
Party ID	Mean
Strong Democrat	
Weak Democrat	
Independent-Dem	
Independent	
Independent-Rep	
Weak Republican	
Strong Republican	
Total	

   C. Generally speaking, does your analysis support the idea that Democrats are more likely than Republicans to support government-funded medical insurance? (circle one)

   Yes   No

   Briefly explain your answer._____

   _____

   _____

   D. Suppose you overheard someone making this claim: "People might say they're 'Independent-Democrats,' but when it comes to opinions about medical insurance, they're closer to 'Independent' than to 'Democrat.'" Based on your analysis, is this claim correct? (circle one)

   Yes   No

Briefly explain your answer. _____

_____

_____

E. Create and print a nicely optioned bar chart of the relationship between inspre_self (dependent variable) and pid_x (independent variable). Here are some suggestions for appropriate options:

bar(1, fcolor(gs12))

graphregion(fcolor(white))

ytitle("Health Insurance Scale")

ytitle(, size(medsmall))

title("Healthcare Opinion, by Party Identification," size(medlarge))

note("Source: 2012 ANES")

F. Create and print a box plot of the inspre_self-pid_x relationship. (Hint: You can apply the same options you used in part E.)

G. In this chapter's guided example of the relationship between Obama_therm and pid_x, we found some interesting anomalies between weak partisans and independent leaners of both parties. Do similar anomalies exist in the inspre_self-pid_x relationship? Briefly explain.

_____

_____

_____

_____

2. (Dataset: nes2012. Variables: gay_marry, relig_attend3, gender, libcon3, [aw=nesw].) Why are some people more likely than others to support gay marriage? One can imagine several characteristics that divide people on this issue. People who regularly attend religious services might be less likely to favor gay marriage than are the less observant. Men may be less likely than women to favor it. Or conservatives may be less open to the idea than liberals.

Dataset nes2012 contains gay_marry, which is coded 0 ("No," gay marriage should not be allowed) or 1 ("Yes"). This is the dependent variable that you will use to test each of the following hypotheses:

Hypothesis 1: In a comparison of individuals, people who have high levels of attendance at religious services will be less likely to favor gay marriage than will people who have lower levels of religious attendance. (The independent variable is relig_attend3.)

Hypothesis 2: In a comparison of individuals, men are less likely than women to favor gay marriage. (The independent variable is gender.)

Hypothesis 3: In a comparison of individuals, conservatives are less likely than liberals to favor gay marriage. (The independent variable is libcon3.)

A. Test these hypotheses by obtaining three cross-tabulations, one for each hypothesis. Be sure to request column percentages. This is dataset nes2012, so remember to weight the analysis. Clean things up with the nofreq and nokey options. For example, the following syntax will permit you to test the first hypothesis: "tab gay_marry relig_attend3 [aw=nesw], col nofreq nokey." In the spaces in the table that follows, record the percentages who say "Yes" when asked about gay marriage:

	Level of religious attendance		
	Low	Middle	High
Percentage "Yes"	?	?	?
	Respondent gender		
	Male		Female
Percentage "Yes"	?		?
	Ideology		
	Liberal	Moderate	Conservative
Percentage "Yes"	?	?	?

B. These findings (circle one)

        support Hypothesis 1.   do not support Hypothesis 1.

Briefly explain your reasoning. _____

_____

_____

_____

_____

C. These findings (circle one)

        support Hypothesis 2.   do not support Hypothesis 2.

Briefly explain your reasoning. _____

_____

_____

_____

_____

D. These findings (circle one)

        support Hypothesis 3.   do not support Hypothesis 3.

Briefly explain your reasoning. _____

_____

_____

_____

_____

_____

Perform the following tasks before proceeding to Part E: (i) Run the following command, which will generate a set of indicator variables (gaydum1 and gaydum2) from gay_marry: "tab gay_marry [aw=nesw], gen(gaydum)." Gaydum2 records the proportion of respondents saying "Yes" to gay marriage. (ii) Convert the proportion to a percentage by running the replace command: "replace gaydum2 = gaydum2 * 100."

E. Create and print a bar chart of the relationship between gaydum2 and relig_attend3. Specify appropriate options for colors, titles, and fonts. For example, you will need descriptive titles for the y-axis ("Percentage Supporting Gay Marriage"), chart title ("Support for Gay Marriage, by Religious Attendance"), and source note.

3. (Dataset: nes2012. Variables: pres_vote12, econ_ecpast, [aw=nesw].) What factors determine how people vote in presidential elections? Political scientists have investigated and debated this question for many years. A particularly powerful and elegant perspective emphasizes voters' *retrospective* evaluations. According to this view, for example, voters who think the country's economy has gotten better during the year preceding the election are likely to reward the candidate of the incumbent party. Voters who believe the economy has worsened, by contrast, are likely to punish the incumbent party by voting for the candidate of the party not currently in power. As political scientist V. O. Key once famously put it, the electorate plays the role of "rational god of vengeance and reward."[2] Does Key's idea help explain how people voted in the 2012 election?

A. Test this hypothesis: In a comparison of individuals, those who thought the economy had improved during the year preceding the 2012 election were more likely to vote for the incumbent, Barack Obama, than were individuals who thought the economy had not improved. Use these two variables from nes2012: pres_vote12 (dependent variable), econ_ecpast (independent variable), and nesw (weight variable). Obtain a cross-tabulation of the relationship. Record the percentages voting for Romney and Obama in the table that follows:

Respondent's Vote, 2012	PRE: National economy better/worse in last year			
	Better	Same	Worse	Total
Obama	?	?	?	?
Romney	?	?	?	?
Total	100.0	100.0	100.0	100.0

B. What do you think? Are the data consistent with the hypothesis? Write a paragraph explaining your reasoning.

_____

_____

_____

_____

C. *Loss aversion* is an interesting psychological phenomenon that can shape the choices people make.[3] One idea behind loss aversion is that losses loom larger than commensurate gains. According to this theory, for example, the psychological pain felt from losing $100 is greater than the pleasure felt from gaining $100. Applied to retrospective voting, loss aversion might suggest that the "vengeance" impulse is stronger than the "reward" impulse—that the anti-incumbent motivation among those who say the economy has worsened will be stronger than the pro-incumbent motivation among those who think it has improved.

With this idea in mind, examine the percentages in the table in Part A. What do you think? Do the data suggest that Key's rational god of vengeance is stronger than his rational god of reward? Answer yes or no, and write a few sentences explaining your reasoning.

_____

_____

_____

_____

4. (Dataset: nes2012. Variables: libcpre_ptyd, libcpre_ptyr, pid_x, [aw=nesw].) Partisan polarization can create some interesting perceptual distortions. Do partisans tend to view themselves as more moderate than they view the opposing party? For example, do Democrats think Republicans are ideologically extreme, yet see themselves are more moderate? By the same token, do Republicans view Democrats as liberal extremists, but perceive themselves as purveyors of middle-of-the-road politics? Where do Independents place the Democrats and Republicans on the left-right continuum? A Pew survey found this thought-provoking asymmetry: All partisans—Democrats, Independents, and Republicans—placed the Republicans at practically the same conservative position on the liberal-conservative scale. However, the placement of the Democrats varied widely: Republicans placed Democrats well toward the liberal side, Independents saw Democrats as somewhat left-of-center, and Democrats placed themselves squarely at the moderate position.[4] In this exercise, you will see if you can replicate the Pew report's findings using nes2012.

The nes2012 variable, libcpre_ptyd, measures respondents' perceptions of the ideological position of the Democratic Party using the standard 7-point scale: 1 ("Extremely liberal"), 2 ("Liberal"), 3 ("Slightly liberal"), 4 ("Moderate"), 5 ("Slightly conservative"), 6 ("Conservative"), and 7 ("Extremely conservative"). Another variable, libcpre_ptyr, asks respondents to place the Republican Party along the same 7-point metric. For the purposes of this exercise, you will treat these two measures as interval-level variables. Thus, lower mean values denote higher perceived liberalism, values around 4 denote perceived moderation, and higher mean values denote higher levels of perceived conservatism. Libcpre_ptyd and libcpre_ptyr are the dependent variables. Our old reliable, pid_x, is the independent variable. If the Pew results are correct, you should find that all partisan groups, from Strong Democrats to Strong Republicans, share very similar conservative perceptions of the Republican Party—but hold very different perceptions of the Democratic Party.

A. Run two mean comparison analyses, one for the libcpre_ptyd-pid_x relationship, and one for the libcpre_ptyr-pid_x relationship. Fill in the means in the following table.

Party ID	Ideol placement of Dems: Mean	Ideol placement of Reps: Mean
StrDem	?	?
WkDem	?	?
IndepDem	?	?
Indep	?	?
IndepRep	?	?
WkRep	?	?
StrRep	?	?

B. Examine your findings. Are the Pew findings borne out by the nes2012 data? Explain your reasoning.

_____

_____

_____

_____

_____

5. (Dataset: gss2012. Variables: polviews, femrole [aw=gssw].) Why do some people hold more traditional views about the role of women in society and politics, whereas others take a less traditional stance? General ideological orientations, liberalism versus conservatism, may play an important role in shaping individuals' opinions on this cultural question. Thus it seems plausible to suggest that ideology (independent variable) will affect opinions about appropriate female roles (dependent variable). The hypothesis: In a comparison of individuals, liberals will be more likely than conservatives to approve of nontraditional female roles.

The gss2012 dataset contains femrole, a scale that measures opinions about the appropriate role of women. You analyzed this variable in Chapter 2. Recall that femrole scores range from 0 (women belong in traditional roles) to 9 (women belong nontraditional roles). That is, higher scores denote less traditional beliefs. This is the dependent variable. The dataset has another familiar variable, polviews, a 7-point ordinal scale measuring ideology. Scores on polviews can range from 1 (extremely liberal) to 7 (extremely conservative). This is the independent variable.

A. According to the hypothesis, as the values of polviews increase, from 1 through 7, mean values of femrole should (circle one)

  decrease.   neither decrease nor increase.   increase.

B. Run tabulate with the summarize option to obtain mean values of femrole across values of polviews. Specify the nost option. Fill in the table that follows.

Summary of female role		
Ideological self-placement	Mean	Freq.*
Extremely liberal	?	?
Liberal	?	?
Slightly liberal	?	?
Moderate	?	?
Slightly conservative	?	?
Conservative	?	?
Extremely conservative	?	?
Total	?	?

*Round weighted frequencies to two decimal places.

C. Do the results support the hypothesis? Write a few sentences explaining your reasoning._____

_____

_____

_____

_____

D. Create and print a bar chart showing mean values of femrole (y-axis) over values of polviews. Provide descriptive titles and fonts. Add a source note. For assistance, refer back to this chapter's examples. Print the chart.

6. (Dataset: gss2012. Variables: egalit_scale3, educ_4, [aw=gssw].) Pedantic pontificator is offering a group of students his thoughts about the relationship between educational attainment and egalitarianism, the belief that government should do more to make sure resources are more equitably distributed in society: "Educated people have a humanistic world view that is sorely lacking among the self-seeking, less-educated classes. They see inequality . . . and want to rectify it! Plus, most colleges and universities are populated with liberal faculty, who indoctrinate their students into left-wing ideologies at every opportunity. Thus, it's really quite simple: As education goes up, egalitarianism increases."

Gss2012 contains egalit_scale3, which measures egalitarian beliefs in three categories: "Less egalitarian," "Middle," and "More egalitarian." Gss2012 also has educ_4, which records educational attainment in four categories: Less than high school ("<HS"), high school ("HS"), some college ("Some Coll"), and college or graduate degree ("Coll+").

A. Run a cross-tabulation analysis that tests pedantic pontificator's idea about the relationship between education and egalitarianism. Obtain column percentages. Use the nofreq option to request uncluttered results. Use the table below to record the percentages you obtained.

	<HS	HS	Some Coll	Coll+	Total
Less egal	?	?	?	?	?
Middle	?	?	?	?	?
More egal	?	?	?	?	?
Total	100.00	100.00	100.00	100.00	100.00

B. Based on your analysis, would it appear that pedantic pontificator is correct? Answer yes or no, and explain.

_____

_____

_____

_____

_____

C. Run tabulate with the generate option to obtain a set of indicator variables for egalit_scale3. Use "egal" and the variable stem. Obtain a nicely optioned bar chart showing the percentage in the "More egalitarian" category across values of educ_4. Print the chart.

7. (Dataset: gss2012. Variables: intethn_2, affrmact2, natrace, [aw=gssw].) Untruthful answers by survey respondents can create big headaches for public opinion researchers. Why might a respondent not tell the truth to an interviewer? Certain types of questions, combined with particular characteristics of the interviewer, can trigger a phenomenon called preference falsification: "the act of misrepresenting one's genuine wants under perceived social pressures."[5] For example, consider the difficulty in gauging opinions on affirmative action, hiring policies aimed at giving preference to black applicants. One might reasonably expect people questioned by an African American interviewer to express greater support for such programs than would those questioned by a white pollster. An affirmative action opponent, not wanting to appear racially insensitive to a black questioner, might instead offer a false pro–affirmative action opinion.[6]

The gss2012 dataset contains intethn_2, coded 1 and labeled "White" for respondents questioned by a white interviewer; and coded 2 and labeled "Black" for those questioned by a black interviewer. This is the independent variable that will allow you to test two preference falsification hypotheses:

Hypothesis 1: In a comparison of individuals, those questioned by a black interviewer will be more likely to express support for affirmative action than will those questioned by a white interviewer. (The dependent variable is affrmact2, coded 1 for "Support" and 2 for "Oppose.")

Hypothesis 2: In a comparison of individuals, those questioned by a black interviewer will be more likely to say that we are spending too little to improve the condition of blacks than will those questioned by a white interviewer. (The dependent variable is natrace, which is coded 1 for respondents saying, "Too little"; 2 for those saying, "About the right amount"; and 3 for "Too much.")

A. Run two cross-tabulation analyses, one analyzing the relationship between intethn_2 and affrmact2 and one analyzing the relationship between intethn_2 and natrace. Make sure to request column percentages. In the table that follows, record the percentages that "Support" affirmative action and the percentages that say we are spending "Too little" to improve the condition of blacks.

	Interviewer's race	
	White	Black
Percent "Support" affirmative action	?	?
Percent spending "Too little" to improve condition of blacks	?	?

These findings (circle one)

support Hypothesis 1.   do not support Hypothesis 1.

Briefly explain your reasoning. _____

_____

_____

_____

_____

B. These findings (circle one)

              support Hypothesis 2.   do not support Hypothesis 1.

Briefly explain your reasoning. _____

_____

_____

_____

_____

Perform two tasks before proceeding to Part D. (i) Generate a set of indicator variables from affrmact2, using the variable handle "affdum." Affdum1 records the proportion of respondents who "Support" affirmative action. (ii) Run the replace command to convert affdum1 from a proportion to a percentage.

C. Create and print a nicely optioned bar chart of the relationship between interviewer race and affirmative action opinions. Be sure to provide a y-axis title, a chart title, and source note.

8. (Dataset: states. Variables: ProLife, region, state.) In this exercise, you will (i) create and print a box plot of the relationship between ProLife (the percentage of public holding a "pro-life" position on abortion) and region; (ii) identify outliers within regions; and (iii) create and print a strip chart of the relationship.

A. Obtain and print a box plot of the relationship between ProLife and region. You will want to apply the options discussed in this chapter. However, you will want to add an option (not discussed previously) that will label outliers using the variable, state, an alpha variable that identifies each state by name. In the box plot options, add the following, just as you see it here. The first character inside the left parentheses is the number one.

```
mark(1, mlab(state))
```

B. The box plot you produced in Part A identifies one outlier in the Northeast and two outliers in the West. (Fill in the blanks that follow.) Which state is the outlier in the Northeast? _____. Which two states are outliers in the West? _____ and _____.

C. Consider this claim: "As measured by the interquartile range, Southern states are less spread out—that is, have less variation in prolife opinions—than states in the Midwest." Is this claim correct? Answer yes or no, and briefly explain.

_____

_____

_____

_____

_____

D. Consider this claim: "Ignoring their outliers, the Northeastern states are more cohesive in their prolife
    opinions than are the Western states." Is this claim correct? Answer yes or no, and briefly explain.

    _____

    _____

    _____

    _____

    _____

E. Use the scatter command to obtain a strip chart of the ProLife-region relationship. Make the chart
    presentable by specifying appropriate options. Make sure to include the jitter option, so the markers do
    not overlap. Print the chart.

9. (Dataset: states. Variables: Smokers12, Cig_tax12_3.) Two policy researchers are debating whether higher
    taxes on cigarettes reduce cigarette consumption:

    Policy Researcher 1: "The demand for cigarettes is highly inelastic—smokers need to consume cigarettes, and
    they will buy them without regard to the cost. Raising taxes on a pack of cigarettes will have no effect on the
    level of cigarette consumption."

    Policy Researcher 2: "Look, any behavior that's taxed is discouraged. If state governments want to discourage
    smoking, then raising cigarette taxes will certainly have the desired effect. Higher taxes mean lower
    consumption."

    Imagine a bar chart of the relationship between cigarette taxes and cigarette consumption. The horizontal axis
    measures state cigarette taxes in three categories, from lower taxes on the left to higher taxes on the right. The
    vertical axis records the percentage of the population who are smokers. Below are two graphic shells, A and B.
    In shell A, you will sketch a bar chart depicting what the relationship would look like if Policy Researcher 1 is
    correct. In shell B, you will sketch a bar chart depicting what the relationship would look like if Policy
    Researcher 2 is correct.

    A. If Policy Researcher 1 were correct, what would the bar chart look like? Sketch three bars inside the
        graphic space, depicting the relationship proposed by Policy Researcher 1.

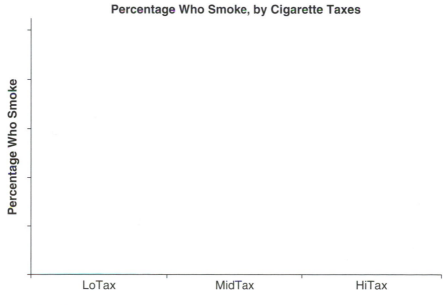

Percentage Who Smoke, by Cigarette Taxes

Source: States Dataset

B. If Policy Researcher 2 were correct, what would the bar chart look like? Sketch three bars inside the graphic space, depicting the relationship proposed by Policy Researcher 2.

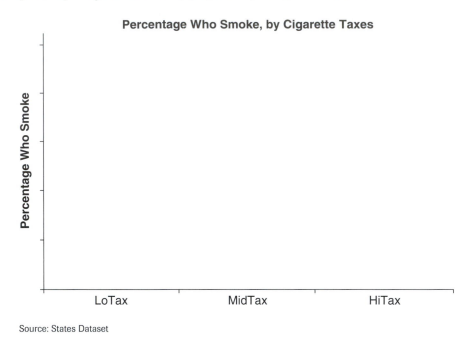

Percentage Who Smoke, by Cigarette Taxes

Source: States Dataset

C. The states dataset contains the variables Smokers12 and Cig_tax12_3. Run a mean comparison analysis, using Smokers12 as the dependent variable and Cig_tax12_3 as the independent variable. Record your results in the table that follows.

Cigarette Taxes	Summary of percentages who smoke, by cigarette taxes	
	Mean	Freq.
LoTax	?	?
MidTax	?	?
HiTax	?	?
Total	21.06	50

D. Create and print a nicely optioned bar chart of the relationship you just analyzed. Be sure to include a descriptive chart title, y-axis title, and source note.

E. Examine the mean comparison table and the line chart. Which policy researcher is more correct? (check one)

❑ Policy Researcher 1 is more correct.

❑ Policy Researcher 2 is more correct.

F. Write a paragraph explaining your reasoning in part E.

_____

_____

_____

_____

_____

10. (Dataset: world. Variables: regime_type3, durable.) Three comparative politics scholars are trying to figure out what sort of institutional arrangement produces the longest-lasting, most stable political system.

Scholar 1: "Presidential democracies, like the United States, are going to be more stable than are any other type of system. In presidential democracies, the executive and the legislature have separate electoral constituencies and separate but overlapping domains of responsibility. The people's political interests are represented both by the president's national constituency and by legislators' or parliament members' more localized constituencies. If one branch does something that's unpopular, it can be blocked by the other branch. The result: political stability."

Scholar 2: "Parliamentary democracies are by far more stable than presidential democracies. In presidential systems, the executive and legislature can be controlled by different political parties, a situation that produces deadlock. Since the leaders of parliament can't remove the president and install a more compliant or agreeable executive, they are liable to resort to a coup, toppling the whole system. Parliamentary democracies avoid these pitfalls. In parliamentary democracies, all legitimacy and accountability resides with the legislature. The parliament organizes the government and chooses the executive (the prime minister) from among its own leaders. The prime minister and members of parliament have strong incentives to cooperate and keep things running smoothly and efficiently. The result: political stability."

Scholar 3: "You two have made such compelling—if incorrect—arguments that I almost hesitate to point this out: Democracies of any species, presidential or parliamentary, are inherently unstable. Any system that permits the clamor of competing parties or dissident viewpoints is surely bound to fail. If it's stability that you value above all else, then dictatorships will deliver. Strong executives, feckless or nonexistent legislatures, powerful armies, social control. The result: political stability."

The world dataset contains the variable durable, which measures the number of years since the last regime transition. The more years that have passed since the system last failed (higher values on durable), the more stable a country's political system. The variable regime_type3 captures system type: dictatorship, parliamentary democracy, or presidential democracy.

A. Perform a mean comparison analysis of the relationship between durable and regime_type3. Based on a comparison of means, which is the apparently correct ranking of regime types, from most stable to least stable?

❑ parliamentary democracies (most stable), presidential democracies, dictatorships (least stable)

❑ parliamentary democracies (most stable), dictatorships, presidential democracies (least stable)

B. Create a box plot of the relationship. Closely examine the box plot. In what way does the graphic evidence support the ranking you chose in Part A?

_____

_____

_____

_____

_____

C. In what way does the graphic evidence NOT support the ranking you chose in Part A?

_____

_____

_____

_____

_____

D. Print the box plot you created in Part B.

11. (Dataset: world. Variables: enpp3_democ, district_size3, frac_eth3.) Two scholars of comparative politics are discussing possible reasons why some democracies have many political parties and other democracies have only a few:

Scholar 1: "It all has to do with the rules of the election game. Some countries, such as the United Kingdom, have single-member electoral districts. Voters in each district elect only one representative. This militates in favor of fewer and larger parties, since small parties have less chance of winning enough votes to gain the seat. Other countries, like Switzerland, have multimember districts. Because voters choose more than one representative per district, a larger number of smaller parties have a chance to win representation. It doesn't surprise me in the least, then, that the UK has fewer political parties than Switzerland."

Scholar 2: "I notice that your explanation fails to mention the single most important determinant of the number of political parties: social structural heterogeneity. Homogeneous societies, those with few linguistic or religious differences, have fewer conflicts and thus fewer parties. Heterogeneous polities, by the same logic, are more contentious and will produce more parties. By the way, the examples you picked to support your case also support mine: The UK is relatively homogeneous and Switzerland relatively heterogeneous. It doesn't surprise me in the least, then, that the UK has fewer political parties than Switzerland."

A. Scholar 1's hypothesis: In a comparison of democracies, those having single-member districts will have (circle one)

fewer political parties   more political parties

than democracies electing multiple members from each district.

B. State Scholar 2's hypothesis:

_____

_____

_____

_____

_____

The world dataset variable enpp3_democ measures, for each democracy, the number of effective parliamentary parties: "1–3 parties," "4–5 parties," or "6–11 parties." Use enpp3_democ as the dependent variable to test each hypothesis. For independent variables, test Scholar 1's hypothesis using district_size3, which measures, for each democracy, the number of members per district: "single-member" districts, more than one but fewer than six members (">1 to 5"), and countries with "6 or more members" per district. Test Scholar 2's hypothesis using frac_eth3, which classifies each country's level of ethnic/ linguistic fractionalization as "Low," "Medium," or "High."

C. In the table that follows, record the percentages of cases falling into the lowest code of the dependent variable, 1–3 parties.

	Average number of members per district		
	Single member	> 1 to 5 members	6 or more members
Percentage having 1–3 parties	?	?	?
	Level of ethnic fractionalization		
	Low	Medium	High
Percentage having 1–3 parties	?	?	?

D. Which of the following statements best summarizes your findings? (check one)

❑ Scholar 1's hypothesis is supported by the analysis, but Scholar 2's hypothesis is not supported by the analysis.

❑ Scholar 2's hypothesis is supported by the analysis, but Scholar 1's hypothesis is not supported by the analysis.

❑ Both hypotheses are supported by the analysis.

❑ Neither hypothesis is supported by the analysis.

E. Making specific reference to your findings, write a paragraph explaining your choice in Part D.

_____

_____

_____

_____

_____

_____

_____

That concludes the exercises for this chapter.

NOTES

1. Stata treats the first-named variable as the row variable and the second-named variable as the column variable. Under this standard setup, the column option will produce percentages of the independent variable. In situations in which the independent variable has many more categories than the dependent variable, the standard setup might create formatting problems, and so you may want to create a cross-tabulation having the dependent variable on the columns and the independent variable on the rows. The following syntax would produce the desired result: tab independent_variable dependent_variable, row. The row option instructs Stata to calculated percentages of the row variable, which in this case is the independent variable.
2. V. O. Key, *Politics, Parties, and Pressure Groups,* 5th ed. (New York: Crowell, 1964), 568.
3. George A. Quattrone and Amos Tversky, "Contrasting Rational and Psychological Analyses of Political Choice," *American Political Science Review* 82, no. 3 (Sept. 1988), 719–736.
4. The Pew Research Center for the People and the Press, "Views of Parties' Ideologies: More Now See GOP as Very Conservative," Monday, September 12, 2011. http://www.people-press.org/2011/09/12/more-now-see-gop-as-very-conservative/.

5. Timur Kuran, *Private Truths, Public Lies: The Social Consequences of Preference Falsification* (Cambridge: Harvard University Press, 1995), 3.
6. It may have occurred to you that this effect might be greater for white respondents than for black respondents, with white subjects more likely to hide their true preferences in the presence of a black interviewer. An exercise in Chapter 5 will give you a chance to investigate this possibility.

5

Making Controlled Comparisons

Commands Covered

bysort *cntrl_var*: tabulate *dep_var indep_var* [*aw=weightvar*], col	Produces, for each value of the control variable, a cross-tabulation of the dependent variable and independent variable with column percentages
tabulate *cntrl_var indep_var* [*aw=weightvar*], summarize (*dep_var*)	Produces a breakdown table showing mean values of the dependent variable for each combination of the control variable and independent variable
graph bar (mean) *dep_var* [*aw=weightvar*], over (*indep_var*) over (*cntrl_var*)	Produces a bar chart showing the relationship between an interval-level dependent variable or an indicator dependent variable and an independent variable for each value of the control variable
graph box *dep_var* [*aw=weightvar*], over (*indep_var*) over (*cntrl_var*)	Produces a box plot showing the relationship between an interval-level dependent variable and an independent variable for each value of the control variable

Political analysis often begins by making simple comparisons using cross-tabulation analysis or mean comparison analysis. Simple comparisons allow the researcher to examine the relationship between an independent variable, X, and a dependent variable, Y. However, there is always the possibility that alternative causes—rival explanations—are at work, affecting the observed relationship between X and Y. An alternative cause is symbolized by the letter Z. If the researcher does not control for Z, then he or she may misinterpret the relationship between X and Y.

What can happen to the relationship between an independent variable and a dependent variable, controlling for an alternative cause? One possibility is that the relationship between the independent variable and the dependent variable is spurious. In a spurious relationship, once the researcher controls for a rival causal factor, the original relationship becomes very weak, perhaps disappearing altogether. The control variable does all of the explanatory work. In another possibility, the researcher observes an additive relationship between the independent variable, the dependent variable, and the control variable. In an additive relationship, two sets of meaningful relationships exist. The independent variable maintains a relationship with the dependent variable, and the control variable helps to explain the dependent variable. A third possibility, interaction, is somewhat more complex. If interaction is occurring, then the effect of the independent variable on the dependent variable depends on the value of the control variable. The strength or tendency of the relationship is different for one value of the control variable than for another value of the control variable.

These situations—a spurious relationship, an additive relationship, and interaction—are logical possibilities. Of course, Stata cannot interpret a set of controlled comparisons for you. But it can produce tabular analysis and graphics that will give you the raw material you need to evaluate controlled comparisons.

In this chapter, you will learn to use the tabulate command to analyze relationships when the independent variable and control variable are categorical and the dependent variable is categorical or interval-level. Because graphic displays are especially valuable tools for evaluating complex relationships, we will demonstrate how to obtain bar charts for controlled comparisons. For interval-level dependent variables, box plots can also add analytic value. All of these skills are natural extensions of the procedures you learned in Chapter 4.

CROSS-TABULATION ANALYSIS WITH A CONTROL VARIABLE

We will begin by working through an example with gss2012. Consider this hypothesis: In a comparison of individuals, those who attend religious services less frequently will be more likely to favor the legalization of marijuana than will those who attend religious services more frequently. In this hypothesis, attend3, which categorizes respondents' church attendance as "Low," "Moderate," or "High," is the independent variable. The dataset contains the variable grass, which records respondents' opinions on the legalization of marijuana. (Code 1 is labeled "Legal," and Code 2 is "Not legal.") First we will look at the uncontrolled relationship between attend3 and grass. Then we will add a control variable.

Open gss2012. Open a new Do-file. Go ahead and run the following tab command, which will produce a cross-tabulation of grass (dependent variable) by attend3 (independent variable) with column percentages: "tab grass attend3 [aw=gssw], col nokey nofreq."

```
.   tab grass attend3 [aw=gssw], col nokey nofreq
```

Legalize Pot?	Religious Attendance			Total
	Low	Moderate	High	
Legal	62.33	45.88	26.67	47.02
Not legal	37.67	54.12	73.33	52.98
Total	100.00	100.00	100.00	100.00

Clearly the hypothesis has merit. Of the low attenders, 62.33 percent favor legalization, compared with 45.88 percent of moderate attenders and 26.67 percent of the highly observant. What other factors, besides church attendance, might account for differing opinions on marijuana legalization? A plausible answer: whether the respondent has children. Regardless of religiosity, people with children may be less inclined to endorse the legalization of marijuana than may people who do not have children. And here is an interesting (if complicating) fact: People who attend church regularly are substantially more likely to have children than are people who rarely or never attend.[1] Thus, when we compare the marijuana opinions of "High" and "Low" attenders, as we have just done, we are also comparing people who are more likely to have children ("High") with people who are less likely to have children ("Low"). It could be that secular individuals are more inclined to favor legalization, not because they are less religious, but because they are less likely to have children. By the same token, those who go to church more often might oppose legalization for reasons unrelated to their religiosity: They're more likely to have children. The only way to isolate the effect of attendance on marijuana opinions is to compare low-attenders who do not have children with high-attenders who do not have children, and to compare low-attenders who have children with high-attenders who have children. In other words, we need to control for the effect of having children by holding it constant.

Dataset gss2012 contains the variable kids, which classifies respondents into one of two categories: those with children (coded 2 and labeled "Yes" on kids) or those without (coded 1 and labeled "No" on kids). Let's run the analysis again, this time adding kids as a control variable.

We need to ask Stata to produce two cross-tabulations. One cross-tab will show the grass-attend3 relationship for people without children, and the other will show the relationship for people with children. Because of the way Stata handles problems such as this—running a command for one value of a control variable (people without children) and rerunning the command for another value of the variable (people with children)—the dataset must first be sorted on the control variable. Conveniently, the user can request this procedure within the tabulate command. Modify the earlier tabulated command as follows:

```
bysort kids: tab grass attend3 [aw=gssw], col nokey nofreq
```

The command prefix "bysort kids:" instructs Stata to sort the dataset according to the values of the control variable, kids, and to produce a cross-tabulation of grass and attend3 for each value of the control. (Stata sometimes calls a sorting variable a "by variable." So, in the current example, kids is the by variable.) Run the modified command, and consider the results:

-> kids = No

Legalize Pot?	Religious Attendance			Total
	Low	Moderate	High	
Legal	71.87	56.17	37.44	62.31
Not legal	28.13	43.83	62.56	37.69
Total	100.00	100.00	100.00	100.00

-> kids = Yes

Legalize Pot?	Religious Attendance			Total
	Low	Moderate	High	
Legal	56.48	42.67	24.92	41.41
Not legal	43.52	57.33	75.08	58.59
Total	100.00	100.00	100.00	100.00

The first cross-tabulation, beneath the label "kids = No," shows the grass-attend3 relationship for people who do not have children. The bottom cross-tabulation shows the relationship for respondents with children, respondents with the value "Yes" on the control variable. (Unless instructed otherwise, Stata will run the command for cases defined as missing on the by variable, as in "kids = ." Generally, these results can be safely ignored. By using the if qualifier, the user can dissuade Stata from producing results for cases defined as missing on the by variable. To learn more about the if qualifier, see "A Closer Look" on page 84.) What is the relationship between church attendance and support for marijuana legalization among respondents who do not have children? For those with children? Is attend3 still related to grass? You can see that attend3 is related to marijuana opinions for both values of kids. Among people without children, 71.87 percent of the low-attenders favor legalization, compared with 56.17 percent of the middle group and 37.44 percent of the high-attenders. The more frequently people attend, the lower the likelihood that they will favor legalization. The same general pattern holds for people with children: 56.48 percent of the "Lows" favor legalization, compared with 42.67 percent of "Moderates" and 24.92 percent of "Highs." So, controlling for kids, attend3 is related to grass in the hypothesized way.

One bonus of control tables is that they permit you to evaluate the relationship between the control variable and the dependent variable, controlling for the independent variable. What is the relationship between the control variable, kids, and marijuana attitudes, controlling for church attendance? We address this question by moving between the top cross-tabulation and the bottom cross-tabulation, comparing marijuana opinions of people who share the same level of attendance but who differ on the control variable, kids. Consider low-attenders. Are "Lows" without kids more likely to favor legalization than are "Lows" with kids? Yes. Among those without children, 71.87 percent favor legalization versus 56.48 percent for those with children. How about "Moderates"? Yes, again. There is a noticeable difference between the percentages favoring legalization among those without children (56.17 percent) and those with children (42.67 percent). For frequent-attenders, too, we see a pronounced "kid effect": 37.44 percent, compared with 24.92 percent.

How would you characterize this set of relationships? Does a spurious relationship exist between grass and attend3? Or are these additive relationships, with attend3 helping to explain legalization opinions, and kids adding to the explanation? Or is interaction going on? Is the grass-attend3 relationship different for

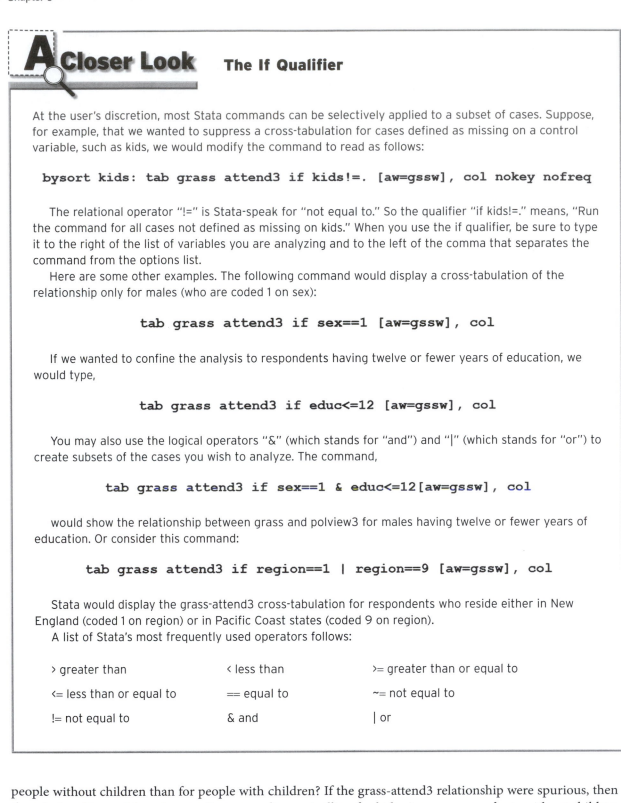

A Closer Look   The If Qualifier

At the user's discretion, most Stata commands can be selectively applied to a subset of cases. Suppose, for example, that we wanted to suppress a cross-tabulation for cases defined as missing on a control variable, such as kids, we would modify the command to read as follows:

```
bysort kids: tab grass attend3 if kids!=. [aw=gssw], col nokey nofreq
```

The relational operator "!=" is Stata-speak for "not equal to." So the qualifier "if kids!=." means, "Run the command for all cases not defined as missing on kids." When you use the if qualifier, be sure to type it to the right of the list of variables you are analyzing and to the left of the comma that separates the command from the options list.

Here are some other examples. The following command would display a cross-tabulation of the relationship only for males (who are coded 1 on sex):

```
tab grass attend3 if sex==1 [aw=gssw], col
```

If we wanted to confine the analysis to respondents having twelve or fewer years of education, we would type,

```
tab grass attend3 if educ<=12 [aw=gssw], col
```

You may also use the logical operators "&" (which stands for "and") and "|" (which stands for "or") to create subsets of the cases you wish to analyze. The command,

```
tab grass attend3 if sex==1 & educ<=12[aw=gssw], col
```

would show the relationship between grass and polview3 for males having twelve or fewer years of education. Or consider this command:

```
tab grass attend3 if region==1 | region==9 [aw=gssw], col
```

Stata would display the grass-attend3 cross-tabulation for respondents who reside either in New England (coded 1 on region) or in Pacific Coast states (coded 9 on region).

A list of Stata's most frequently used operators follows:

> greater than	< less than	>= greater than or equal to
<= less than or equal to	== equal to	~= not equal to
!= not equal to	& and	| or

people without children than for people with children? If the grass-attend3 relationship were spurious, then the relationship would weaken or disappear after controlling for kids. Among respondents without children, low-, moderate-, and high-attenders would all hold the same opinion about marijuana legalization. Similarly, for people with children, attendance would not play a role in explaining the dependent variable. Because the relationship persists after controlling for kids, we can rule out spuriousness. Now, it is sometimes difficult to distinguish between additive relationships and interaction relationships, so let's dwell on this question. In additive relationships, the effect of the independent variable on the dependent variable is the same or quite similar for each value of the control variable. In interaction relationships, by contrast, the effect of the independent variable on the dependent variable varies in strength or direction for different values of the control variable.

Return to the cross-tabulation results. The grass-attend3 relationship has the same tendency—it "runs in the same direction"—for people with and without children: For both values of the control, "Lows" are more prolegalization than are "Moderates," who in turn are more prolegalization than "Highs." What is more, the size of this effect is very similar at both values of the control variable. For individuals without kids, the percentage favoring legalization drops by 34.43 points across the full range of the independent variable: 71.87 − 37.44 = 34.43. So the "attendance effect" is about 34 points for people without children. For people with kids, the attendance effect would be 56.48 − 24.92 = 31.56, or about 32 points. And notice that the "kid effect," though perhaps a bit stronger for low-attenders, is quite similar across values of church attendance: 15.39 for "Lows" (71.87 − 56.48), 13.5 for "Moderates" (56.17 − 42.67), and 12.52 for "Highs" (37.44 − 24.92). Now, if someone were to ask, "What is the effect of church attendance on marijuana opinions?," we would not be misrepresenting the results to reply, "Low church attenders are about 30 percentage points more likely to favor legalization than are high-attenders." If asked about the role of children, we would be well within the boundaries of the data to say, "People without kids are about 13 points more likely to favor legalization than are people who have children." All additive relationships share this straightforward simplicity: Same tendency, same or similar strengths, at all values of the control variable. Interaction relationships are more challenging, because they can take a number of different forms. So that you can learn to recognize interaction, we will analyze another relationship using gss2012.

For this example, we'll keep the same independent variable (attend3) and control variable (kids), but change the dependent variable to homosex2, a two-category measure of respondents' view of homosexuality. Respondents are measured as saying that homosexuality is "Wrong" (coded 0) or "Not wrong" (coded 1). Copy/paste the earlier "bysort kids:" line onto a new line of your Do-file, change "grass" to "homosex2," and run the analysis:

```
bysort kids: tab homosex2 attend3 [aw=gssw], col nokey nofreq

-> kids = No
```

Homosexuality Wrong?	Religious Attendance			Total
	Low	Moderate	High	
Wrong	29.63	47.40	74.99	42.83
Not wrong	70.37	52.60	25.01	57.17
Total	100.00	100.00	100.00	100.00

```
-> kids = Yes
```

Homosexuality Wrong?	Religious Attendance			Total
	Low	Moderate	High	
Wrong	45.42	61.96	77.97	61.06
Not wrong	54.58	38.04	22.03	38.94
Total	100.00	100.00	100.00	100.00

Focus on the percentage of respondents saying "Not wrong." Clearly enough, religious attendance has a big effect on the dependent variable for people without children, as well as for people with children. As the independent variable changes from "Low" to "Moderate" to "High," the "Not wrong" percentages decline. So, just as with grass, the homosex2-attend3 relationship has the same tendency for both values of the control, kids. Now take a closer look at the size of this effect. For respondents without kids, the drop is on the order of 45 points, from 70.37 percent to 25.01 percent. For respondents with kids, the decline, though still noteworthy, is nonetheless weaker—about 32 points (from 54.58 percent to 22.03 percent). Keep practicing reading the control table and identifying the interaction pattern. Is the "kid effect" the same for low-attenders, moderate-attenders, and high-attenders? No, it is not. There is about a

16-percentage-point difference on the dependent variable between "Lows" without kids (70.37 percent) and "Lows" with kids (54.58 percent). For "Moderates," the kid effect shrinks slightly (about 14 points). Among "Highs," however, the effect of having children virtually disappears: 25.01 – 22.03 = 2.98, or about 3 percentage points. Thus, high-attenders share very similar opinions of homosexuality, regardless of whether they have children. For low- and moderate-attenders, by contrast, having kids makes a sizable difference in opinions on this issue.

Bar Charts for Controlled Comparisons with a Categorical Dependent Variable

Take a few moments to examine Figure 5-1, a bar chart of the relationship, analyzed earlier, between marijuana opinions and church attendance, controlling for whether respondents have children. The values of the control variable, kids, appear along the x-axis: "No" and "Yes." The y-axis records the percentage of each group falling into the "Legal" category of the dependent variable, grass. There are three bars at each value of kids. The lighter bars denote lower values of attend3, and the darker bars denote higher values of attend3. Appreciate the symmetry that bespeaks a set of additive relationships. For both sets of bars, the lightest bar stands about 30 points higher than the darkest bar. And, for bars of the same color, the one on the "No" sides stands about 13 points higher than the one on the "Yes" side. Clearly, this graphic greatly facilitates interpretation of the relationship. To reproduce Figure 5-1, follow two steps:

Figure 5-1   Bar Chart with a Control Variable (indicator dependent variable)

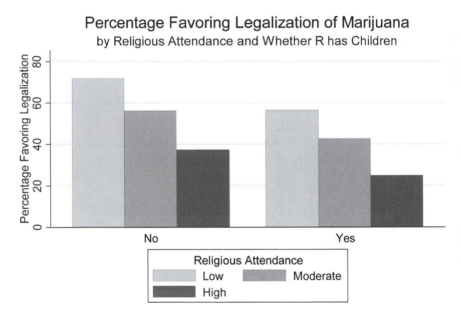

SOURCE: 2012 General Social Survey.

Step 1. Generate an indicator variable from the dependent variable. The dependent variable, grass, is a categorical variable. As discussed in Chapter 4, Stata will graph a categorical dependent variable after it has been transformed into an indicator variable. Because we want to graph the first-coded value of grass (code 1, "Legal"), we will be interested in the first indicator, grassdum1, generated by the following command: "tab grass, gen(grassdum)." To convert to percentages, type "replace grassdum1 = grassdum1 * 100":

```
tab grass, gen(grassdum)
replace grassdum1 = grassdum1 * 100
```

Step 2. Type and run the graph bar command. The following syntax contains some new elements, along with the usual suspects:

```
#delimit ;
graph bar (mean) grassdum1 [aw=gssw], over(attend3) over(kids)
  graphregion(fcolor(white))
asyvars
bar(1, fcolor(gs15))
bar(2, fcolor(gs10))
bar(3, fcolor(gs5))
ytitle("Percentage Favoring Legalization")
title("Percentage Favoring Legalization of Marijuana")
subtitle("by Religious Attendance and Whether R has Children")
note("Source: 2012 General Social Survey")
legend(title("Religious Attendance", size(medsmall)));
```

Annotations:
- over(attend3) — Independent variable
- over(kids) — Control variable
- asyvars — Enhances chart's appearance
- bar(1, fcolor(gs15)) / bar(2, fcolor(gs10)) / bar(3, fcolor(gs5)) — Requests a different grayscale ("gs") shade for each bar
- subtitle(...) — A subtitle is usually needed for controlled comparisons

This syntax adds necessary extensions to the basic graph bar procedure you learned in Chapter 4. Notice that the independent variable, attend3, is the first-mentioned "over" group, "over(attend3)," and the control variable comes second, "over(kids)." When Stata sees this ordering, it will first create a graph of the relationship between independent and dependent variables, and then create subsets on the basis of the second-mentioned variable, the control variable. This setup makes the graph directly analogous to the cross-tabulation analysis, in which we sorted on the control variable, kids, and then requested two cross-tabulations, one for each value of kids. The asyvars option is as influential as it is weird. When you specify this option, Stata applies three appearance-enhancing features: (1) The bars depicting categories of the independent variable will touch, (2) the bars will be of different colors (unless you specify colors, as we have done), and (3) the bars will be identified by a legend beneath the x-axis. Bar colors are largely a matter of taste. Even so, Stata's grayscale palette provides a reliable go-to. Higher "gs" values are lighter ("gs16" is white); lower "gs" values are darker ("gs0" is black). For ordinal variables, it makes sense to shade darker for higher values of the independent variable. Finally, the subtitle option allows for the longer titles that are usually required for complex relationships.

Write out the syntax, and run the command. Depending on your font size and bar color choices, the bar chart should look very similar to Figure 5-1.

MEAN COMPARISON ANALYSIS WITH A CONTROL VARIABLE

We now consider a situation in which the dependent variable is interval-level, and the independent variable and the control variable are nominal or ordinal. Three examples follow. The first (which uses an nes2012 variable, married, that you created in Chapter 3) analyzes a set of interaction relationships. In the second, you will identify an additive pattern. In the third example, you will create graphic displays for controlled mean comparisons—tasks that are recapitulations of the skills you have already gained. Before beginning the next example, save gss2012, and open nes2012.

An Example of Interaction

It has become an article of faith that women are more strongly attracted to the Democratic Party than are men. Indeed, on nes2012's Democratic Party feeling thermometer (ft_dem), women's ratings are five "degrees" warmer than men's: 54 degrees versus 49 degrees. We might wonder, however, whether this gap is the same for married and unmarried people. Plausibly, shared beliefs and values (perhaps including party affiliation) are of key importance to couples who marry. And evidence suggests that married couples become politically more similar over time.[2] Let's investigate the relationship between Democratic ratings and gender, controlling for marital status.

Stata provides a concise way to perform mean comparison analyses with a control variable. The following command will create a Stata *breakdown table*, a single table of summary statistics for each combination of values of the independent variable and the control variable:

```
tab  married gender[aw=nesw], sum(ft_dem) nost noobs nofreq
```

In this setup, the control variable is typed first (right after the tab command), followed by the independent variable (and weight variable), a comma, and the summarize option, which will return descriptive statistics on the variable enclosed in parentheses. By default, the summarize option will report means, standard deviations, weighted frequencies, and unweighted numbers of observations for each combination of variables named in the tab command. The syntax shown above suppresses all statistics except for means. Consider the results:

Is R Married?	Gender Male	Female	Total
No	53.07	62.08	57.71
Yes	46.14	48.03	47.13
Total	49.13	54.04	51.67

Breakdown tables are compact and readable. The values of the control variable, married, mentioned first in the syntax, define the rows. The values of the independent variable, gender, which appears second in the syntax, define the columns. Table entries are mean Democratic Party thermometer ratings for respondents having each combination of married and gender. The "Total" row and "Total" column report the overall means of the dependent variable for respondents of each gender (bottom-most row) and marital status (right-most column). For example, the mean rating for all women, unmarried and married mixed together, is 54.04. All unmarried respondents rated the Democrats at 57.71, on average.

To evaluate the effect of the independent variable, we would compare the mean ratings of women with the mean ratings of men for unmarried and for married respondents. What do these comparisons reveal? Consider respondents who are not married. The mean Democratic Party rating for unmarried men is 53.07. This mean increases to 62.08 for unmarried women. So, for the unmarried, the thermometer gets 9 degrees warmer as we move from males to females. Now shift your attention to married respondents. Here we see a gender gap of less than 2 degrees: 46.14 for men and 48.03 for women. Does the gender-Democratic thermometer relationship have the same tendency at both values of the control? Yes, for both unmarried and married respondents, women feel more warmly toward the Democratic Party than do men. Do the relationships have the same (or similar) strengths at both values of the control? No, the gender gap is almost five times larger for unmarried people than for married people. A situation such as this—same tendency, different strength—is a common form of interaction.

Confirm the interaction interpretation by determining how the control variable, married, affects Democratic ratings for each gender. For males, for instance, there is a difference of about 7 degrees: 53.07 for unmarried men compared with 46.14 for married men. The "marriage effect," however, is 14 degrees for women: 62.08 compared with 48.03. Again, same tendency (unmarried people rate the Democrats higher than do married people), but different strengths (the effect is substantially larger for women than for men).

An Example of an Additive Relationship

Nes2012 contains several measures of "linked fate," the extent to which individual members of identifiable groups feel attached to other members of the same group. For example, link_wom_scale measures the extent to which female respondents sense a connection between themselves and other women in society. Female respondents are measured as feeling "Weak," "Moderate," or "Strong" ties to other females. Nes2012 also contains modsex_scale, which measures the extent to which individuals perceive that women are discriminated against and have few opportunities for achievement. Modsex_scale runs from 0 (the respondent perceives little discrimination against women and more opportunities for achievement) to 16 (a great deal of discrimination, few opportunities). It seems reasonable to hypothesize that women with a stronger sense of linked fate (higher values on link_wom_scale) will be more likely to perceive higher levels of sexism (higher values on modsex_scale) than will women with a weaker sense of linked fate. It is an interesting question, however, whether the relationship will be the same for white females and black females. Blacks are likely to perceive greater discrimination than are whites, regardless of their feelings of a linked fate with other women. In this example, you will analyze the modsex_scale-link_wom_scale relationship, controlling for race (dem_raceeth2). In keeping with the mean comparison protocol, the following syntax will produce the analysis we are after:

```
#delimit ;
tab dem_raceeth2 link_wom_scale [aw=nesw],
  sum(modsex_scale) nofreq noobs nost ;
```

Means of Modern sexism

| White/Black | Linked fate: other Women | | | |
	Weak	Moderate	Strong	Total
White	7.99	8.60	9.34	8.57
Black	8.99	9.73	10.36	9.61
Total	8.16	8.75	9.50	8.73

Does linked fate work as hypothesized? Yes. For both whites and blacks, mean values of modsex_scale ascend as we move from "Weak" to "Moderate" to "Strong." Indeed, the magnitude of the end-to-end increase is virtually identical for both races: 1.35 for white females (9.34 − 7.99) and 1.37 for black females (10.36 − 8.99). And notice the consistent effects of race. At each value of the independent variable, black women are about 1 point higher on the discrimination scale than their white counterparts: 1 point among those having "Weak" linked fate, 1.13 points among the "Moderate" group, and 1.02 points among women who feel "Strong" ties to other women. Additive relationships are the soul of symmetry.

Bar Charts and Box Plots for Controlled Mean Comparisons

The procedures for creating bar charts based on cross-tabulations (categorical dependent variables) and bar charts for controlled mean comparisons (interval-level dependent variables) are the same, except that in the latter case we avoid the necessity of generating a set of indicator variables. Furthermore, for interval-level dependent variables, we can request box plots. In fact, it is so easy to obtain a box plot from a nicely optioned bar chart syntax, a box plot is almost always worth exploring. Easy? Stata? Sometimes it happens.

Consider Figure 5-2, a bar chart of the ft_dem-gender relationship, controlling for married. This is a fine visual complement to the mean comparison analysis. For unmarried respondents, the darker bar (females) is about 9 units taller than the lighter bar (males); for married people, there is only about a 2-point difference. For males, the left-hand bar stands about 7 units taller than the right-hand bar. For females, the difference is much larger, 14 points. Following is the increasingly familiar syntax that created Figure 5-2:

```
#delimit ;
 graph bar (mean) ft_dem [aw=nesw],
 over(gender) over(married) asyvars
 graphregion(fcolor(white))
 bar(1, fcolor(gs15))
 bar(2, fcolor(gs7))
 ytitle("Thermometer Rating")
 title("Democratic Party Thermometer Ratings",
  size(medlarge))
 subtitle("by Gender and Marital Status")
 note("Source: 2012 National Election Study")
 legend(title("Gender", size(medsmall)));
```

Now, do this. Copy/paste the bar chart syntax into empty space in your Do-file. In the pasted syntax, delete "bar (mean)" and replace it with "box":

Figure 5-2 Bar Chart with a Control Variable (interval-level dependent variable)

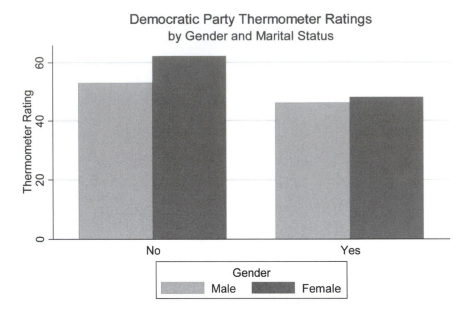

SOURCE: 2012 National Election Study

```
#delimit ;
```
Replace "bar (mean)" with "box"
```
graph box ft_dem [aw=nesw],
over(gender) over(married) asyvars
graphregion(fcolor(white))
bar(1, fcolor(gs15))
bar(2, fcolor(gs7))
ytitle("Thermometer Rating")
title("Democratic Party Thermometer Ratings",
 size(medlarge))
subtitle("by Gender and Marital Status")
note("Source: 2012 National Election Study")
legend(title("Gender", size(medsmall)));
```

Figure 5-3 Box Plot with a Control Variable (interval-level dependent variable)

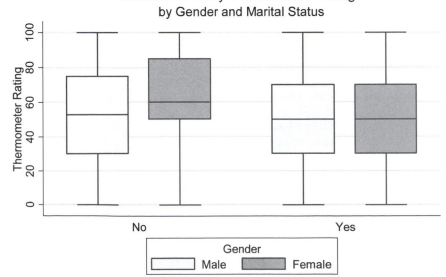

SOURCE: 2012 National Election Study

Create the plot, and see if anything interesting turns up (Figure 5-3). In terms of medians and interquartile ranges, married people are exact copies: Both medians are equal to 50, and the middle halves of both distributions fall between ratings of 30 and 70. The unmarried male distribution is flat and wide, with the longest interquartile range in the plot, between 30 and 75. Even so, despite a slightly higher median than married men—and a somewhat more stretched-out distribution—unmarried males and married males are similar in appearance. Unmarried females, by contrast, are distinct. They are the most cohesive group, with three fourths of them rating the Democratic Party between 50 and 85 (which is the highest upper quartile in the graph). Notice, too, the sizable number of unmarried women above the median of 60 degrees.

EXERCISES

1. (Dataset: world. Variables: world.dta, democ, gdpcap08_2, frac_eth3.) Some countries have democratic regimes, and other countries do not. What factors help to explain this difference? One idea is that the type of government is shaped by the ethnic and religious diversity in a country's population. Countries that are relatively homogeneous, with most people sharing the same language and religious beliefs, are more likely to develop democratic systems than are countries having more linguistic conflicts and religious differences. Consider the ethnic heterogeneity hypothesis: In a comparison of countries, countries with lower levels of ethnic heterogeneity will be more likely to be democracies than will countries with higher levels of ethnic heterogeneity.

   A. According to the ethnic heterogeneity hypothesis, if you were to compare countries having lower heterogeneity with countries having higher heterogeneity, you should find (check one)

      ❏ a lower percentage of democracies among countries having lower heterogeneity.

      ❏ a higher percentage of democracies among countries having lower heterogeneity.

      ❏ no difference between the percentage of democracies among countries having lower heterogeneity and the percentage of democracies among countries with higher heterogeneity.

   B. The world dataset contains the variable democ, "Democracy?," which classifies each country as a democracy ("Yes," coded 100) or a dictatorship ("No," coded 0). (Note: The 0/100 coding will make democ easier to graph in Part F below.) Democ is the dependent variable. The dataset also contains frac_eth3, which classifies countries according to their level of ethnic heterogeneity: "Low" (coded 1), "Medium" (coded 2), or "High" (coded 3). This is the independent variable. Run tabulate, testing the ethnic heterogeneity hypothesis. Fill in the percentages of democracies in the table.

	Ethnic heterogeneity		
	Low	Medium	High
Percentage of democracies	?	?	?

   C. Based on these results, you could say that (check one)

      ❏ as ethnic heterogeneity increases, the percentage of democracies increases.

      ❏ as ethnic heterogeneity increases, the percentage of democracies decreases.

      ❏ as ethnic heterogeneity increases, there is little change in the percentage of democracies.

   D. A country's level of economic development also might be linked to its type of government. According to this perspective, countries with higher levels of economic development will be more likely to be democracies than will countries with lower levels. The world dataset contains the variable gdpcap08_2. This variable, based on gross domestic product per capita, is an indicator of economic development. Countries are classified as "Low" (coded 0) or "High" (coded 1). Use the bysort prefix to obtain a cross-tabulation analysis of the democ-frac_eth3 relationship, controlling for gdpcap08_2. Fill in the percentages of democracies in the table.

	Ethnic heterogeneity		
	Low	Medium	High
Low GDP per capita Percentage of democracies	?	?	?
High GDP per capita Percentage of democracies	?	?	?

E. Examine the relationship between ethnic heterogeneity and democracy in high-GDP countries and low-GDP countries.

Consider the democ-frac_eth3 relationship for low-GDP countries. Are ethnic heterogeneity and democracy related? Answer yes or no and briefly explain.

_____

_____

_____

_____

_____

Now consider the democ_regime-frac_eth3 relationship for high-GDP countries.

Are ethnic heterogeneity and democracy related? Answer yes or no and briefly explain.

_____

_____

_____

_____

_____

F. Obtain and print a presentation-quality bar chart of the democ-frac_eth3 relationship, controlling for gdpcap08_2. Because non-democracies are coded 0 on democ, and democracies are coded 100, you do not need to generate a set of indicator variables in order to produce the chart. Remember to specify the independent variable as the first over group and the control variable as the second over group. Specify the asyvars option. Here are some suggestions for text elements: ytitle("Percentage of Democracies"), title("Percentage of Democracies"), subtitle("by Ethnic Heterogeneity and GDP Per Capita"), note("Source: World Dataset"), legend(title("Ethnic Heterogeneity", size(medsmall))).

G. Think about the set of relationships you just analyzed. Consider all the numeric and graphic evidence. How would you describe the relationship between ethnolinguistic heterogeneity and democracy, controlling for GDP per capita? (circle one)

spurious   additive   interaction

Explain your reasoning.

_____

_____

_____

_____

_____

2. (Dataset: world. Variables: women13, womyear2, pr_sys.) In Chapter 2 you analyzed the distribution of the variable women13, the percentage of women in the lower house of the legislatures in a number of countries. In this exercise you will analyze the relationship between women13 and two variables that could have an impact on the number of women serving in national legislatures.

First consider the role of the type of electoral system. Many democracies have proportional representation (PR) systems. PR systems foster multiple parties having diverse ideological positions—and, perhaps, having diverse demographic compositions as well. Non-PR systems, like the system used in US elections, militate in favor of fewer and more homogeneous parties. Thus you might expect that non-PR countries will have fewer women in their national legislatures than will countries with PR-based electoral systems.

Now consider the role of history and tradition. In some countries, women have had a long history of political empowerment. New Zealand, for example, gave women the right to vote in 1893. In other countries, such as Switzerland (where women were not enfranchised until 1971), women have had less experience in the electoral arena. Thus it seems reasonable to hypothesize that countries with longer histories of women's suffrage (say, that enfranchised women before 1944) will have higher percentages of women in their national legislatures than will countries in which women's suffrage is a more recent development (since 1944). In this exercise you will isolate the effect of the type of electoral system on the percentage of women in parliament, controlling for the timing of women's suffrage. However, before running any analyses, you will graphically depict different possible scenarios for the relationships you might discover.

Parts A and B contain graphic shells showing the percentage of women in parliament along the vertical axis and the type of electoral system along the horizontal axis. Countries without PR systems are represented by "No," and countries with PR systems by "Yes." For each shell, you will draw four bars within the graphic space: a bar for "1944 or before" countries without PR systems ("No"), a bar for "1944 or before" countries with PR systems ("Yes"), a bar for "After 1944" countries without PR systems ("No"), and a bar for "After 1944" countries with PR systems ("Yes").

A. Draw an additive relationship fitting this description: Countries with PR systems have higher percentages of women in parliament than do countries with non-PR systems, and countries with a longer history of women's suffrage have higher percentages of women in parliament than do countries with a shorter history of women's suffrage. (Hint: In additive relationships, the strength and tendency of the relationship is the same or very similar for all values of the control variable.)

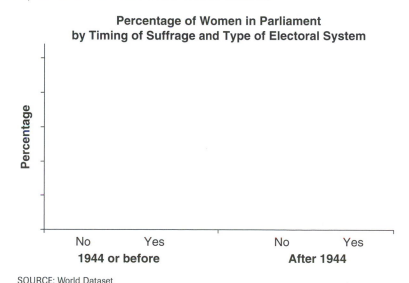

Percentage of Women in Parliament by Timing of Suffrage and Type of Electoral System

SOURCE: World Dataset

B. Draw a set of interaction relationships fitting this description: For countries with a longer history of women's suffrage, those with PR systems have higher percentages of women in parliament than do countries with non-PR systems. For countries with a shorter history of women's suffrage, the type of electoral system has no effect on the percentage of women in parliament.

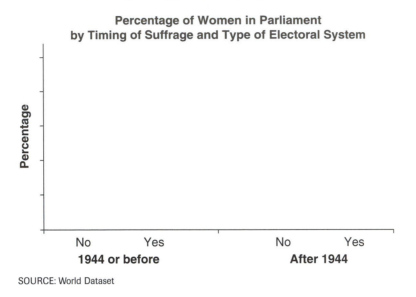

**Percentage of Women in Parliament
by Timing of Suffrage and Type of Electoral System**

SOURCE: World Dataset

In addition to the dependent variable, women13, the world dataset contains pr_sys, labeled "No" and coded 0 for countries with non-PR systems and labeled "Yes" and coded 1 for those having PR systems. Use pr_sys as the independent variable. World also contains womyear2, which measures the timing of women's suffrage by two values: "1944 or before" (coded 0) and "After 1944" (coded 1). Use womyear2 as the control variable.

C. Obtain a breakdown table showing mean values of women13 for each value of pr_sys, controlling for womyear2. Refer to the results. In the table below, record the mean values of women13 next to each question mark:

Women's suffrage	PR system?		Total
	No	Yes	
1944 or before	?	?	?
After 1944	?	?	?
Total	?	?	?

D. Obtain a bar chart of the relationship between women13 and pr_sys, controlling for womyear2. Use the titles and labeling shown in the graphic shells. Make sure to include the asyvars option, and specify a legend title (in medium small font), such as "PR system?".

E. Examine the numeric data (Part C) and the chart (Part D). Consider the women13-pr_sys relationship for countries that enfranchised women in 1944 or before. Examine the difference between the means for non-PR countries and PR countries. This difference shows that the mean for PR countries is _____ points (circle one)

lower than   higher than

the mean for non-PR countries.

Now consider the women13-pr_sys relationship for countries that enfranchised women after 1944. Examine the difference between the means for non-PR countries and PR countries. This difference shows that the mean for PR countries is _____ points (circle one)

lower than   higher than

the mean for non-PR countries.

F. Which of the following best characterizes the women13-pr_sys relationship, controlling for womyear2? (check one)

❑ The women13-pr_sys relationships have the same tendency and very similar strength at both values of womyear2.

❑ The women13-pr_sys relationships have the same tendency but very different strengths at each value of womyear2.

❑ The women13-pr_sys relationships have different tendencies at each value of womyear2.

G. Review your artistic work in parts A and B. Examine the table (Part C) and the chart (Part D). Consider your conclusions in parts E and F. Which possible scenario—the bar chart you drew in part A or B—resembles more closely the pattern shown in the data? (circle one)

The chart in Part A   The chart in Part B

H. As you know, box plots reveal distributional properties that are sometimes obscured by mean comparisons. Obtain a box plot of the relationships you have just analyzed. Do this by copy/pasting the bar chart syntax to an empty space in your Do-file. Replace "bar (mean)" with "box." Print the box plot. The box plot supports which of the following statements? Check all that apply.

_____A comparison of median values of women13 supports the findings of the mean comparison analysis.

_____"1944 or before" countries with PR systems show the most variation in women13.

_____"After 1944" countries without PR systems have the lowest median but outliers with extremely high values of women13.

3. (Dataset: nes2012. Variables: polknow3, dhs_threat3, ftgr_tea, [aw=nesw].) Given the tea party movement's deep skepticism of government activism, it seems plausible to hypothesize that individuals who regard the government as a threat would have warmer feelings toward the tea party than would those who do not think the government poses a threat. Of course, persons would need to be reasonably well informed about politics to make the connection between their assessment of government threat and their evaluation of the tea party. When we control for political knowledge (control variable), we may find that the relationship between tea party ratings (dependent variable) and perceptions of government threat (independent variable) gets stronger as knowledge increases. In other words, interaction could be occurring in this set of relationships. Consider two propositions and an ancillary hypothesis.

Proposition 1: At all levels of political knowledge (nes2012 variable, polknow3), individuals who perceive the government as a threat (dhs_threat3) will give the tea party higher ratings (ftgr_tea) than will people who do not regard the government as a threat.

Proposition 2: The relationship between perceived threat and tea party ratings will be weaker for lower-knowledge respondents than for those with higher knowledge.

Ancillary hypothesis: In a comparison of individuals, those with higher levels of political knowledge are less likely to regard the government as a threat than are those with lower levels of political knowledge.

The dependent variable: the tea party feeling thermometer (ftgr_tea), which runs from 0 (cold or negative feelings) to 100 (warm or positive feelings). The independent variable: dhs_threat3, which captures assessments of government's threat with three ordinal values—government represents no threat ("None"), a moderate threat ("Mod"), or an extreme threat ("Extrm"). Political knowledge is also a three-category ordinal: low ("Low know"), moderate ("Mid know"), and high knowledge ("High know").

A. Obtain a breakdown table of mean values of ftgr_tea for each combination of dhs_threat3 and polknow3. Record the means next to the question marks in the following table.

Pol Knowledge	Federal Government a Threat?			Total
	None	Moderate	Extreme	
Low know	?	?	?	?
Mid know	?	?	?	?
High know	?	?	?	?
Total	?	?	?	?

B. Obtain a presentation-quality bar chart of the relationship between the tea party thermometer and dhs_threat3 (first over group), controlling for polknow3 (second over group). Make sure to use the asyvars option. Request appropriate titles and fonts. Print the chart.

C. Consider the numeric table and the graph. Do the results support Proposition 1? Answer yes or no, and explain.

_____

_____

_____

_____

_____

_____

_____

D. Do the results support Proposition 2? Answer yes or no, and explain.

_____

_____

_____

_____

_____

_____

E. Test the ancillary hypothesis using dhs_threat3 as the dependent variable and polknow3 as the independent variable. Obtain column percentages. Do the results support the hypothesis? Answer yes or no, and explain, making specific reference to the cross-tabulation percentages.

_____

_____

_____

_____

_____

4. (Dataset: nes2012. Variables: ft_rep, south, dem_raceeth2, [aw=nesw].) Two political analysts are discussing reputed partisan differences between southern and non-southern states.

Political Analyst 1: "Media pundits and confused academics tend to exaggerate the South's reputation as a stronghold of Republican sentiment. In fact, people who live outside the South and people who live in the South don't differ that much in their ratings of the Republican Party. Look at my latest Stata analysis. When I ran 'tab south [aw=nesw], sum(ft_rep) nost' I found this: Non-southerners rated the Republicans at 43.40 on the feeling thermometer; this compared with a slightly warmer 46.66 for southerners. That's a paltry 3-point difference on the 100-point scale!"

Political Analyst 2: "Hmmm…that's interesting. But did you control for race? I wonder what happens to the relationship between region and Republican ratings after you take race into account. After all, blacks are less strongly attracted to the Republicans than are whites. And since southern states have a higher proportion of blacks than do non-southern states, racial differences in Republican ratings could affect regional differences in Republican ratings."

A. According to Political Analyst 2, why did Political Analyst 1's analysis find a small difference between the Republican ratings of non-southerners and the Republican ratings of southerners? (check two)

❑ Because southern respondents are more likely to be white than are non-southern respondents

❑ Because southern respondents are more likely to be black than are non-southern respondents

❑ Because blacks give the Republican Party lower ratings than do whites

❑ Because blacks give the Republican Party higher ratings than do whites

B. Obtain a breakdown table showing mean thermometer ratings of the Republican Party (ft_rep) by race (dem_raceeth2) and by non-southern/southern region of residence (south). The independent variable is south. Non-southern respondents are coded 0 on south, and southern respondents are coded 1. Use dem_raceeth2 as the control variable: "White" is coded 1, and "Black" is coded 2. Note: You will report weighted frequencies in this exercise, so do not specify the nofreq option. In the following table, fill in the mean values (Mean) and weighted frequencies (rounded to two decimal places) next to each question mark.

Means and Frequencies of Feeling Thermometer: Republican Party

Race:			
White		South	
Black	Non-South	South	Total
White Mean	?	?	?
Weighted Freq.	?	?	4136.55
Black Mean	?	?	?
Weighted Freq.	?	?	691.64
Total Mean	44.34	48.03	45.51
Weighted Freq.	3299.99	1528.19	4828.18

C. Refer to the right-most "Total" column of the table in Part B. This column shows you the mean values of ft_rep for all ~4,137 whites in the sample and all ~692 blacks in the sample. According to these numbers, whites are _____ points (circle one)

cooler   warmer

toward the Republican Party than are blacks.

D. Now figure out if the group of southern respondents has proportionately more blacks than the group of non-southern respondents. According the table in Part B, there are ~1,528 southern respondents in the data set. About what percentage of these 1,528 southern respondents are black? (circle one)

about 25 percent   about 35 percent   about 45 percent

About what percentage of the ~3,300 non-southern respondents are black? (circle one)

about 10 percent   about 20 percent   about 30 percent

E. Evaluate the ft_rep-south relationship, controlling for dem_raceeth2. When you compare southern whites with non-southern whites, you find that southern whites are _____ points (circle one)

cooler   warmer

toward the Republican Party than are non-southern whites.

When you compare southern blacks with non-southern blacks, you find that southern blacks are _____ points (circle one)

cooler   warmer

toward the Republican Party than are non-southern blacks.

F. Obtain a presentation-quality bar chart of the relationship between ft_rep and south (first over group), controlling for dem_raceeth2 (second over group). Make sure to use the asyvars option. Request appropriate titles and fonts. Print the chart.

G. Consider all of the evidence you have obtained in this exercise. How would you characterize this set of relationships? (circle one)

spurious   additive   interaction

Explain your reasoning:

_____

_____

_____

_____

_____

_____

_____

5. (Dataset: gss2012. Variables: race_2, intethn_2, natrace, natfare, natsci, [aw=gssw].) For an exercise in Chapter 4, you tested for the presence of preference falsification, the tendency for respondents to offer false opinions that they nonetheless believe to be socially desirable under the circumstances. You evaluated the hypothesis that respondents are more likely to express support for government policies aimed at helping blacks (such as "government spending to improve the conditions of blacks") when questioned by a black interviewer than when questioned by a white interviewer. But you did not control for the respondent's race. That is, you did not look to see whether whites are more (or less) likely than blacks to misrepresent their support for racial policies, depending on the race of the interviewer.[3]

Furthermore, it may be that whites, and perhaps blacks as well, will engage in the same preference-falsifying behavior for policies that do not explicitly reference race but that may *symbolize* race, such as "government spending for welfare." Although "welfare" does not mention "blacks," it may be that whites see "welfare" through a racially tinged lens and will respond *as if* the question refers to a racial policy. Of course, some policies, such as "government spending for scientific research," do not evoke such symbolic connections. Questions about these race-neutral policies should not show the same race-of-interviewer effects as questions that make explicit—or implicit—reference to race.[4]

In this exercise you will extend your Chapter 4 analysis in two ways. First, you will analyze the relationship between interviewer race (intethn_2, the independent variable) and three dependent variables: opinions on an explicitly racial policy (natrace, which measures attitudes toward spending to improve the conditions of blacks), a symbolically racial policy (natfare, opinions on spending for welfare), and a race-neutral policy (natsci, spending for scientific research). Second, you will perform these analyses while controlling for respondent's race (race_2).

Based on previous research in this area, what might you expect to find? Here are two plausible expectations:

Expectation 1: For both white and black respondents, the race-of-interviewer effect will be strongest for the explicitly racial policy (natrace), weaker for the symbolically racial policy (natfare), and weakest for the race-neutral policy (natsci).

Expectation 2: For the explicitly racial policy (natrace) and for the symbolically racial policy (natfare), the race-of-interviewer effect will be greater for white respondents than for black respondents. For the race-neutral policy (natsci), the race-of-interviewer effect will be the same (or close to 0) for both white respondents and black respondents (see Expectation 1).

A. Run the appropriate cross-tabulation analyses. In the table that follows, record the percentages of respondents saying that we are spending "too little" in each of the policy areas. For each policy, obtain the race-of-interviewer effect by subtracting the percentage of respondents saying "too little" when interviewed by a white questioner from the percentage saying "too little" when interviewed by a black questioner. (For example, if 50.0 percent of respondents said we are spending "too little" when questioned by a white and 70.0 percent said "too little" when questioned by a black, then the race-of-interview effect would be 70.0 percent minus 50.0 percent, or 20.0 percent.)

| Race of respondent | Percent saying we are spending "too little" on: | Race of interviewer | | |
		White	Black	Race-of-interviewer effect (black % - white %)
White	Improving the conditions of blacks (natrace)	?	?	?
	Welfare (natfare)	?	?	?
	Supporting scientific research (natsci)	?	?	?
Black	Improving the conditions of blacks (natrace)	?	?	?
	Welfare (natfare)	?	?	?
	Supporting scientific research (natsci)	?	?	?

B. Examine the data closely. Among white respondents, would you say that Expectation 1 is or is not supported by the evidence? (circle one)

Expectation 1 is not supported.   Expectation 1 is supported.

Explain your reasoning.

_____

_____

_____

_____

_____

_____

Among black respondents, would you say that Expectation 1 is or is not supported by the evidence? (circle one)

Expectation 1 is not supported.   Expectation 1 is supported.

Explain your reasoning.

_____

_____

_____

_____

_____

_____

C. Now compare the race-of-interviewer effects between respondents of different races. That is, compare the race-of-interviewer effect on natrace among white respondents with the race-of-interviewer effect on natrace among black respondents. Do the same for natfare and natsci. Generally speaking, would you say that Expectation 2 is supported or is not supported by the evidence? (circle one)

Expectation 2 is not supported.   Expectation 2 is supported.

Explain your reasoning.

_____

_____

_____

_____

_____

_____

_____

D. Produce a presentable bar chart of the relationship between natrace and intethn_2, controlling for race_2. You will need to generate an indicator variable that is coded 1 for respondents saying we are spending "too little" and 0 for respondents giving other responses. Use the replace command to multiply the indicator by 100. Make sure to use the asyvars option. Request appropriate titles and fonts. Print the chart.

That concludes the exercises for this chapter. Before exiting Stata, be sure to save your Do-file.

NOTES

1. According to gss2012, 82.83 percent of high-attenders have children, compared with 62.06 percent of low-attenders—a 20-percentage-point difference.
2. Laura Stoker and M. Kent Jennings, "Political Similarity and Influence Between Husbands and Wives," in _The Social Logic of Politics_, ed. Alan S. Zuckerman (Philadelphia: Temple University Press, 2005).
3. See Darren W. Davis and Brian D. Silver, "Stereotype Threat and Race of Interviewer Effects in a Survey of Political Knowledge," _American Journal of Political Science_ 47, no. 1 (2003), 33–45.
4. There is a large body of literature on "symbolic racism." For an excellent review and analysis, see Stanley Feldman and Leonie Huddy, "Racial Resentment and White Opposition to Race-Conscious Programs: Principles or Prejudice?" _American Journal of Political Science_ 49, no. 1 (2005), 168–183.

6

Making Inferences about Sample Means

Commands Covered

mean *varname* [pw=*probability_weightvar*] lincom [*varname*] - *test_value*	Performs a one-sample t-test
mean *dep_var* [pw=*probability_weightvar*], over(*indep_var*) lincom [*dep_var*]*indepvar_label1* - [*dep_var*]*indepvar_label2*	Performs a two-sample t-test

Political research has much to do with observing patterns, creating explanations, framing hypotheses, and analyzing relationships. In interpreting their findings, however, researchers often operate in an environment of uncertainty. This uncertainty arises, in large measure, from the complexity of the political world. As we have seen, when we infer a causal connection between an independent variable and a dependent variable, it is hard to know for sure whether variation in the independent variable is causing the variation we observe in the dependent variable. Other, uncontrolled variables might be affecting the relationship, too. Yet uncertainty arises, as well, from the simple fact that research findings are often based on random samples. In an ideal world, we could observe and measure the characteristics of every element in the population of interest—every voting-age adult, every student enrolled at a university, every bill introduced in every national legislature, and so on. In such an ideal situation, we would enjoy a high degree of certainty that the variables we have described and the relationships we have analyzed mirror what is really going on in the population. But of course we often do not have access to every member of a population. Instead we rely on a sample, a subset drawn at random from the population. By taking a random sample, we introduce random sampling error. In using a sample to draw inferences about a population, therefore, we never use the word *certainty*. Rather, we talk about *confidence* or *probability*. We know that the measurements we make on the sample will reflect the characteristics of the population, within the boundaries of random sampling error.

What are those boundaries? If we calculate the mean income of a random sample of adults, for example, how confident can we be that the mean income we observe in our sample is the same as the mean income in the population? The answer depends on the standard error of the sample mean, the extent to which the mean income of the sample departs by chance from the mean income of the population. If we use a sample to calculate a mean income for women and a mean income for men, how confident can we be that the difference between these two sample means reflects the true income difference between women and men in the population? Again, the answer depends on the standard error—in this case, the standard error of the *difference* between the sample means, the extent to which the difference in the sample departs from the difference in the population.

In this chapter you will use the mean and lincom commands to explore and apply inferential statistics. First, you will use the mean command to obtain the 95 percent confidence interval—the boundaries within which there is a .95 probability that the true population mean falls. Using one of Stata's postestimation commands, lincom ("linear combination"), you will learn to test hypotheses about a single sample mean. Supplied with the over option, the mean command also permits you to compare two sample means, and the lincom command will test for statistically significant differences between them.

DESCRIBING A SAMPLE MEAN

To gain insight into the properties and application of inferential statistics, we will work through an example using nes2012. The dataset contains egal_scale, a measure of egalitarian beliefs that ranges from 0 (low egalitarianism) to 24 (high egalitarianism). Stata syntax does not get much simpler than the mean command:

mean *varname* [pw = *probability_weightvar*]

Type "mean," followed by the name of the variable of interest and, in brackets, an optional probability weight "[pw=…]." Probability weight? Haven't we been using analytic weights, "[aw=…]," in this book? Yes, but now our aim is different. Analytic weights give us accurate estimates of *sample* statistics, such as means and percentages. Probability weights allow us to figure out how closely a sample statistic reflects a *population* parameter.[1] As a practical matter, we simply substitute "pw" for "aw" and use the dataset's weight variable:

```
mean egal_scale [pw=nesw]
```

Stata responds:

```
Mean estimation                    Number of obs    =    5456
```

	Mean	Std. Err.	[95% Conf. Interval]	
egal_scale	14.0839	.0898937	13.90767	14.26013

In the sample of 5,456 respondents, egal_scale has a mean equal to 14.0839, or 14.08.[2] How closely does the mean of 14.08 reflect the true mean in the population from which this sample was drawn? If we had measured egal_scale for every US adult and calculated a population mean, how far off the mark would our sample estimate of 14.08 be? The answer depends on the standard error of the sample mean, equal to .0898937, or .09. This number, .09, tells us the extent to which the sample mean of 14.08 departs by chance from the population mean. It is an established statistical rule that, if we were to calculate the sample means of an infinite number of random samples drawn from an unseen population, the mean of all those sample means would be equal to the population mean, give or take a standard error or two. More precisely, there is a 95 percent probability that the true population mean falls in the interval between the sample mean minus 1.96 standard errors and the sample mean plus 1.96 standard errors. However, because random processes can produce fluke samples, there is a .05 probability that the population mean falls outside the 95 percent confidence interval—a .025 chance that it lies below the lower boundary, and a .025 chance that it lies above the upper boundary. Using Stata's classic display command (abbreviated "dis"), and armed only with the standard error, we could arrive at the 95 percent confidence interval on our own (accurate to three decimal places):

```
. dis 14.0839 - 1.96*.0898937   ← The sample mean minus 1.96 standard errors
13.907708
```

```
. dis 14.0839 + 1.96*.0898937   ← The sample mean plus 1.96 standard errors
14.260092
```

Confidence intervals provide a foolproof tool for inference and hypothesis testing. Suppose someone claimed that egal_scale's true population mean is 13.5, not 14.08, the estimate we obtained. Because only .025, or 2.5 percent, of all possible population means fall below 13.91, we know that it is highly unlikely—a probability less than .025—that the true mean is 13.5. Similarly, if someone hypothesized that the population mean is equal to 14.2, we would not reject this claim. The proposed mean of 14.2 falls within the high-probability zone defined by 13.91 at the low end and 14.26 at the high end. We accept all hypothetical claims within this zone and reject all hypothetical claims outside this zone.

The confidence interval approach is quick and easy to apply, but it is blunt. In the P-value approach, implemented using the lincom command, the researcher determines the exact probability associated with a hypothetical claim about the population mean. Let's run the command and then review what Stata has done:

```
lincom [egal_scale] - 13.5
```

- Subtracts the hypothetical population mean from the sample mean
- Tells Stata to recall from memory egal_scale's mean, 14.08

In the Results Window:

Mean	Coef.	Std. Err.	t	P>|t|	[95% Conf. Interval]	
(1)	.5838985	.0898937	6.50	0.000	.4076709	.7601261

To test the hypothetical claim that egal_scale's true mean is equal to 13.5, lincom first calculated the difference between the observed sample mean (14.08) and the hypothetical population mean (13.5). The difference, 14.08 minus 13.5, is recorded in the "Coef." column: .5838985, or .58. Lincom then provides a t-statistic or t-ratio, equal to 6.50. A t-ratio is a *test statistic*, a number used for making statistical inferences.

Stata computes a t-ratio by subtracting the hypothetical population mean from the observed sample mean and dividing by the standard error:

t = (observed mean − hypothetical mean) / standard error.

In the current example:

t = (14.0839 − 13.5) / .0898937 ≈ 6.50.

When you compare two means that are equal or nearly equal, the numerator in the first expression above will be close to zero, resulting in a low magnitude for t. (In using t-ratios to make inferences, ignore the sign, "+" or "-," and focus on the absolute value of t.) Low t-ratios produce high probability values, or P-values. P-values, which can range from 0 to 1, communicate the probability that the two means were drawn from the same population of means. When we can say, with 95 percent confidence, that two means could have been drawn from the same population of means, then we conclude that they are not significantly different. Low t-ratios and their accompanying high P-values communicate a strong likelihood that the two means came from the same population—therefore, that they are not statistically different from each other. As the difference between the sample mean and the hypothetical mean grows in size, the numerator in the above expression increases, resulting in higher t-ratios. High t-ratios produce low P-values, communicating a lower probability that the two means were drawn from the same population of means—thus, that they are statistically different from each other.

Our current example returned a t-ratio equal to 6.50 and a P-value equal to 0.000. The P-value may be interpreted like this: If, as the hypothetical claim asserts, the true population mean is equal to 13.5, then a random sample from that population would yield the observed sample mean (14.08) 0.000 percent of the time, by chance. In other words, it is highly unlikely that the true population is equal to 13.5. [3] Therefore, we reject the hypothetical mean and infer that the observed mean, 14.08, is closer to the true population mean.

The ".05 rule" defines a widely accepted standard for interpreting P-values. For P-values of greater than .05, do not reject the hypothetical claim. There is a likelihood of greater than .05 that the observed mean and the proposed mean were both drawn from the same population. For P-values that are equal to or less than .05, reject the hypothetical claim. The probability is low—5 percent or less—that both values, the observed mean and the hypothetical mean, were drawn from the same population. To reemphasize, the .05 benchmark is the standard for testing your hypothesis. If the P-value is less than or equal to .05, you can infer that the hypothetical mean is significantly different from the sample mean. If the P-value is greater than .05, you can infer that the hypothetical mean is not significantly different from the observed sample mean.

So that you can become comfortable thinking about P-values, let's run through another example. This time we test the claim that the true population mean is equal to 14.2. Recall that, because 14.2 falls within egal_scale's 95 percent confidence interval, 13.91–14.26, we cannot reject the 14.2 claim. A P-value will lend more precision to this inference. Because lincom is a postestimation command, by default it will analyze only the most recent results it holds in memory. To ensure that the egal_scale estimates are the most recent, we will quickly rerun the mean command, followed by "lincom [egal_scale] – 14.2":

```
mean egal_scale [pw=nesw]
```

Mean estimation   Number of obs   =   5456

	Mean	Std. Err.	[95% Conf. Interval]	
egal_scale	14.0839	.0898937	13.90767	14.26013

```
lincom [egal_scale] - 14.2
```

Mean	Coef.	Std. Err.	t	P>|t|	[95% Conf.	Interval]
(1)	-.1161015	.0898937	-1.29	0.197	-.2923291	.0601261

Lincom returns the difference, -.12; a t-ratio of small magnitude, -1.29; and a P-value of .197, which is greater than .05. If the true population mean is 14.2, then a random sample would yield the observed mean, 14.08, .197 (or 19.7 percent) of the time by chance. So, yes, the true population mean could be 14.2. A P-value of .197 represents a fairly high probability that 14.08 and 14.2 were drawn from the same population of means. Therefore, do not reject the claim that the true mean is 14.2.

TESTING THE DIFFERENCE BETWEEN TWO SAMPLE MEANS

We now turn to a common hypothesis-testing situation: comparing the sample means of a dependent variable for two groups that differ on an independent variable. Someone investigating the gender gap, for example, might test the hypothesis that women are more egalitarian than men: In a comparison of individuals, women score higher on the egalitarian scale than do men. The hypothesis asserts that, in the unobserved population of individuals, women and men form distinct subpopulations. For women, the true subpopulation mean of the egalitarianism scale is higher than the true subpopulation mean for men.

The researcher always tests his or her hypotheses against a skeptical foil, the *null hypothesis*. The null hypothesis claims that, regardless of any group differences that a researcher observes in a random sample, no group differences exist in the population from which the sample was drawn. Thus, the null hypothesis states that distinct subpopulation means do not exist, that the mean for women and the mean for men were drawn from the same population. How does the null hypothesis explain systematic patterns that might turn up in a sample, such as a mean difference between women and men on egal_scale? Random sampling error. In essence the null hypothesis says, "You observed such and such a difference between two groups in your random sample. But, in reality, no difference exists in the population. When you took the sample, you introduced random sampling error. Thus, random sampling error accounts for the difference you observed."

For the gender-egal_scale hypothesis, the null hypothesis says that there is no real difference between men and women in the population, that men do not score lower than women on egal_scale. The null hypothesis further asserts that any observed differences in the sample can be accounted for by random sampling error. The null hypothesis, abbreviated H_0, is so central to the methodology of statistical inference that we always begin by assuming it to be correct. We then set a fairly high standard for rejecting it. The researcher's hypothesis is considered the alternative hypothesis, abbreviated H_A. In the current case, H_A is the hypothesis that women are more egalitarian than men.

The mean command's over option permits us to compare means of a dependent variable for groups defined by an independent variable. The lincom command returns a t-ratio and P-value for the mean difference. Nes2012 contains female, an indicator variable coded 0 for males ("Male") and 1 for females ("Female"). First let's run the mean command with the over option:

```
mean egal_scale [pw=nesw], over(female)
```

Over	Mean	Std. Err.	[95% Conf. Interval]	
egal_scale				
Male	13.69738	.1288302	13.44482	13.94993
Female	14.44775	.1250026	14.2027	14.69281

Women score 14.45 on the scale, about .75 higher than men, who average 13.70. Is the difference statistically significant? Although the lincom command will give us a precise answer (this analysis is performed below), a comparison of the confidence intervals counsels us to reject the null hypothesis. Notice the upper boundary of the male range, 13.95. This represents the highest plausible male mean in the population. Now notice the lower boundary for women, 14.20. This number represents the lowest plausible female mean in the population. Because the lowest plausible female mean (14.20) is higher than the highest plausible male mean (13.95), we can be quite confident that women and men do indeed compose distinction subpopulations within the population.

There is one note of caution when making inferences using the confidence interval approach. To be sure, if two 95 percent confidence intervals do not overlap, then rest assured that the two sample means are significantly different. The difference between them is large enough to safely reject the null hypothesis. However, the converse is not always true. That is, sometimes two confidence intervals may overlap slightly, yet the mean difference remains statistically significant. For this reason, it is always a good idea to run lincom and obtain precise P-values for mean comparisons you find interesting. For example, following is the lincom syntax that tests the gender difference on egal_scale:

```
lincom [egal_scale]Male - [egal_scale]Female
```

Value label for code 0 on female: "Male"	Value label for code 1 on female: "Female"

This command asks lincom to subtract the female mean from the male mean, and to evaluate the difference. You must use the exact value labels in identifying the subsample means.[4]

Mean	Coef.	Std. Err.	t	P>|t|	[95% Conf. Interval]	
(1)	-.7503768	.1795073	-4.18	0.000	-1.102283	-.3984709

Lincom reports the mean difference, -.75; the standard error of the difference, .18; a t-ratio (t = -4.18); and the probability (P-value) that the difference was produced by random sampling error, 0.000. Under the assumption that the null hypothesis is correct, we would observe a mean difference of -.75 zero percent of the time, by chance. Reject the null hypothesis.

EXTENDING THE MEAN AND LINCOM COMMANDS

Adapt the mean-lincom duo to other mean comparison situations. Suppose that the independent variable is not a 0-1 indicator (such as female) but a multicategory nominal or ordinal. The mean command will return statistics for each value of the independent variable, and lincom will allow you to test for statistically significant differences between pairs of means. For example, the following command requests means, standard errors, and confidence intervals for each value of party identification (pid_3)—"Dem," "Ind," and "Rep":

```
mean egal_scale [pw=nesw], over(pid_3)
```

Over	Mean	Std. Err.	[95% Conf.	Interval]
egal_scale				
Dem	16.51603	.1271447	16.26677	16.76528
Ind	13.86404	.140833	13.58795	14.14013
Rep	11.2396	.1627034	10.92064	11.55856

Democrats average 16.52, Independents 13.86, and Republicans 11.24. Thus, as partisanship changes from "Dem" to "Ind" to "Rep," mean values of egal_scale decline. Interestingly, none of the 95 percent confidence intervals overlap. Therefore, any comparison of mean differences—Democrats compared with Independents, Independents compared with Republicans, or Democrats compared with Republicans—will yield P-values that beat the null hypothesis. Comparing Democrats with Independents, we have the following:

```
lincom [egal_scale]Dem - [egal_scale]Ind
```

Mean	Coef.	Std. Err.	t	P>|t|	[95% Conf.	Interval]
(1)	2.651984	.1897359	13.98	0.000	2.280026	3.023943

Lincom returns the mean difference (2.65), a gargantuan t-ratio (13.98), and a miniscule P-value (0.000). Reject the null hypothesis, and conclude that, in the population, Democrats are significantly more egalitarian than Independents.

The mean-lincom combo can also compare the means of subpopulations defined by differences on two (or more) variables. Suppose we are exploring egalitarian beliefs among four groups: white males, white females, black males, and black females. We would enter two variables in the over option—black (coded 0 and labeled "No" for whites; coded 1 and labeled "Yes" for blacks), and female (0 = "Male," 1 = "Female"):

```
mean egal_scale [pw=nesw], over(black female)
```

```
       Over: black female
  _subpop_1: No Male
  _subpop_2: No Female
  _subpop_3: Yes Male
  _subpop_4: Yes Female
```

> Stata labels each subpopulation sequentially and associates the labels with the mean estimates

Over	Mean	Std. Err.	[95% Conf.	Interval]
egal_scale				
_subpop_1	13.25594	.1364503	12.98844	13.52343
_subpop_2	13.99917	.1326688	13.73908	14.25925
_subpop_3	17.15763	.3399296	16.49123	17.82403
_subpop_4	17.50795	.286485	16.94632	18.06957

White males (labeled "_subpop_1") have the lowest mean score, 13.26, about .74 below white females ("_subpop_2"), who average 13.999, or 14.0. As a substantive matter, a mean difference of .74 on egal_scale, which runs from 0 to 24, may not seem particularly noteworthy. However, according to the nonoverlapping confidence intervals, the mean difference is statistically significant. More interesting is the substantial distance—between 3 and 4 points—between the means for whites and the means for blacks. Black males ("_subpop_3") average 17.16, only about .35 lower than black females ("_subpop_4"), who show a mean value of 17.51. Indeed, the highest plausible black-male mean, 17.82, is well within the confidence band of the black-female mean, suggesting that the difference between the two means is statistically indistinguishable from zero.

Lincom confirms our confidence-interval work for whites and for blacks. In using lincom to compare subpopulation means, use Stata's labels, including the leading underscore. Thus, to compare the white-male and white-female means:

```
lincom [egal_scale]_subpop_1 - [egal_scale]_subpop_2
```

Mean	Coef.	Std. Err.	t	P>|t|	[95% Conf. Interval]	
(1)	-.7432322	.1903147	-3.91	0.000	-1.116325	-.3701391

The mean difference (-.74) and standard error (.19) combine to produce a sizable t-ratio (-3.91) and small P-value (0.000). The null hypothesis's idea that, in the population, white males and white females do not differ on egal_scale does not hold up. Reject the null hypothesis. H_0 prevails, however, in the comparison between black males and black females:

```
lincom [egal_scale]_subpop_3 - [egal_scale]_subpop_4
```

Mean	Coef.	Std. Err.	t	P>|t|	[95% Conf. Interval]	
(1)	-.3503158	.4445513	-0.79	0.431	-1.221814	.5211828

If the null hypothesis is correct that the black-male mean and black-female mean are drawn from the same population—that the gender gap among blacks is equal to zero—then we would observe a mean difference of -.35 about 43 percent of the time, by chance. Do not reject the null hypothesis.

EXERCISES

1. (Dataset: gss2012. Variables: spend10, [pw=gssw].) Dataset gss2012 contains spend10, which records the number of government policy areas where respondents think spending should be increased. Scores range from 0 (the respondent does not want to increase spending on any of the policies) to 10 (the respondent wants to increase spending on all ten policies). The 2012 GSS, of course, polls a random sample of US adults. In this exercise you will analyze spend10 using the mean and lincom commands. You then will draw inferences about the population mean. (Remember to specify gssw as the probability weight.)

   A. Spend10 has a sample mean of _____.

   B. There is a probability of .95 that spend10's true population mean falls between a score of _____ at the low end and a score of _____ at the high end.

   C. A student researcher hypothesizes that political science majors will score significantly higher on spend10 than the typical adult. The student researcher also hypothesizes that business majors will score significantly lower on the spend10 than the average adult. Using the same questions asked in the GSS, the researcher obtains scores on spend10 from a number of political science majors and a group of business majors. Here are the results: political science majors' mean, 3.11; business majors' mean, 2.85. Using the confidence interval approach, you can infer that (check one)

      ❑ political science majors do not score significantly higher on spend10 than US adults.

      ❑ political science majors score significantly higher on spend10 than US adults.

      Using the confidence interval approach, you can infer that (check one)

      ❑ business majors do not score significantly lower on spend10 than US adults.

      ❑ business majors do score significantly lower on spend10 than US adults.

D. Run lincom to evaluate the difference between the GSS spend10 mean and the business majors' mean. The mean difference is equal to _____. The t-ratio of the mean difference is equal to _____. The P-value is equal to _____.

E. Interpret the P-value you recorded in Part D. Suppose someone hypothesized that the business majors' mean was drawn from the same population that produced the GSS spend10 mean. Applying the .05 rule, you would (circle one)

reject   not reject

this claim because (fill in the blank) _____.

2. (Dataset: gss2012. Variables: spend10, sex, [pw=gssw].) In discussing the gender gap, two scholars of public opinion observe that there are gender differences "on issues relating to jobs, education, income redistribution, and protection of the vulnerable in society."[5] In this exercise, you will analyze values of spend10 to test this idea. Recall that spend10 ranges from 0 (the respondent does not want to increase spending on any of ten government programs) to 10 (the respondent wants to increase spending on all ten programs). Gss2012 also contains sex, with categories "Male" and "Female." Now, consider the following hypothesis: In a comparison of individuals, women will score significantly higher on spend10 than will men.

A. The null hypothesis for the relationship between sex and spend10 is as follows (fill in the blanks): In the population from which the sample is drawn, the difference between the mean value of spend10 for men and the mean value of spend10 for women is equal to _____. Any difference observed in the sample was produced by _____ when the sample was drawn.

B. Run the mean command with the over option. Run lincom to evaluate the mean difference between women and men. Fill in the blanks:

Male mean: _____

Female mean: _____

Mean difference: _____

t-ratio: _____   P-value: _____

C. Which two of the following statements are supported by your findings? (check two)

❑ In the population, women probably do not score higher on spend10 than do men.

❑ The statistical evidence supports the alternative hypothesis.

❑ If the null hypothesis is correct, a random sample would produce the observed mean difference more than 5 percent of the time, by chance.

❑ Reject the null hypothesis.

3. (Dataset: gss2012. Variables: spend10, sex, married [pw=gssw].) Consider two claims about the relationship between opinions on government spending (dependent variable), sex (independent variable), and marital status (control variable).

Claim 1. Among unmarried people, women will be significantly more likely than men to favor government spending—a statistically significant gender gap exists among the unmarried.

Claim 2. Among married people, women and men will have similar views on government spending—no statistically significant gender gap exists among the married.

Again you will use spend10 as the dependent variable. Spend10 ranges from 0 (the respondent does not want to increase spending on any of ten government programs) to 10 (the respondent wants to increase spending on all ten government programs). Use sex as the independent variable (1 = "Male" and 2 = "Female"), and married as the control (0 = "No" and 1 = "Yes"). Test Claim 1 and Claim 2 by running the mean command on spend10 with the over option, using married and sex. Specify this order: "over (married sex)."

A. Make two lincom runs: One comparing unmarried men with unmarried women, the second comparing married men with married women. Fill in the following table.

Unmarried male mean	?	Married male mean	?
Unmarried female mean	?	Married female mean	?
Mean difference	?	Mean difference	?
t-ratio	?	t-ratio	?
P-value	?	P-value	?

B. Consider the statistical evidence you assembled in Part D. Does the statistical evidence support Claim 1? Answer yes or no, and explain.

_____

_____

_____

_____

C. Does the evidence support Claim 2? Answer yes or no, and explain.

_____

_____

_____

_____

4. (Dataset: gss2012. Variables: authoritarianism, sibs, sex, relig2, [pw=gssw].) Here are two bits of conventional wisdom, beliefs that are widely accepted as accurate descriptions of the world. Conventional Wisdom 1: Catholics have bigger families than do Protestants. Conventional Wisdom 2: Men have stronger authoritarian tendencies than do women. In this exercise you will test these ideas and see how well they stand up to the statistical evidence. Test Conventional Wisdom 1 by comparing the average number of siblings (gss2012 variable sibs) for Protestants and Catholics (relig2). Test Conventional Wisdom 2 by comparing mean authoritarianism scale scores (authoritarianism) for males and females (sex). The authoritarianism scale ranges from 0 (low authoritarianism) to 7 (high authoritarianism). Run the analyses. Record the results in the following table.

	Conventional Wisdom 1	Conventional Wisdom 2
Mean difference	?	?
t-ratio	?	?
P-value	?	?
Is conventional wisdom supported? (yes or no)	?	?

That concludes the exercises for this chapter.

NOTES

1. For a discussion of Stata weights, see William Scribney's entry on StataCorp's FAQ, "Probability weights, analytic weights, and summary statistics," updated July 2009, http://www.stata.com/support/faqs/statistics/weights-and-summary-statistics/.
2. To simplify the presentation of the material in this chapter, all mean values have been rounded to two decimal places.
3. Of course, because random processes are at work, P-values are never exactly equal to zero. There is always some chance, however remote, that the sample mean represents a rare event. Ttail, one of Stata's statistical functions, returned a P-value of 4.373^{-11} for the current example. That is .00000000004373.
4. You can save typing by running the mean command with the nolabel option, and then using numeric codes instead of value labels in the lincom command: mean egal_scale [pw=nesw], over(female, nolabel). The following lincom command uses code 0 (males) and code 1 (females): lincom [egal_scale]0 – [egal_scale]1
5. Robert S. Erikson and Kent L. Tedin, *American Public Opinion: Its Origins, Content, and Impact,* 7th ed. (New York: Pearson Longman, 2005), 209.

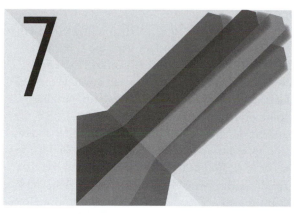

7

Chi-Square and Measures of Association

In the preceding chapter you learned how to test for mean differences on an interval-level dependent variable. But what if we are not dealing with interval-level variables? What if we are doing cross-tabulation analysis, and we are trying to figure out whether an observed relationship between two nominal or ordinal variables mirrors the true relationship in the population? Just as with mean differences, the answer depends on the boundaries of random sampling error, the extent to which our observed results happened by chance when we took the sample. The tabulate command—and for weighted survey data, a specialized version of Stata's tabulate command, svy: tabulate—will provide the information we need to test the statistical significance of nominal or ordinal relationships. A command written by Roger Newson, somersd, will provide an appropriate measure of association for determining the strength of the relationship between ordinal-level independent and dependent variables.[1] A special function that you will write and save in a Do-file will help you gauge the strength of nominal-level relationships.

You know how to use Stata's tabulate command to produce cross-tabulations. However, this familiar classic has an important limitation: It does not permit probability weights. As we saw in Chapter 6, to assess statistical significance—that is, to estimate the degree to which a sample reflects the population from which it was drawn—we need to use probability weights. To be sure, tabulate works fine for unweighted data, such as states or world. For weighted data, one of the survey (svy) commands, svy: tabulate, will give us the sort of results we are after. Actually, svy is a command *prefix*. The user first runs the svyset command, which defines a dataset as a survey dataset. In svyset, we specify the appropriate probability weight. Thereafter, each time Stata sees the svy prefix, it will apply the probability weight and return the correctly weighted results.

Svy: tabulate (and plain old tabulate) provide the oldest and most widely applied test of statistical significance in cross-tabulation analysis, the Pearson chi-square test. With rare exceptions, chi-square can always be used to determine whether an observed cross-tab relationship departs significantly from the expectations of the null hypothesis. In the first guided example, you will be introduced to the logic behind chi-square, and you will learn how to interpret svy: tabulate's chi-square results. You also will learn how to obtain measures of association for the relationships you are analyzing. If both variables you are using are ordinal-level variables, then Somers' d is the appropriate measure of association. Somers' d is an asymmetrical measure. It reports different measures of the strength of a relationship, depending on whether the independent variable is used to predict the dependent variable, or the dependent variable is used to predict the independent variable. Asymmetrical measures of association generally are preferred over symmetrical measures, which yield the same value, regardless of whether the independent variable is used to predict the dependent variable or the dependent variable is used to predict the independent variable.[2]

Somers' d is a proportional reduction in error (PRE) measure of the strength of a relationship. A PRE measure tells you the extent to which the values of the independent variable predict the values of the dependent variable. A value close to 0 says that the independent variable provides little predictive leverage; the relationship is weak. Values close to the poles—to –1 for negative associations or to +1 for positive relationships—tell you that the independent variable provides a lot of help in predicting the dependent variable; the relationship is strong.[3]

For measuring the strength of nominal-level relationships, the choices are more limited. A nominal-level PRE measure, lambda, is sometimes used. Granted, PRE measures are generally preferred over measures that do not permit a PRE interpretation. Even so, lambda frequently underestimates the strength of relationships, a problem that is especially acute when one of the variables has low variation. Therefore, when you are analyzing a relationship in which one or both of the variables are nominal, you will calculate Cramer's V. Cramer's V, one of a variety of chi-square–based measures, does not measure strength by the PRE criterion. However, it is bounded by 0 (no relationship) and 1 (a perfect relationship). Cramer's V is particularly useful in evaluating controlled comparisons.

ANALYZING ORDINAL-LEVEL RELATIONSHIPS

We will begin by using nes2012 to analyze an ordinal-level relationship. Consider this hypothesis: In a comparison of individuals, those having higher levels of education will have stronger pro-environmental attitudes than will those having lower levels of education. Dataset nes2012 has envjob_3, an ordinal variable that measures the extent to which respondents think that we should "regulate business to protect the environment and create jobs," or have "no regulation, because it will not work and will cost jobs."[4] Responses are classified as pro-environment ("Envir," coded 1), a middle position ("Mid," 2), or pro-jobs ("Jobs," 3). Envjob_3 is the dependent variable. Nes2012 variable, dem_educ3, is the independent variable. Dem_educ3's ordinal categories are high school or less ("HS or less," 1), some college ("Some coll," 2), or college degree or higher ("Coll+," 3). Open nes2012, begin a Do-file, and let's perform the analysis.

First we will test the envjob_3-dem_educ3 hypothesis the old-fashioned way—by getting a cross-tabulation and comparing column percentages. Before we do so, however, we need to run svyset, which will define nes2012 as a survey dataset by specifying a sampling weight. The simplified syntax:

svyset [pw = *probability_weightvar*]

Applied to nes2012:[5]

```
svyset [pw=nesw]
```

Stata responds:

```
         pweight: nesw
             VCE: linearized
     Single unit: missing
        Strata 1: <one>
            SU 1: <observations>
           FPC 1: <zero>
```

All right. Now run the svy: tabulate command. The main command follows the same syntactical conventions as the standard tabulate command.

svy: tabulate *dep_var indep_var,* col percent count pearson

Applied to the example:

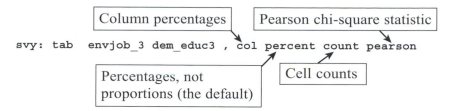

```
                    Column percentages        Pearson chi-square statistic

svy: tab  envjob_3 dem_educ3 , col percent count pearson

             Percentages, not          Cell counts
             proportions (the default)
```

With the exception of the svy prefix, the setup to the left of the comma is straightforward tabulate (which, of course, may be abbreviated "tab"). However, the options for tabulate and svy: tabulate are not always the same. By default, svy: tabulate will produce proportions. Specify the percent option to obtain percentages, which are more visually appealing. The count option asks for cell frequencies, which Stata will omit otherwise. Oddly enough, if you fail to request pearson, the Pearson chi-square test statistic, Stata will give it to you anyway; it's the default. It is shown here for emphasis.

Consider the Results window:

Envir or Jobs?	Education			
	HS or le	Some col	Coll+	Total
Envir	693.9	570.9	656.2	1921
	38.08	37.81	41.33	39.05
Mid	646.2	562.2	561.3	1770
	35.46	37.24	35.36	35.97
Jobs	482.2	376.7	370.1	1229
	26.46	24.95	23.31	24.98
Total	1822	1510	1588	4920
	100	100	100	100

```
  Key:   weighted counts
         column percentages

  Pearson:
    Uncorrected   chi2(4)            =      7.5544
    Design-based  F(3.98, 19746.22)=      1.0570    P = 0.3759
```

How would you evaluate the envjob_3-dem_educ3 hypothesis in light of this analysis? Focus on the column percentages in the "Envir" row. According to the hypothesis, as we move along this row, from lower education to higher education, the percentage of pro-environment respondents should increase. Is this what happens? The percentages run from 38.08 among the least educated, drop slightly, to 37.81, among the middle group, and then rise again, to 41.33, among those with a college education or higher. So, there is something on the order of a 3-percentage-point difference between the least- and most-educated respondents, not a terribly robust relationship between the independent and dependent variables. The 3-point gradient is similar—perhaps slightly more systematic—along the "Jobs" row: 26.46 percent, 24.95 percent, 23.31 percent. Indeed, two political analysts might offer conflicting interpretations of these results. The first analyst might conclude that, yes, as education increases, pro-environment sentiments grow stronger, and pro-jobs attitudes become weaker. The other might declare the relationship too weak to support the hypothesis. Inferential statistics, of course, is designed to settle such arguments.

Let's reconsider the envjob_3-dem_educ3 cross-tabulation in the way that the chi-square test of statistical significance would approach it. Chi-square begins by looking at the "Total" column, which contains the distribution of the entire sample across the values of the dependent variable, envjob_3. Thus 39.05 percent of the sample is pro-environment, 35.97 percent takes a middle position, and 24.98 percent is pro-jobs. Chi-square then frames the null hypothesis, which claims that, in the population, envjob_3 and dem_educ3 are not related to each other—that individuals' levels of education are unrelated to their opinions about the environment. If the null hypothesis is correct, then a random sample of people with a high school education or less would produce the same distribution of opinions as the total distribution: 39.05 percent "Envir" / 35.97 percent "Mid" / 24.98 percent "Jobs." By the same token, a random sample of people with some college would yield a distribution that looks just like the total distribution: 39.05 percent "Envir" / 35.97 percent "Mid" / 24.98 percent "Jobs." A random sample of individuals with college or higher would produce the same result: 39.05 percent "Envir" / 35.97 percent "Mid" / 24.98 percent "Jobs." Thus, if the null hypothesis is correct, then the distribution of cases down each column of the table will be the same as the distribution in the "Total" column. Of course, the null hypothesis asserts that any departures from this monotonous pattern resulted from random sampling error.

Now reexamine the table and make a considered judgment. Would you say that the observed distribution of cases within each category of dem_educ3 conforms to the expectations of the null hypothesis? For those with high school or less, the distribution is very close to the total distribution, with modest departures—for example, a somewhat lower percentage in the "Envir" category than the null would expect and a slightly higher percentage in the "Jobs" category. The distribution for those with some college corresponds quite well to the total distribution, as does the distribution for the most-educated respondents. Thus, for each value of dem_educ3, there is fairly close conformity to what we would expect to find if the null hypothesis is true. The small departures from these expectations, furthermore, might easily be explained by random sampling error.

Now let's consider the statistics beneath the cross-tabulation, reproduced here, and see if the numbers bear out our judgment call:

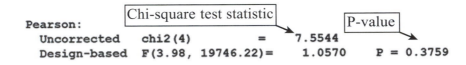

The first computed value in the "Pearson chi2" row, 7.5544, is the chi-square test statistic.[6] If the observed data perfectly fit the expectations of the null hypothesis, this test statistic would be 0. As the observed data depart from the null's expectations, this value grows in size. For the envjob_3-dem_educ3 cross-tabulation, Stata calculated a chi-square test statistic equal to 7.5544. Is this number, 7.5544, statistically different from 0, the value we would expect to obtain if the null hypothesis is true? Put another way, under the assumption that the null hypothesis is correct, how often would we obtain a test statistic of 7.5544 by chance? The answer is contained in the entry: "P = 0.3759," the P-value for the chi-square test statistic. How would you interpret a P-value of .3759? Assuming that the null hypothesis is correct in its assertion that there is no relationship between the independent and dependent variables, we will obtain a test statistic of 7.5544, by chance, 37.59 percent of the time. The null hypothesis is on safe inferential ground. From our initial comparison of percentages, we were unsure whether the relationship was strong enough to trump the null hypothesis. Maybe it was or maybe it wasn't. The chi-square test has given us the inferential leverage we needed in order to make a decision. If the null hypothesis is correct, the observed pattern would occur by chance more frequently than 5 times out of 100. Do not reject the null hypothesis.

Chi-square is a test of statistical significance. It tells you whether random sampling error could plausibly account for the observed results. For ordinal-by-ordinal tables we can augment our analysis with Somers' d, a measure of association that gives a precise reading of the strength of the relationship. The somersd package is not part of "official" Stata. It needs to be installed separately. Before proceeding, find out whether somersd is installed by clicking in the Command window and entering "which somersd." If somersd is installed, Stata will give you this response:

```
. which somersd
c:\ado\plus\s\somersd.ado
*! Author: Roger Newson
*! Date: 20 May 2013
```

If somersd is not installed, type "ssc install somersd." Stata will respond:

```
. ssc install somersd
checking somersd consistency and verifying not already installed...
installing into c:\ado\plus\...
installation complete.
```

The general syntax for the somersd command is as follows:

somersd *indep_var dep_var* [pw = *probability_weightvar*]

Somers' d is an asymmetrical measure of association—that is, it is sensitive to the causal order of the variables. In typing the variables, make sure to type the independent variable first, followed by the dependent variable(s):[7]

somersd dem_educ3 envjob_3 [pw=nesw]

dem_educ3	Coef.	Jackknife Std. Err.	z	P>|z|	[95% Conf. Interval]	
envjob_3	-.0290591	.0171899	-1.69	0.091	-.0627507	.0046324

Stata returns a Somers' d of −.0290591, or about −.03, for the envjob_3-dem_educ3 relationship. Ignore for the moment its puny magnitude, and consider its negative sign. How does Somers' d determine whether a relationship is positive or negative? If increasing codes of the independent variable are associated with increasing codes of the dependent variable, then somersd returns a positive coefficient. If, as in the current example, increasing codes of the independent variable—from lower to higher levels of education—are associated with decreasing codes of the dependent variable—from pro-jobs to pro-environment—then somersd returns a negative coefficient. By being alert to how the variables are coded, you will know which sign is implied by your hypothesis, a positive sign or a negative sign. Placing that issue aside, you can focus on the magnitude of the Somers' d statistic.

What does the magnitude of Somers' d ($|-.03| = .03$) tell us about our ability to predict values of the dependent variable based on knowledge of the independent variable? It tells us this: Compared with how well we can predict individuals' environmental opinions without knowing their levels of education, knowledge of their education level improves our prediction by 3 percent.

Summary

Svy: tab, and tabulate, report a chi-square test statistic. Values close to 0 are within the domain of the null hypothesis. As chi-square increases in magnitude (the chi-square statistic cannot assume negative values), the null's explanation for the observed data—"it all happened by chance"—becomes increasingly implausible. The chi-square statistic is accompanied by a P-value. Here is a template for writing an interpretation of the P-value:

"If the null hypothesis is correct that there is no relationship between [independent variable] and [dependent variable], then random sampling error will produce the observed data [P-value] of the time."

For our example: "If the null hypothesis is correct that there is no relationship between education and environmental attitudes, then random sampling error will produce the observed data 0.3759 of the time." (Percentages may sound better: ". . . will produce the observed data 37.6 percent of the time.") Use the .05 benchmark. If the P-value is less than or equal to .05, then reject the null hypothesis. If the P-value is greater than .05, accept the null hypothesis.

For ordinal-by-ordinal relationships, run somersd. Somers' d is a directional measure, ranging from −1 to +1. Somers' d has a PRE interpretation. Here is a template for writing an interpretation of Somers' d or, for that matter, any PRE measure:

"Compared to how well we can predict [dependent variable] by not knowing [independent variable], we can improve our prediction by [value of PRE measure] by knowing [independent variable]."

Our example: "Compared to how well we can predict environmental attitudes by not knowing respondents' levels of education, we can improve our prediction by .03 by knowing respondents' education levels." (Substituting percentages: ". . . we can improve our prediction by 3 percent by knowing respondents' incomes.") Note that a negative sign on a PRE measure imparts the direction of the relationship, but it does not affect the PRE interpretation.

ANALYZING AN ORDINAL-LEVEL RELATIONSHIP WITH A CONTROL VARIABLE

The education-environmental attitudes hypothesis did not fare well against the null hypothesis. Here is a hypothesis that sounds more promising: In a comparison of individuals, liberals will be more supportive of gay rights than will conservatives. For the dependent variable, we will use gay_rights3, which measures attitudes toward gay rights by three categories: "Low" support (coded 1), a middle position ("Mid," 2), and "High" support (3). The independent variable is libcon3: liberal ("Lib," 1), moderate ("Mod," 2), and conservative ("Cons," 3). Because education might also affect attitudes toward gay rights, we will use dem_educ3 (from the previous example) as the control variable.

For this analysis, we want Stata to produce three ordinal-by-ordinal cross-tabulations—a cross-tab showing the gay_rights3-libcon3 relationship for each value of dem_educ3. Unlike the tabulate command (and the somersd command), svy: tabulate does not allow the bysort prefix. We will use the if qualifier to create subsets for three education cross-tabs. The somersd command, combined with the bysort prefix, will give us the appropriate measure of strength for the gay_rights3-libcon3 relationship separately for respondents at each education level. The following suite of commands uses an acceptable abbreviation for the percent option ("per"), and does not request cell counts. Also, note that we can drop "pearson" from the options list. Stata will still report it:

```
svy: tab  gay_rights3 libcon3 if dem_educ3==1, col per
svy: tab  gay_rights3 libcon3 if dem_educ3==2, col per
svy: tab  gay_rights3 libcon3 if dem_educ3==3, col per
```

Gay Rights Support	Lib	Ideology Mod	Cons	Total
Low	20.91	44.4	51.54	41.22
Mid	33.93	33.82	33.84	33.86
High	45.16	21.77	14.62	24.92
Total	100	100	100	100

Key: column percentages

Pearson:
Uncorrected   chi2(4)   =   102.1159
Design-based   F(3.96, 3704.70)=   14.9676   P = 0.0000

Gay Rights Support	Lib	Ideology Mod	Cons	Total
Low	17.61	33.88	53.81	38.54
Mid	30.63	32.47	34.7	32.99
High	51.76	33.65	11.49	28.47
Total	100	100	100	100

Key: column percentages

Pearson:
Uncorrected   chi2(4)   =   163.6015
Design-based   F(3.97, 3607.46)=   23.6405   P = 0.0000

Gay Rights Support	Ideology			Total
	Lib	Mod	Cons	
Low	9.823	20.67	49.69	30.56
Mid	24.5	41.57	38.63	33.65
High	65.68	37.76	11.67	35.79
Total	100	100	100	100

Key: column percentages

Pearson:
  Uncorrected   chi2(4)   =   273.7580
  Design-based F(3.93, 3522.96)=   41.9279   P = 0.0000

Do peoples' gay rights opinions depend on their ideology? At all three levels of education, the answer is yes. The chi-square statistics in the first cross-tabulation (chi-square = 102.1159, P-value = 0.0000), in the second (chi-square = 163.6015, P-value = 0.0000), and in the third (chi-square = 273.7580, P-value = 0.0000) easily defeat the null hypothesis. All of the observed relationships depart significantly from the null hypothesis's version of events.

Take a closer look at the percentages, and figure out what is going on—spuriousness, additive relationships, or interaction. In the least-educated group, there is a sizable decline of about 30 points in the percentages professing "High" support across the values of libcon3, from 45.16 among liberals to 14.62 percent among conservatives. Yet the drop is even steeper among those with some college: from 51.75 percent to 11.49 percent, a 40-point drop. The gap increases to over 50 points among the most highly educated: 65.68 percent for liberals and 11.67 percent for conservatives. Thus, the "ideology effect" is either 30 points, 40 points, or over 50 points, depending on education level.[8] Although the direction of the gay_rights3-dem_educ3 relationship is the same at all levels of education—conservatives are less supportive than liberals—the relationship becomes stronger as education increases. Interaction would seem the best way to describe this set of relationships.

Let's see if this interpretation is supported by Somers' d, which will provide a precise PRE measure of the strength of the gay_rights3-libcon3 relationship at each value of dem_educ3.

Use the bysort prefix to obtain Somers' d for the gay_rights3-libcon3 relationship at each level of education:

Tells Stata not to run somersd for missing cases

`bysort dem_educ3: somersd libcon3 gay_rights3 if dem_educ3 !=. [pw=nesw]`

libcon3	Coef.	Jackknife Std. Err.	z	P>|z|	[95% Conf. Interval]	
gay_rights3	-.2765834	.0375382	-7.37	0.000	-.3501568	-.20301

libcon3	Coef.	Jackknife Std. Err.	z	P>|z|	[95% Conf. Interval]	
gay_rights3	-.3834642	.0361181	-10.62	0.000	-.4542544	-.3126739

libcon3	Coef.	Jackknife Std. Err.	z	P>|z|	[95% Conf. Interval]	
gay_rights3	-.5149742	.0340236	-15.14	0.000	-.5816592	-.4482892

Again note the negative signs on the Somers' d statistics. At each education level, as the coded values of libcon3 increase from "Lib" to "Cons," gay_rights3's codes decline from "High" support to "Low" support. Thus the negative signs are consistent with the hypothesis that conservatives are less supportive of gay rights than are liberals.

Focus on the Somers' d magnitudes. Somers' d has a magnitude (absolute value) of .2765834 (or .28) for the least-educated, .38 for the middle group, and .52 for the most-educated. So the values of Somers' d capture the strengthening relationship between gay_rights3 and libcon3 as education increases. Plus, because Somers' d is a PRE measure, we can give a specific answer to the "how strong?" question. For least-educated respondents we would say that, compared to how well we can predict their opinions on gay rights without knowing their ideology, we can improve our prediction by 28 percent by knowing their ideology. The predictive leverage of the independent variable strengthens to 38 percent for the middle group, and increases to 52 percent for those at the highest level of educational attainment.

ANALYZING NOMINAL-LEVEL RELATIONSHIPS

All of the variables analyzed thus far have been ordinal-level. Many social and political characteristics, however, are measured by nominal categories—gender, race, region, or religious denomination, to name a few. In this example, we will use race to help frame the following hypothesis: In a comparison of individuals, blacks are more likely than are whites to be Democrats. To make this rather pedestrian hypothesis marginally more interesting, we will control for another variable that might also affect partisanship, whether the respondent resides in the South. Would the racial difference on partisanship be the same for southerners and non-southerners? Or might the racial divide be stronger in the South than the non-South? Let's investigate.

Dataset nes2012 contains pid_3, with values "Dem" (code 1), "Ind" (2), and "Rep" (3). Pid_3 is the dependent variable. The independent variable is dem_raceeth2: "White" (1) and "Black" (2). For the control variable we will use south: "Non-South" (0) and "South" (1). The analytic task at hand is, by now, abundantly familiar: Use the if qualifier to obtain two subsets for cross-tabulations of the pid_3-dem_raceeth2 relationship, one for each value of south:

```
svy: tab pid_3 dem_raceeth2 if south==0, col per
svy: tab pid_3 dem_raceeth2 if south==1, col per
```

Party ID: 3 cats	White/Black		
	White	Black	Total
Dem	29.54	71.17	33.5
Ind	39.26	26.24	38.02
Rep	31.19	2.591	28.48
Total	100	100	100

Key: column percentages

Pearson:
Uncorrected   chi2(2)   =   220.7038
Design-based F(1.79, 5413.22)=   91.4466   P = 0.0000

Party ID: 3 cats	White/Black		
	White	Black	Total
Dem	18.01	76.9	32.65
Ind	41.93	20.85	36.69
Rep	40.07	2.255	30.66
Total	100	100	100

Key: column percentages

Pearson:
Uncorrected   chi2(2)   =   453.0306
Design-based F(1.91, 2806.40)=   111.4618   P = 0.0000

Not surprisingly, the chi-square statistics tell us to reject the null hypothesis for both regions: 220.7038 (P = 0.0000) for the non-South, and 453.0306 (P = 0.0000) for the South. Are there interregional differences in the patterns of the relationships? Among non-southerners, 29.54 percent of whites are Democrats, compared with 71.17 percent of blacks—more than a 40 percentage-point gap. What happens when we switch to respondents who reside in the South? Among southerners, the percentage of blacks who are Democrats increases to 76.9, while the percentage of whites who are Democrats drops by about 11 points, to 18.08 percent. These dynamics produce a racial gap that is considerably wider in the South (about 60 points) than in the non-South (about 40 points). Because the effect of race on partisanship is stronger in the South than in the non-South, we can conclude that interaction best describes this situation.

A chi-square based, nominal-level measure of strength, Cramer's V, gives you an additional interpretive tool. That's the good news. The not-so-good news is that you will need to type out V's tedious formula. The not-so-bad news is that, once you have it correctly typed and saved in a Do-file, you can access it whenever you need it, and you will never have to type it again. Space to a new line in your active Do-file, and type the following, precisely as you see it here:

```
dis "Cramer's V = " sqrt(e(cun_Pear)/(e(N)*min((e(r)-1),(e(c)-1))))
```

Each time Stata runs an estimation command, such as svy: tab, it temporarily stores the results in "e-class" estimators. For example, "e(cun_Pear)," is the chi-square statistic from the most recent svy: tab run. Similarly, "e(N)" is the number of cases in the cross-tabulation, "e(r)" is the number of rows, and "e(c)" is the number of columns. The "dis" (for "display") command, plus the text, "Cramer's V =," instructs Stata to send a nicely labeled value of V to the Results window.[9]

Now, each time Stata runs an estimation command, it overwrites the stored results from any previous estimation command. This means that you will need to invoke Cramer's V after each svy: tab analysis of nominal-level data. You can do this by clicking around the Do-file—click-run the first svy: tab statement, click-run the Cramer's V command, click-run the next svy: tab statement, and so on. Or, you can copy/paste Cramer's V and sandwich it in wherever you need it:

```
svy: tab pid_3 dem_raceeth2 if south==0, col percent

dis "Cramer's V = " sqrt(e(cun_Pear)/(e(N)*min((e(r)-1),(e(c)-1))))

svy: tab pid_3 dem_raceeth2 if south==1, col percent

dis "Cramer's V = " sqrt(e(cun_Pear)/(e(N)*min((e(r)-1),(e(c)-1))))
```

For the non-South cross-tab we obtain:

```
. dis "Cramer's V = " sqrt(e(cun_Pear)/(e(N)*min((e(r)-1),(e(c)-1))))
Cramer's V = .27024503
```

For the South cross-tab we obtain:

```
. dis "Cramer's V = " sqrt(e(cun_Pear)/(e(N)*min((e(r)-1),(e(c)-1))))
Cramer's V = .5551433
```

Cramer's V does not have a PRE interpretation. However, it varies between 0 (weak relationship) and 1 (strong relationship). V is particularly useful in interpreting controlled comparisons. In reassuring support of our interaction interpretation, the V for southern respondents (.56) is much stronger than the V for non-southern respondents (.27).

ANALYZING UNWEIGHTED DATA WITH THE TABULATE COMMAND

For unweighted data, such as states or world, we return to Stata's classic tabulate command:

```
tabulate dep_var indep_var, col chi2 V
```

With unweighted data, there are few complications and little drama. For all tabulate analyses, request chi-square by specifying the chi2 option. For nominal data, request Cramer's V with the V option. For ordinal data, omit "V" and run the somersd command without the weight parameter: "somersd *indep_var dep_var*." Unlike svy: tab, tabulate allows the bysort prefix, which helps out when you are comparing cross-tabs across the values of a control variable.

The following command uses the states dataset to analyze the relationship between religiosity (each state is classified as "Low," "Mid," or "High" on Religiosity3) and region. Because region is nominal-level, we would request Cramer's V:

```
tab Religiosity3 region, col nokey chi2 V
```

Religiosity	Census region				
	Northeast	Midwest	South	West	Total
Low	8	0	0	9	17
	88.89	0.00	0.00	69.23	34.00
Mid	1	9	5	2	17
	11.11	75.00	31.25	15.38	34.00
High	0	3	11	2	16
	0.00	25.00	68.75	15.38	32.00
Total	9	12	16	13	50
	100.00	100.00	100.00	100.00	100.00

```
      Pearson chi2(6) =   41.8592   Pr = 0.000
          Cramér's V =    0.6470
```

The percentage of states with high levels of religiosity varies by region: from none in the Northeast to 68.75 percent in the South. The data depart significantly from the null's expectations (chi-square = 41.86, $P = 0.000$). With V = .65, we can safely conclude that the relationship is fairly strong.

EXERCISES

1. (Dataset: states. Variables: Abort_rank3, Gun_rank3, cook_index3.) Pedantic pontificator is pondering a potential partisan paradox of public policy.

   "Think about two sorts of policies that figure prominently in cultural debate: laws restricting abortion and laws restricting guns. For both policies, fewer restrictions mean more choices and greater freedom, while more restrictions mean fewer choices and less freedom. Because choice and freedom are the touchstone values, one would think that partisan elites would be consistent in their positions on these policies. If Republicans favor fewer gun restrictions, then they ought to favor fewer abortion restrictions, too. By the same logic, if Democrats favor fewer abortion restrictions, then they should also support less gun control. As a keen observer of state politics, however, it is my impression that Republican-controlled states have less-restrictive gun laws but more-restrictive abortion laws. Democrat-controlled states are just the reverse: less-restrictive abortion laws and more-restrictive gun laws. I am sure that when you analyze the states dataset, you will discover this odd partisan paradox."

   The states dataset contains these two policy measures, which will serve as dependent variables: Abort_rank3 and Gun_rank3. Both variables are identically coded, three-category ordinals. Codes range from 1 (states having more restrictions) to 3 (states having fewer restrictions). Another three-category ordinal, cook_index3, measures states' partisan balance in three codes: 1 (Republican states), 2 (states with even balance), and 3 (Democratic states). This is the independent variable.

   A. If pedantic pontificator is correct, as you compare states across increasing values of cook_index3—from Republican states, to even states, to Democratic states—the percentage of states having more-restrictive abortion policies should (circle one)

   decrease.   stay the same.   increase.

The percentage of states having more-restrictive gun policies should (circle one)

decrease.   stay the same.   increase.

B. If pedantic pontificator is correct, you should find that states having higher codes on cook_index3 will have (circle one)

lower   higher

codes on Abort_rank3. You should also find that states having higher codes on cook_index3 will have (circle one)

lower   higher

codes on Gun_rank3.

C. Think about how Stata calculates Somers' d. If pedantic pontificator is correct, the Somers' d statistic for the Abort_rank3-cook_index3 relationship will have a (circle one)

negative   positive

sign. The Somers' d statistic for the Gun_rank3-cook_index3 relationship will have a (circle one)

negative   positive

sign.

D. The states dataset is unweighted, so you can analyze the data using Stata's classic tabulate command. Run two tabulate analyses, one for the Abort_rank3-cook_index3 relationship and one for the Gun_rank3-cook_index3 relationship. Make sure to request chi-square ("chi2"). Obtain Somers' d for both relationships. (Hint: Because the somersd command permits the user to specify more than one dependent variable, only one somersd run is required: "somersd cook_index3 Abort_rank3 Gun_rank3.") Browse the cross-tabulation results. In the table below, enter the percentage of Democratic states, even states, and Republican states having more-restrictive policies. In the Abort_rank3 row, for example, record the percentage of states that are "More restrictive." Similarly, in the Gun_rank3 row, enter the percentage of states that are "More restrictive." For each relationship, record chi-square, chi-square's P-value, and Somers' d.

Dependent variable:	More Rep	Even	More Dem	Chi-square	P-value	Somers' d
Abort_rank3 % more restrictive	?	?	?	?	?	?
Gun_rank3 % more restrictive	?	?	?	?	?	?

E. Consider Somers' d for the Gun_rank3-cook_index3 relationship. This value of Somers' d means that, compared to how well we can predict Gun_rank3 without knowing cook_index3, (complete the sentence) _____.

F. Consider the chi-square P-value for the Abort_rank3-cook_index3 relationship. This P-value means that, under the assumption that the null hypothesis is correct, (complete the sentence) _____ _____. Therefore, you should (circle one)

reject   not reject

the null hypothesis.

G. Consider all the evidence from your analysis. The evidence suggests that pedantic pontificator is (circle one)

correct.   incorrect.

Explain your reasoning:

_____

_____

_____

_____

_____

2. (Dataset: gss2012. Variables: abhlth, femrole2, sex, "svyset[pw=gssw]".) Interested student has joined pedantic pontificator in a discussion of the gender gap in US politics.

Interested student: "On what sorts of issues or opinions are men and women most likely to be at odds? What defines the gender gap, anyway?"

Pedantic pontificator: "That's easy. A couple of points seem obvious, to me anyway. First, we know that the conflict over abortion rights is the defining gender issue of our time. Women will be more likely than men to take a strong prochoice position on this issue. Second—and pay close attention here—on more mundane cultural questions, such as whether women should take nontraditional roles outside the home, men and women will not differ at all."

A. Pedantic pontificator has suggested the following two hypotheses about the gender gap: (check two)

❑ In a comparison of individuals, women will be less likely than men to think that abortion should be allowed.

❑ In a comparison of individuals, women and men will be equally likely to think that abortion should be allowed.

❑ In a comparison of individuals, women will be more likely than men to think that abortion should be allowed.

❑ In a comparison of individuals, women will be less likely than men to think that women should play nontraditional roles.

❑ In a comparison of individuals, women and men will be equally likely to think that women should play nontraditional roles.

❑ In a comparison of individuals, women will be more likely than men to think that women should play nontraditional roles.

B. Open gss2012. Run "svyset [pw=gssw]" to define gss2012 as a survey dataset. Run svy: tabulate to test pedantic pontificator's hypotheses. Gss2012 contains two variables that will serve as dependent variables. Abhlth, which asks respondents whether an abortion should be allowed if the pregnancy endangers the woman's health, is coded "Yes" and "No." The variable femrole2, which measures attitudes toward the role of women, has values labeled "Traditional" and "NonTrad." The independent variable is sex, "Male" or "Female." This is svy: tab, so Stata will return chi-square by default. Sex is a nominal variable, so be sure to run the Cramer's V formula you constructed in this chapter. In the abhlth-sex cross-tabulation, focus on the percentage saying "Yes." In the femrole2-sex cross-tabulation, focus on the "NonTrad" category. Record your results in the table that follows.

Dependent variable	Male	Female	Chi-square	P-value	Cramer's V
Percent "Yes" (abhlth)	?	?	?	?	?
Percent "NonTrad" (femrole2)	?	?	?	?	?

C. Based on these results, you may conclude that (check three)

❑ a statistically significant gender gap exists on abortion opinions.

❑ pedantic pontificator's hypothesis about the femrole2-sex relationship is not supported by the analysis.

❑ under the assumption that the null hypothesis is correct, the abhlth-sex relationship could have occurred by chance more frequently than 5 times out of 100.

❑ pedantic pontificator's hypothesis about the abhlth-sex relationship is supported by the analysis.

❑ a higher percentage of females than males think that women belong in nontraditional roles.

D. The P-value of the chi-square statistic in the femrole2-sex cross-tabulation tells you that, under the assumption that the null hypothesis is correct, (complete the sentence)

_____.

3. (Dataset: gss2012. Variables: polview3, racial_liberal3, social_cons3, spend3, "svyset [pw=gssw]".) While having lunch together, three researchers are discussing what the terms *liberal, moderate,* and *conservative* mean to most people. Each researcher is touting a favorite independent variable that may explain the way survey respondents describe themselves ideologically.

Researcher 1: "When people are asked a question about their ideological views, they think about their attitudes toward government spending. If people think the government should spend more on important programs, they will respond that they are 'liberal.' If they don't want too much spending, they will say that they are 'conservative.'"

Researcher 2: "Well, that's fine. But let's not forget about social policies, such as abortion and pornography. These issues must influence how people describe themselves ideologically. People with more permissive views on these sorts of issues will call themselves 'liberal.' People who favor government restrictions will label themselves as 'conservative.'"

Researcher 3: "Okay, you both make good points. But you're ignoring the importance of racial issues in American politics. When asked whether they are liberal or conservative, people probably think about their opinions on racial policies, such as affirmative action. Stronger proponents of racial equality will say they are 'liberal,' and weaker proponents will say they are 'conservative.'"

In Chapter 3 you created an ordinal measure of ideology, polview3, which is coded 1 for "Liberal," 2 for "Moderate," and 3 for "Conservative." This is the dependent variable. Gss2012 also contains Researcher 1's favorite independent variable, spend3, a three-category ordinal measure of attitudes toward government spending. Spend3 is coded 1 ("Conserv," spend on fewer programs), 2 ("Mod," middle position), or 3 ("Liberal," spend on more programs). Researcher 2's favorite independent variable is social_cons3, a three-category ordinal measure of attitudes on social issues. Social_cons3 is coded 1 ("Liberal," respondent has the most permissive views social issues), 2 ("Mod," middle), or 3 ("Conserv," respondent has the least permissive views). Researcher 3's favorite independent variable is racial_liberal3, also a three-category ordinal variable. Racial_liberal3 is coded 1 ("Conserv," respondent has least liberal positions on racial policies), 2 ("Mod," middle), or 3 ("Liberal," respondent has the most liberal positions on racial policies).

A. Think about how Stata calculates Somers' d. Assuming that each researcher is correct, Stata should report (check all that apply)

❑ a negative sign on Somers' d for the polview3-spend3 relationship.

❑ a positive sign on Somers' d for the polview3-social_cons3 relationship.

❑ a negative sign on Somers' d for the polview3-racial_liberal3 relationship.

B. Run an svy: tabulate analysis for each of the relationships, using polview3 as the dependent variable and spend3, social_cons3, and racial_liberal3 as independent variables. (If you did not perform Exercise 2, then make sure to run "svyset [pw=gssw]." If you performed Exercise 2, then you are all set to analyze the data using svy: tab.) Obtain Somers' d for each relationship. Summarize your results in the following table. In the first three columns, enter the percent of self-identified "conservatives" on polview3 for each value of the independent variable. For example, from the spend3 cross-tab, record the percentage of conservatives among respondents taking the "Conserv" position (code 1 of spend3), the percentage of conservatives among respondents taking the "Mod" position (code 2 on spend3), and the percentage of conservatives among respondents taking the "Liberal" position (code 3 on spend3). For each relationship, record chi-square, chi-square's P-value, and Somers' d.

	Code on independent variable*					
	1	2	3	Chi-square	P-value	Somers' d
Percent "Conservative" (spend3 cross-tab)	?	?	?	?	?	?
Percent "Conservative" (social_cons3 cross-tab)	?	?	?	?	?	?
Percent "Conservative" (racial_liberal3 cross-tab)	?	?	?	?	?	?

*For spend3, code 1= "Conserv," code 2 = "Mod," and code 3 = "Liberal." For social_cons3, code 1 = "Liberal," code 2 = "Mod," and code 3 = "Conserv." For racial_liberal3, code 1= "Conserv," code 2 = "Mod," and code 3 = "Liberal."

C. Consider the evidence you have assembled. Your analysis supports which of the following statements? (Check three.)

❑ As values of spend3 increase, the percentage of respondents describing themselves as conservatives decreases.

❑ As values of social_cons3 increase, the percentage of respondents describing themselves as conservative increases.

❑ The polview3-racial_liberal3 relationship is not statistically significant.

❑ If the null hypothesis is correct, you will obtain the polview3-spend3 relationship less frequently than 5 times out of 100 by chance.

❑ If the null hypothesis is correct, you will obtain the polview3-racial_liberal3 relationship more frequently than 5 times out of 100 by chance.

D. Somers' d for the polview3-social_cons3 relationship is equal to (fill in the blank) _____. Thus, compared with how well we can predict polview3 by not knowing, (complete the sentence) _____

_____.

E. The three researchers make a friendly wager. The researcher whose favorite independent variable does the worst job predicting values of the dependent variable has to buy lunch for the other two. Who pays for lunch? (circle one)

Researcher 1   Researcher 2   Researcher 3

4. (Dataset: gss2012. Variables: partyid_3, egalit_scale3, educ_2, "svyset [pw=gssw]".) Certainly you would expect partisanship and egalitarian attitudes to be related: In a comparison of individuals, those with stronger egalitarian beliefs are more likely to be Democrats than those with weaker egalitarian beliefs. Yet it also seems reasonable to hypothesize that the relationship between egalitarianism (independent variable) and party identification (dependent variable) will not be the same for all education groups (control variable). It may be that, among people with less education, the party identification-egalitarianism relationship will be weaker than among those with higher levels of education. This idea suggests a set of interaction relationships: As education increases, the relationship between the independent variable and the dependent variable becomes stronger. In this exercise, you will test for this set of interaction relationships.

Gss2012 contains partyid_3, which measures party identification: "Dem," "Ind," and "Rep." This is the dependent variable. (For this exercise, treat partyid_3 as an ordinal-level variable, with higher codes denoting stronger Republican identification.) The independent variable is egalit_scale3: "Less egal," "Middle," or "More egal." The control variable is educ_2: "0–12 yrs" (coded 1) and "13+ yrs" (coded 2).

Run svy: tab using partyid_3 as the dependent variable, egalit_scale3 as the independent variable, and educ_2 as the control. (If you did not perform Exercise 2 or Exercise 3, then make sure to run "svyset [pw=gssw]." If you performed Exercise 2 or 3, then you are all set to analyze the data using svy: tab.) This is svy: tab, so the bysort prefix is not allowed. Use the if qualifier to create subsets for separate cross-tabulations for each value of educ_2: "if educ_2==1," and "if educ_2==2." Run somersd with the bysort prefix to obtain Somers' d statistics separately for each education group. (Be sure to include the weight parameter, "[pw=gssw].")

A. In the controlled comparison cross-tabulations, focus on the percentages of Democrats across the values of egalit_scale3. Fill in the table that follows.

Education level	Less egal (% Dem)	Middle (% Dem)	More egal (% Dem)	Chi-square	P-value	Somers' d
0–12 years	?	?	?	?	?	?
13+ years	?	?	?	?	?	?

B. Which of the following inferences are supported by your analysis? (check all that apply)

❑ At both levels of education, people with stronger egalitarian beliefs are more likely to be Democrats than are people with weaker egalitarian beliefs.

❑ For the less-educated group, random sampling error would produce the observed relationship between egalitarianism and partisanship less frequently than 5 times out of 100.

❑ The partisanship-egalitarianism relationship is stronger for the more-educated group than for the less-educated group.

C. Focus on the value of Somers' d for those who have 13 or more years of education. This value of Somers' d

says that, compared to how well you can predict _____

_____.

D. Based on your analysis of these relationships, you can conclude that (check one)

❑ The partisanship-egalitarianism-education relationships are not a set of interaction relationships.

❑ The partisanship-egalitarianism-education relationships are a set of interaction relationships.

Explain your reasoning._____

_____

_____

_____

_____

_____

5. (Dataset: world. Variables: protact3, gender_equal3, vi_rel3, pmat12_3.) Ronald Inglehart offers a particularly elegant and compelling idea about the future of economically advanced societies. According to Inglehart, the cultures of many postindustrial societies have been going through a value shift—the waning importance of materialist values and a growing pursuit of postmaterialist values. In postmaterialist societies, economically based conflicts—unions versus big business, rich versus poor—are increasingly supplanted by an emphasis on self-expression and social equality. Postmaterialist societies also are marked by rising secularism and elite-challenging behaviors, such as boycotts and demonstrations. In this exercise you will investigate Inglehart's theory.[10]

The World variable pmat12_3 measures the level of postmaterial values by a three-category ordinal measure: low postmaterialism (coded 1), moderate postmaterialism (coded 2), and high postmaterialism (coded 3). Higher codes denote a greater prevalence of postmaterial values. Use pmat12_3 as the independent variable. Here are three dependent variables, all of which are three-category ordinals: gender_equal3, which captures gender equality (1 = low equality, 2 = medium equality, 3 = high equality); protact3, which measures citizen participation in protests (1 = low, 2 = moderate, 3 = high); and vi_rel3, which gauges religiosity by the percentage of the public saying that religion is "very important" (1 = less than 20 percent, 2 = 20–50 percent, 3 = more than 50 percent). Higher codes on the dependent variables denote greater gender equality (gender_equal3), more protest activity (protact3), and higher levels of religiosity (vi_rel3).

A. Using pmat12_3 as the independent variable, three postmaterialist hypotheses can be framed:

Gender equality hypothesis (fill in the blanks): In a comparison of countries, those with higher levels of postmaterialism will have _____ levels of gender equality than will countries having lower levels of postmaterialism.

Protest activity hypothesis (fill in the blanks): In a comparison of countries, those with _____ levels of postmaterialism will have _____ levels of protest activity than will countries having _____ levels of postmaterialism.

Religiosity hypothesis (complete the sentence): In a comparison of countries, those with _____

_____.

B. Consider how the independent variable is coded and how each dependent variable is coded. In the way that Stata calculates the Somers' d, which one of the three hypotheses implies a negative sign on the measure of association? (check one)

❏ The gender equality hypothesis

❏ The protest activity hypothesis

❏ The religiosity hypothesis

C. The world dataset is unweighted, so you can test each hypothesis using the tabulate command. Obtain chi-square ("chi2") and Somers' d. In the table that follows, record the percentages of countries falling into the highest category of each dependent variable. Also, report chi-square statistics, P-values, and Somers' d.

Dependent variable	Level of postmaterialism			Chi-square	P-value	Somers' d
	Low	Moderate	High			
Percentage high gender equality	?	?	?	?	?	?
Percentage high protest activity	?	?	?	?	?	?
Percentage high religiosity	?	?	?	?	?	?

D. Which of the following inferences are supported by your analysis? (check all that apply)

❏ The gender equality hypothesis is supported.

❏ Compared with how well we can predict gender equality by not knowing the level of postmaterialism, we can improve our prediction by 20.03 percent by knowing the level of postmaterialism.

❏ The protest activity hypothesis is supported.

❏ If the null hypothesis is correct, the postmaterialism-protest activity relationship would occur, by chance, less frequently than 5 times out of 100.

❏ The religiosity hypothesis is supported.

❏ If the null hypothesis is correct, the postmaterialism-religiosity relationship would occur, by chance, less frequently than 5 times out of 100.

That concludes the exercises for this chapter. Before exiting Stata, be sure to save your Do-file.

NOTES

1. Roger Newson, May 20, 2013. In this chapter you will install Newson's somersd package from the Statistical Software Components (SSC) archive.
2. Asymmetry is the essence of hypothetical relationships. Thus one would hypothesize that income causes opinions on welfare policies, but one would not hypothesize that welfare opinions cause income. We would prefer a measure of association that tells us how well income (independent variable) predicts welfare opinions (dependent variable), not how well welfare opinions predict income. Or, to cite Warner's tongue-in-cheek example: "There are some situations where the ability to make predictions is asymmetrical; for example, consider a study about gender and pregnancy. If you know that an individual is pregnant, you can predict gender (the person must be female) perfectly. However, it you know that an individual is female, you cannot assume that she is pregnant." Rebecca M. Warner, *Applied Statistics* (Thousand Oaks, CA: SAGE, 2008), 316.

3. Somers' d may be used for square tables (in which the independent and dependent variables have the same number of categories) and for nonsquare tables (in which the independent and dependent variables have different numbers of categories). Because of its other attractive properties, some methodologists prefer Somers' d to other measures, such as gamma, Kendall's tau-b, or Kendall's tau-c. See George W. Bohrnstedt and David Knoke, *Statistics for Social Data Analysis,* 2nd ed. (Itasca, IL: Peacock, 1988), 325.

4. This question wording represents a noteworthy departure from the traditional "environment versus jobs" tradeoff question in the American National Election Studies. In the 2008 ANES (question V083154), the strongest pro-environment position on the 7-point scale is "protect environment, *even if it costs jobs* & standard of living," and the strongest pro-jobs position is "jobs & standard of living more important than environment" (emphasis added). The 2012 ANES 7-point scale on which envjob_3 is based, envjob_self, allows the respondent to support the protection of the environment *and* the creation of jobs: "regulate business to protect the environment *and create jobs*" (emphasis added). This have-your-cake-and-eat-it-too proposition was hard to resist. In 2012, 20.6 percent took the strongest pro-environment position, compared with only 8.1 percent in 2008.

5. The 2012 ANES was administered in two survey modes: face-to-face and online. The face-to-face subsample contains three design parameters: primary sampling unit (2012 ANES variable, sample_ftfpsu), sampling weight (weight_ftf), and strata (strata_ftf). The online subsample has a sampling weight only (weight_web). Because this book analyzes the combined face-to-face and online samples, we use one full-sample weight, nesw, which is identical to the 2012 ANES variable, weight_full. However, if you wish to analyze the face-to-face sample only, you should specify all three design parameters in the svyset command: "svyset sample_ftfpsu [pw=weight_ftf], strata(strata_ftf)."

6. Notice that the "education effect" is quite pronounced for liberals, yet virtually nonexistent for conservatives. For liberals, gay rights support increases from 45.16 percent, to 51.75 percent, to 65.68 percent—about 20 points from low education to high education. By contrast, education has practically no effect for conservatives: 14.62 percent, 11.49 percent, and 11.67 percent.

7. See this Statalist thread: http://www.stata.com/statalist/archive/2008–08/msg00581.html.

8. Stata reports degrees of freedom in parentheses. The envjob_3-dem_educ3 table has 4 degrees of freedom, which is displayed in the label, "chi2(4)."

9. The somersd command pairs the first-named variable (the independent variable) with each succeeding variable (modeled as dependent variables) and returns the value of Somers' d for each pair. Thus the command, "somersd x y1 y2," will report values of Somers' d for the x-y1 relationship and for the x-y2 relationship.

10. Ronald Inglehart has written extensively about cultural change in postindustrial societies. For example, see his *Culture Shift in Advanced Industrial Society* (Princeton: Princeton University Press, 1990).

8

Correlation and Linear Regression

Commands Covered

correlate *varlist* [aw = *weightvar*]	Reports Pearson's correlation coefficients
regress *dep_var indep_var₁ … indep_var_n* [pw = *probability_weightvar*]	Performs bivariate regression and multiple regression
twoway (scatter *dep_var indep_var*) (lfit *dep_var indep_var*)	Creates a scatterplot with a linear prediction line
twoway (scatter *dep_var indep_var₁*) (lfit *dep_var indep_var₁*) [aw = *indep_var₂*]	Creates a bubble plot with a linear prediction line

Correlation and regression are powerful and flexible techniques used to analyze interval-level relationships. Pearson's correlation coefficient (Pearson's r) measures the strength and direction of the relationship between two interval-level variables. Pearson's r is not a proportional reduction in error (PRE) measure, but it does gauge strength on an easily understood scale—from -1, a perfectly negative association between the variables, to +1, a perfectly positive relationship. A correlation of 0 indicates no relationship. Researchers often use correlation techniques in the beginning stages of analysis to get an overall picture of the relationships between interesting variables.

Regression analysis produces a statistic, the regression coefficient, that estimates the effect of an independent variable on a dependent variable. Regression also produces a PRE measure of association, R-square, which indicates how completely the independent variable (or variables) explain(s) the dependent variable. In regression analysis the dependent variable is measured at the interval level, but the independent variable can come in any variety—nominal, ordinal, or interval. Regression is more specialized than correlation. Researchers use regression analysis to model causal relationships between one or more independent variables and a dependent variable.

In this chapter you will learn to perform correlation analysis using the correlate command. You will run bivariate regression and multiple regression using the regress command. Bivariate regression uses one independent variable to predict a dependent variable, whereas multiple regression uses two or more independent variables to predict a dependent variable. Using the graph twoway command, you will learn to overlay a scatterplot with a regression prediction line. These graphic techniques will help you interpret your findings and will greatly enhance the presentation of your results.

THE CORRELATE COMMAND AND THE REGRESS COMMAND

Suppose that a student of state politics is interested in the gender composition of state legislatures. Running the summarize command on a variable (womleg_2011) in the states dataset, this student finds that state legislatures range from 9.4 percent female to 41.0 percent female. Why is there such variation in this variable? The student researcher begins to formulate an explanation. Perhaps states with lower percentages of college graduates have lower percentages of women legislators than do states with more college-educated residents. And maybe a traditionally cultural variable, the percentage of highly religious people, plays a role. Perhaps states with higher levels of religiosity have lower percentages of female lawmakers. Correlation analysis would give this researcher an overview of the relationships among these variables.

Open the states dataset, and start a Do-file. First we will use correlate to get a general idea about the direction and strength of the relationships among three variables: the percentage of highly religious (Relig_high), the percentage of college graduates (BA_or_more), and the percentage of female state legislators (womleg_2011). Stata commands don't get much simpler than correlate. The user types "correlate" (or "cor" for short) and then types or clicks the variables into the Command window:

```
cor womleg_2011 Relig_high BA_or_more

                  wom~2011 Relig~gh BA_or_~e

  womleg_2011       1.0000
   Relig_high      -0.6351    1.0000
   BA_or_more       0.5865   -0.5948    1.0000
```

Stata produces a table, called a correlation matrix, that shows the correlation of each variable with each of the other variables—it even shows the correlation between each variable and itself. The correlation between Relig_high and womleg_2011 is -.6351, or about -.64, which tells us that increasing values of one of the variables is associated with decreasing values of the other variable. So as the percentage of highly religious people goes up, the percentage of female legislators goes down. How strong is the relationship? We know that Pearson's r is bracketed by -1 and +1, so we could say that this relationship is a fairly strong negative association. The correlation between BA_or_more and womleg_2011, at about .59, indicates a positive relationship: As states' percentages of college graduates increase, so do their percentages of women legislators. This is a fairly strong association—nearly as strong as the womleg_2011-Relig_high relationship. Finally, Relig_high and BA_or_more, with a Pearson's r of -.59, are also strongly related. As we compare states with fewer college graduates to states with more college graduates, we are also comparing states with more highly religious residents to states with fewer highly religious residents. (This relationship becomes important later.)

Correlation analysis is a good place to start when analyzing interval-level relationships. Even so, a correlation coefficient is agnostic on the question of which variable is the cause and which the effect. Does an increase in the percentage of college graduates somehow cause higher percentages of women in state legislatures? Or do increasing percentages of women in state legislatures somehow cause states to have higher percentages of college graduates? Either way, correlation analysis reports the same measure of association, a Pearson's r of .59.

Regression is more powerful than correlation, in part because it helps the researcher investigate causal relationships—relationships in which an independent variable is thought to affect a dependent variable. Regression analysis will (1) reveal the precise nature of the relationship between an independent and dependent variable, (2) test the null hypothesis that the observed relationship occurred by chance, and (3) provide a PRE measure of association between the independent variable and the dependent variable. To illustrate these and other points, we will run two separate bivariate regressions. First we will examine the relationship between Relig_high and womleg_2011, and then we will analyze the relationship between BA_or_more and womleg_2011.

For simple bivariate regression, the general syntax of the regress command is as follows:

regress *dep_var indep_var*

Using the permissible command abbreviation "reg," we would analyze the effect of Relig_high on womleg_2011 by typing and running the following:

```
reg womleg_2011 Relig_high
```

Source	SS	df	MS
Model	870.648396	1	870.648396
Residual	1288.2084	48	26.8376751
Total	2158.8568	49	44.058302

Number of obs =	50
F(1, 48) =	32.44
Prob > F =	0.0000
R-squared =	0.4033
Adj R-squared =	0.3909
Root MSE =	5.1805

womleg_2011	Coef.	Std. Err.	t	P>|t|	[95% Conf. Interval]	
Relig_high	-.4694007	.0824128	-5.70	0.000	-.6351028	-.3036986
_cons	42.30051	3.32837	12.71	0.000	35.60837	48.99265

In the bottom-most table, Stata reports values ("Coef.") for the Y-intercept or constant, _cons, and for the regression coefficient on the independent variable, Relig_high. According to these coefficients, the regression equation for estimating the effect of Relig_high on womleg_2011 is:

Percent of state legislators who are women = 42.30 – 0.47 * Relig_high.

The constant, 42.30, is the estimated value of Y when X equals 0. If you were using this equation to estimate the percentage of women legislators for a state, you would start with 42.30 percent and then subtract .47 for each percentage of the state's population who are highly religious. So your estimate for a state with, say, 50 percent highly religious would be 42.30 – .47*(50) = 42.30 – 23.50 ≈ 19 percent female legislators. The main statistic of interest, then, is the regression coefficient, -.47, which estimates the average change in the dependent variable for each unit change in the independent variable. A regression coefficient of -.47 tells us that, for each one-unit increase in the percentage of highly religious residents, there is a .47-unit decrease in the percentage of female legislators. So a 1-percentage-point increase in Relig_high is associated with a decrease in womleg_2011 of about half a percentage point.[1]

What would the null hypothesis have to say about all this? Of course, we are not analyzing a random sample here, since we have information on the entire population of fifty states. But let's assume, for illustrative purposes, that we have just analyzed a random sample and that we have obtained a sample estimate of the effect of Relig_high on womleg_2011. The null hypothesis would say what it always says: In the population from which the sample was drawn, there is no relationship between the independent variable (in this case, the percentage of highly religious residents) and the dependent variable (the percentage of female legislators). In the population, the true regression coefficient is equal to 0. Furthermore, the regression coefficient that we obtained, -.47, occurred by chance.

In Stata regression results, you test the null hypothesis by examining two columns in the bottom table—the column labeled "t," which reports t-ratios, and the column labeled "P>| t |," which reports P-values. Informally, in order to safely reject the null hypothesis, the researcher generally looks for t-ratios with magnitudes (absolute values) of 2 or greater. According to the results of our analysis, the regression coefficient for Relig_high has a t-ratio of -5.70, well above the informal |2|-or-greater rule. A P-value, which tells you the probability of obtaining the results if the null hypothesis is correct, helps you to make more precise inferences about the relationship between the independent variable and the dependent variable. If the figure in the "P>| t |" column is greater than .05, then the observed results would occur too frequently by chance, and you must not reject the null hypothesis. By contrast, if the figure in the "P>| t |" column is equal to or less than .05, then the null hypothesis represents an unlikely occurrence and may be rejected. The t-ratio for Relig_high has a corresponding P-value of 0.000. If the null is correct, it is highly unlikely that we would obtain these results. Reject the null hypothesis. It depends on the research problem at hand, of course, but for most applications you can ignore the t-ratio and P-value for the constant.[2]

How strong is the relationship between Relig_high and womleg_2011? The answer is provided by the R-squared statistics, which appear on the right-hand side of the results, above the table of coefficients, t-ratios, and P-values. Stata reports two values, one labeled "R-squared," and one labeled "Adj R-squared." Which one should you use? Most research articles report the adjusted value, so let's rely on "Adj R-square" to provide the best overall measure of the strength of the relationship. (See "A Closer Look.") Adjusted R-squared is equal to .3909. What does this mean? R-square communicates the proportion of the variation in the dependent variable that is explained by the independent variable. Like any proportion, R-square can assume any value between 0 and 1. Thus, of all the variation in womleg_2011 between states, .3909, or 39.1 percent, is explained by Relig_high. The rest of the variation in womleg_2011, 60.9 percent, remains unexplained by the independent variable.

So that you can become comfortable with bivariate regression—and to address a potential source of confusion—let's perform another regression analysis, this time using BA_or_more as the independent

R-Squared and Adjusted R-Squared: What's the Difference?

Most data analysis programs, Stata included, provide two values of R-squared—a plain version, which Stata labels "R-squared," and an adjusted version, "Adj R-squared." Adjusted R-squared is often about the same as (but is always less than) plain R-squared. What is the difference? Just like a sample mean, which provides an estimate of the unseen population mean, a sample R-squared provides an estimate of the true value of R-squared in the population. And just like a sample mean, the sample R-squared is equal to the population R-squared, give or take random sampling error. However, unlike the random error associated with a sample mean, R-squared's errors can assume only positive values—squaring any negative error, after all, produces a positive number—introducing upward bias into the estimated value of R-squared. This problem, which is more troublesome for small samples and for models with many independent variables, can be corrected by adjusting plain R-squared "downward." For a sample of size N and a regression model with k predictors, adjusted R-squared is equal to: $1 - (1 - R\text{-squared})[(N - 1)/(N - k - 1)]$. See Barbara G. Tabachnick and Linda S. Fidell, *Using Multivariate Statistics*, 3rd ed. (New York: HarperCollins, 1996), 164–165.

variable. In your Do-file, copy/paste "reg womleg_2011 Relig_high" onto a new line, and modify it to read "reg womleg_2011 BA_or_more":

reg womleg_2011 BA_or_more

Source	SS	df	MS
Model	742.49059	1	742.49059
Residual	1416.36621	48	29.5076294
Total	2158.8568	49	44.058302

Number of obs =	50
F(1, 48) =	25.16
Prob > F =	0.0000
R-squared =	0.3439
Adj R-squared =	0.3303
Root MSE =	5.4321

womleg_2011	Coef.	Std. Err.	t	P>|t|	[95% Conf. Interval]
BA_or_more	.8226485	.163997	5.02	0.000	.4929103 1.152387
_cons	1.454996	4.521861	0.32	0.749	-7.636814 10.54681

What is the regression line for the effect of BA_or_more on womleg_2011? It is

Percent female state legislators = 1.45 + 0.82 * BA_or_more.

First, consider the puny magnitude of the constant, 1.45. For states in which 0 percent of residents have college degrees, the estimated percentage of female legislators is merely 1.45 percent, an implausibly low number.[3] In fact, you will sometimes obtain regression results in which the constant is a negative number, which leaves the realm of the implausible and enters the realm of the impossible, at least for dependent variables, such as womleg_2011, that cannot assume negative values. (In one of this chapter's exercises, you will obtain a negative constant, even though the dependent variable cannot take on negative values.) Simply stated, Stata anchors the line at the Y-intercept that produces the best estimates for the data. Of course, you can use the equation to arrive at a more realistic estimate for cases having the lowest observed value on the independent variable. For example, for states in which 20 percent of the population have a college degree—a value that is quite close to the actual minimum of BA_or_higher—we would estimate a value on womleg_2011 of about 18 percent: 1.45 + .82*20 ≈ 18 percent.

The regression coefficient, .82, says that for each percentage-point increase in BA_or_more, there is an average increase of .82 of a percentage point in the percentage of female legislators. Again, increase the percentage of BA_or_more graduates by 1, and the percentage of women legislators goes up by .8, on average. In the population, could the true value of the regression coefficient be 0? Probably not, according to the t-ratio (5.02) and the P-value (0.000). And, according to adjusted R-squared, the independent variable does a fair amount of work in explaining the dependent variable. About 33 percent of the variation in womleg_2011 is explained by BA_or_more. As bivariate regressions go, that's not too bad.

CREATING A SCATTERPLOT WITH A LINEAR PREDICTION LINE

For unweighted datasets, such as states or world, a versatile graphing command, twoway, adds a visual dimension to correlation and regression. This helps you paint a richer portrait of a relationship. Consider Figure 8-1, which overlays two graphic forms: a scatterplot (scatter) and a linear prediction or linear fit line (lfit). The scatterplot displays the states in a two-dimensional space according to their values on the two variables. The horizontal axis is defined by the independent variable, BA_or_more, and the vertical axis is defined by a dependent variable, womleg_2011. We know from our correlation analysis that Pearson's r for this relationship is .59. We can now see what the correlation "looks like." Based on the figure, states with lower percentages of college graduates tend to have lower percentages of women legislators, with values on the y-axis that range from 10 percent to about 25 percent or so. The percentages of women legislators for states at the higher end of the x-axis, furthermore, fall between 15–20 percent and around 35 percent. So as you move from left to right along the x-axis, values on the y-axis generally increase, just as the positive correlation coefficient suggested. The dots have been overlaid by the linear prediction line obtained from the analysis we just performed: Estimated percentage of women legislators = 1.45 + 0.82 * BA_or_more. Thanks to this visual depiction, one can see that the linear summary of the relationship, while reasonably coherent, is far from perfect. Obviously, this graph adds depth and interest to our description of the relationship.

A basic overlay can be created with a few simple parameters:

```
#delimit ;
twoway (scatter womleg_2011 BA_or_more)  ←  Requests a scatterplot

   (lfit womleg_2011 BA_or_more ),  ←  Overlays a linear prediction line

  legend(off) ;  ←  Suppresses the legend
```

The first parenthetical, "scatter womleg_2011 BA_or_more," creates the scatterplot. The second parenthetical, "lfit womleg_2011 BA_or_more," overlays a linear prediction (regression) line. In accordance with Stata's rules, the dependent variable or y-axis variable (womleg_2011) is named first, and the independent variable or x-axis variable (BA_or_more) is named second. Unless instructed otherwise, Stata will include a legend that distinguishes the different plotted elements in its graphic overlays. For the kind of straightforward plotting we are doing here—a scatter plus a linear prediction line—a legend adds unnecessary clutter. The option, "legend(off)," ensures a tidier display. The scatter-overlay in Figure 8-1 adds a number of tweaks and options, which are annotated in Figure 8-2. (Figure 8-2 also reveals a quirk of Stata graphing syntax.)

Figure 8-1 Scatterplot with Regression Line

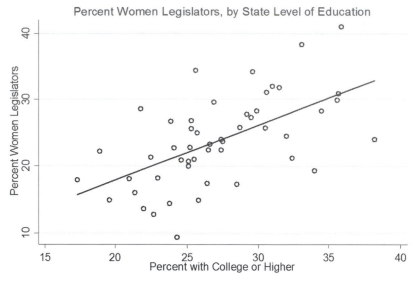

SOURCE: States Dataset

Figure 8-2 Creating a Scatterplot with Regression Line

MULTIPLE REGRESSION

Before proceeding, let's review what we have learned thus far about the womleg_2011-Relig_high and womleg_2011-BA_or_more relationships. The womleg_2011-Relig_high regression revealed a statistically significant negative relationship: The percentage of female legislators declines by .47 of a percentage point, on average, for every one percentage-point increase in high religiosity. The womleg_2011-BA_or_more regression revealed a significantly positive relationship: The percentage of female legislators increases by .82 of a percentage point, on average, for every one percentage-point increase in college graduates. A researcher who performed these analyses to test two separate hypotheses, the "religiosity hypothesis" and the "college hypothesis," might be tempted to conclude that each coefficient— -.47 for religiosity and .82 for college degrees—captures the true effect of each variable on the dependent variable. However, this conclusion would be unwarranted. Recall this result, revealed in the correlation analysis: The two independent variables are themselves rather strongly related (r = -.59). How might this relationship affect the analysis?

Consider Figure 8-3, a "bubble plot" that helps us visualize the relationships we have been discussing. (To learn how to add the bubble feature to a scatterplot, see "A Closer Look.") In its essential two-dimensional character, Figure 8-3 re-expresses the Figure 8-1 relationship—states with higher percentages of college graduates have higher percentages of female legislators—except that, instead of a dot, each state is represented by a circle. The size of each circle represents the second independent variable, Relig_high—the bigger the circle, the higher the state's religiosity.

Figure 8-3 Bubble Plot

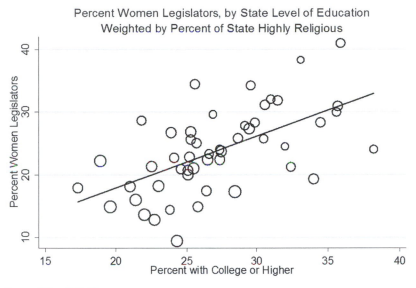

Source: States Dataset

Take a few minutes to examine the bubble plot. To visualize the womleg_2011-Relig_high relationship, imagine collapsing the circles onto the y-axis, stacking them up as they would fall, from low values of womleg_2011 to high values of womleg_2011. The lower range of the dependent variable would be populated with larger circles, the higher range with smaller ones. Now imagine collapsing the circles onto the x-axis. As BA_or_more increases, from left to right, the circles decrease in size, from high-religiosity states to low-religiosity states. Thus, when we compare states having lower percentages of college graduates with states having higher percentages of college graduates, we are also comparing states having more highly religious residents with states having fewer highly religious residents. Do states with more college graduates have higher percentages of female legislators because they have more college graduates, or because they have lower religiosity? How much of the "college effect" is attributable to the "religiosity effect"? Multiple regression analysis is designed to disentangle the confounding effects of two (or more) independent variables. Multiple regression will estimate the effect of each independent variable on the dependent variable, controlling for the effects of all other independent variables in the model.

To perform multiple regression, simply type the names of additional independent variables at the end of the regression command:

```
reg womleg_2011 BA_or_more Relig_high
```

Source	SS	df	MS		
Model	1016.17707	2	508.088537		
Residual	1142.67973	47	24.3123346		
Total	2158.8568	49	44.058302		

Number of obs = 50
F(2, 47) = 20.90
Prob > F = 0.0000
R-squared = 0.4707
Adj R-squared = 0.4482
Root MSE = 4.9308

womleg_2011	Coef.	Std. Err.	t	P>|t|	[95% Conf. Interval]
BA_or_more	.4530699	.1851843	2.45	0.018	.0805271 .8256128
Relig_high	-.3273943	.0975793	-3.36	0.002	-.5236986 -.13109
_cons	24.39521	7.974693	3.06	0.004	8.352198 40.43822

This analysis provides the information we need to isolate the partial effect of each independent variable on the dependent variable. The multiple regression equation is as follows:

percent female state legislators = 24.40 + .45*BA_or_more − .33*Relig_high

Let's focus on the regression coefficients for each of the independent variables. The coefficient on BA_or_more, .45, tells us the effect of BA_or_more on womleg_2011, controlling for Relig_high. Recall that in the bivariate analysis, a 1-percentage-point increase in BA_or_more was associated with a .82-unit increase in the percentage of female legislators. When we control for Relig_high, however, we find a reduction in this effect—to a .45-unit increase in womleg_2011. Even so, the regression coefficient on BA_or_more, with a t-statistic of 2.45 and a P-value of .018, remains statistically significant. The partial effect of Relig_high tells a similar story. The uncontrolled effect of religious attendance, -.47, weakens to -.33 but remains significant (t = -3.36, P-value = .002). In multiple regression, adjusted R-squared communicates how well all of the independent variables explain the dependent variable. So by knowing two things about states—percentage of college graduates and level of religiosity—we can account for about 45 percent of the variation across states in the percentage of female legislators. This is an improvement over the explanatory leverage of Relig_high (.39) or BA_or_more (.33) considered separately.

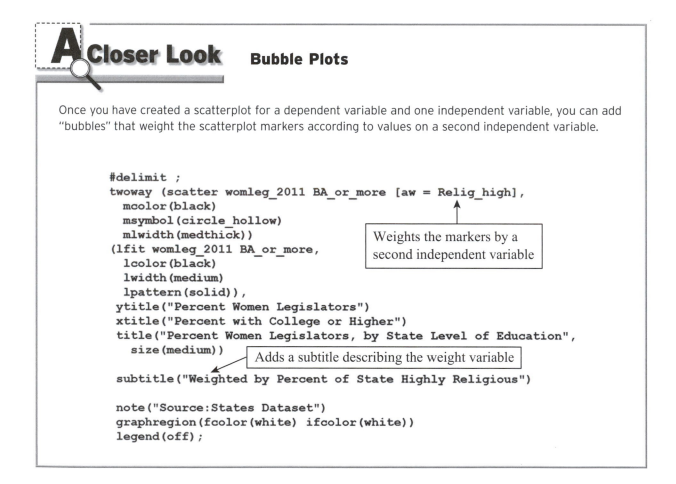

A Closer Look   Bubble Plots

Once you have created a scatterplot for a dependent variable and one independent variable, you can add "bubbles" that weight the scatterplot markers according to values on a second independent variable.

```
#delimit ;
twoway (scatter womleg_2011 BA_or_more [aw = Relig_high],
  mcolor(black)
  msymbol(circle_hollow)
  mlwidth(medthick))
(lfit womleg_2011 BA_or_more,
  lcolor(black)
  lwidth(medium)
  lpattern(solid)),
 ytitle("Percent Women Legislators")
 xtitle("Percent with College or Higher")
 title("Percent Women Legislators, by State Level of Education",
   size(medium))

subtitle("Weighted by Percent of State Highly Religious")

note("Source:States Dataset")
graphregion(fcolor(white) ifcolor(white))
legend(off);
```

Weights the markers by a second independent variable

Adds a subtitle describing the weight variable

CORRELATION AND REGRESSION WITH WEIGHTED DATA

We now turn to the analysis of weighted data, an increasingly common situation, especially in survey research. Stata's correlate command allows analytic weights, [aw = *weightvar*], although probability weights are not permitted. This book does not cover questions of statistical inference for correlation coefficients—how closely does an observed correlation coefficient reflect the true correlation coefficient in the population?—so analytic weights are all we need.[4]

The regress command allows probability weights, albeit with a Stata-esque complication. We explore these points by analyzing gss2012. Before proceeding, close states and open gss2012.

Gss2012 contains the variable, abortion, which records the number of conditions under which respondents think an abortion should be permitted, from 0 conditions to 7 conditions. The dataset also has educ, which measures educational attainment, from "None" (coded 2) to "8 years of college" (coded 22). Another familiar variable, femrole, gauges respondents' beliefs about the role of women, from 0 ("Traditional") to 9 ("NonTraditional"). To get an overall picture of the relationships between these variables, run correlate with the weight variable:

```
cor abortion educ femrole [aw=gssw]
```

	abortion	educ	femrole
abortion	1.0000		
educ	0.2107	1.0000	
femrole	0.3209	0.2838	1.0000

As education increases, and as femrole shades toward nontraditional beliefs, abortion opinions become more permissive. Educ and femrole, as well, are positively associated.

Now let's run a multiple regression, using abortion as the dependent variable and educ and femrole as independent variables. Type the regress command as you would for unweighted data, but add "[pw=gssw]" at the end of the command:

```
reg abortion educ femrole [pw=gssw]
```

Linear regression

```
Number of obs =      518
F( 2,    515) =    34.13
Prob > F      =   0.0000
R-squared     =   0.1185
Root MSE      =   2.4243
```

abortion	Coef.	Robust Std. Err.	t	P>|t|	[95% Conf.	Interval]
educ	.1104601	.0414937	2.66	0.008	.0289424	.1919778
femrole	.3688799	.0577176	6.39	0.000	.255489	.4822708
_cons	.295546	.6230502	0.47	0.635	-.9284867	1.519579

Remember that the dependent variable is measured in whole numbers that range from 0 (allow abortion under no conditions) to 7 (allow under all seven conditions). The coefficient on educ, .11, says that each 1-year increment in educational attainment is associated with an increase of about a tenth of a condition. More meaningfully, we could say that every 10-year increment is associated with an increase of a bit more than one condition on the 0-7 abortion scale. According to the statistical tests, the effect of educ is significant (t = 2.66, P = .008). Femrole, too, posts a strong positive effect (t = 6.39, P = 0.000).

How completely do both independent variables explain the dependent variable? We have R-squared, which is equal to .1185, but regress with probability weights does not return adjusted R-squared. However, Stata temporarily stores adjusted R-squared as an e-return estimate, named "e(r2_a)."[5] To retrieve this estimate, type and keep the following command in the Do-file:

```
dis "Adjusted R2 = " e(r2_a)
```

Run the command after each reg run that uses probability weights:

```
. dis "Adjusted R2 = " e(r2_a)
Adjusted R2 = .11511404
```

Taken together, both independent variables account for 11.5 percent of the variation in the abortion scale.

EXERCISES

1. (Dataset: states. Variables: demHR11, demstate13, union10.) Consider a plausible scenario for the relationships between three variables: The percentages of a state's US House and US Senate delegations who are Democrats, the percentage of state legislators who are Democrats, and the percentage of workers in the state who are unionized. One could hypothesize that, compared with states with few Democrats in their state legislatures, states having larger percentages of Democratic legislators would also have greater proportions of Democrats in their US congressional delegations. Furthermore, because unions tend to support Democratic candidates, one would also expect more heavily unionized states to have higher percentages of Democratic legislators at the state and national levels. Dataset states contains three variables: demHR11, the percentage of House and Senate members who are Democrats; demstate13, the percentage of state legislators who are Democrats; and union10, the percentage of workers who are union members.

A. Run correlate to find the Pearson correlation coefficients among demHR11, demstate13, and union10. Next to the question marks, write in the correlation coefficients.

		Percent US House and Senate Democratic (demHR11)	Percent of state legislators who are Democrats (demstate13)	Percent workers who are union members (union10)
Percent US House and Senate Democratic (demHR11)	Pearson Correlation	1		
Percent of state legislators who are Democrats (demstate13)	Pearson Correlation	?	1	
Percent workers who are union members (union10)	Pearson Correlation	?	?	1

B. According to the correlation coefficient, as the percentage of unionized workers increases, the percentage of Democratic US representatives and US senators (circle one)

increases.   decreases.

C. According to the correlation coefficient, as the percentage of unionized workers decreases, the percentage of Democratic US representatives and US senators (circle one)

increases.   decreases.

D. Which two of the following statements describe the relationship between the percentage of unionized workers and the percentage of state legislators who are Democrats (check two)?

❏ The relationship is negative.

❏ The relationship is positive.

❏ The relationship is stronger than the relationship between the percentage of unionized workers and the percentage of Democratic US representatives and US senators.

❑ The relationship is weaker than the relationship between the percentage of unionized workers and the percentage of Democratic US representatives and US senators.

2. (Dataset: states. Variables: HR_conserv11, Conserv_public.) Two congressional scholars are discussing the extent to which members of the US House of Representatives stay in touch with the voters in their states.

Scholar 1: "When members of Congress vote on important public policies, they are closely attuned to the ideological makeups of their states. Members from states having lots of liberals will tend to cast votes in the liberal direction. Representatives from states with mostly conservative constituencies, by contrast, will take conservative positions on important policies."

Scholar 2: "You certainly have a naïve view of congressional behavior. Once they get elected, members of congress adopt a 'Washington, DC, state of mind,' perhaps voting in the liberal direction on one policy and in the conservative direction on another. One thing is certain: The way members vote has little to do with the ideological composition of their states."

Think about an independent variable that measures the percentage of self-described "conservatives" among the mass public in a state, with low values denoting low percentages of conservatives and high values denoting high percentages of conservatives. And consider a dependent variable that gauges the degree to which the state's House delegation votes in a conservative direction on public policies. Low scores on this dependent variable tell you that the delegation tends to vote in a liberal direction, and high scores say that the delegation votes in a conservative direction.

A. Below is an empty graphic shell showing the relationship between the independent variable and the dependent variable. Draw a regression line inside the shell that depicts what the relationship should look like if Scholar 1 is correct.

B. Below is another graphic shell showing the relationship between the independent variable and the dependent variable. Draw a regression line inside the shell that depicts what the relationship should look like if Scholar 2 is correct.

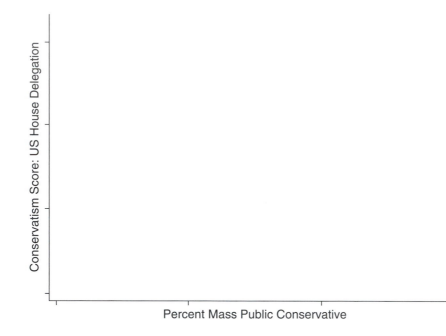

C. Dataset states contains the variable Conserv_public, the percentage of the mass public calling themselves conservative. This is the independent variable. The dataset also contains HR_conserv11, a measure of conservative votes by states' House members. Scores on this variable can range from 0 (low conservatism) to 100 (high conservatism). This is the dependent variable. Run regress.

  According to the regression equation, a 1-percentage-point increase in conservatives in the mass public is associated with (check one)

  ❑ about a 27-point decrease in House conservatism scores.

  ❑ about a 2-point increase in House conservatism scores.

  ❑ about an 8-point increase in House conservatism scores.

D. If you were to use this regression to estimate the mean House conservatism score for states having 30 percent conservatives, your estimate would be (circle one)

  a score of about 29.   a score of about 39.   a score of about 49.

E. The adjusted R-squared for this relationship is equal to _____. This tells you that about_____ percent of the variation in HR_conserv11 is explained by Conserv_public.

F. Run twoway to obtain a scatterplot with a linear prediction overlay. Remember that HR_conserv11 is the y-axis variable, and Conserv_public is the x-axis variable. Suppress the legend. Add the following elements: (i) add a y-axis title ("Conservatism score, House delegation"); (ii) add a source note ("Source: States dataset"); (iii) add a chart title ("House Conservatism, by Percent Mass Public Conservative"); and (iv) change the pattern of the linear prediction line. If you prefer, make other enhancements to the graph's appearance. Print the graph.

G. Based on your inspection of the regression results, the scatterplot and linear prediction line, and adjusted R-squared, which congressional scholar is more correct?

  ❑ Scholar 1 is more correct because _____

  _____.

❑ Scholar 2 is more correct because _____

_____.

3. (Dataset: states. Variables: TO_0812, Obama2012.) An article of faith among Democratic Party strategists (and a source of apprehension among Republican strategists) is that high voter turnouts help Democratic candidates. Why should this be the case? According to the conventional wisdom, Democratic electorates are less likely to vote than are Republican voters. Thus low turnouts naturally favor Republican candidates. As turnouts push higher, the reasoning goes, a larger number of potential Democratic voters will go to the polls, creating a better opportunity for Democratic candidates. Therefore, as turnouts go up, so should the Democratic percentage of the vote.[6]

A. Use the regress command to test this conventional wisdom. The states dataset contains TO_0812, the percentage-point change in presidential election turnout between 2008 and 2012. States in which turnout declined between 2008 and 2012 have negative values on TO_0812, while states in which turnout increased have positive values on TO_0812. (For example, Utah's turnout increased by a bit more than two percentage points between 2008 and 2012, giving Utah a score of 2.1 on TO_0812. Florida's turnout dropped by four points, giving a value of -4 on TO_0812.) TO_0812 is the independent variable. Another variable, Obama2012, the percentage of the vote cast for Democratic candidate Barack Obama, is the dependent variable.

Based on your results, the regression equation for estimating the percentage voting for Obama is (put the constant, _cons, in the first blank):

_____ + _____ * TO_0812.

B. The P-value for the regression coefficient on TO_0812 is _____, and adjusted R-squared is _____.

C. Consider your findings in A and B. One may conclude that

❑ The conventional wisdom is correct because _____

_____.

❑ The conventional wisdom is incorrect because _____

_____.

4. (Dataset: states. Variables: abortlaw10, ProChoice.) As you are no doubt aware, in its momentous decision in *Roe v. Wade* (1973) the US Supreme Court declared that states may not outlaw abortion. Even so, many state legislatures have enacted restrictions and regulations that, while not banning abortion, make an abortion more difficult to obtain. Other states, however, have few or no restrictions. What factors might explain these differences in abortion laws among the states? We know that the public remains divided on this issue. Public opinion in some states is more favorable toward permitting abortion, while in other states public opinion is less favorable. Does public opinion guide state policy on this issue?

The dataset states contains abortlaw10, which measures the number of abortion restrictions a state has enacted into law. Values on abortlaw10 range from 0 (least restrictive) to 10 (most restrictive). This is the dependent variable. The dataset also has the variable, ProChoice, the percentage of the mass public that is prochoice. This is the independent variable.

A. If you were to use regression analysis to test the idea that public opinion on abortion affects state abortion policy, you would expect to find (check one)

❑ A negative sign on ProChoice's regression coefficient.

❑ A positive sign on ProChoice's regression coefficient.

B. Using regression, analyze the abortlaw10-ProChoice relationship. According to the results, the regression equation for estimating the number of abortion restrictions is (fill in the blanks)

_____ _____*ProChoice.
  (constant)   (regression coefficient)

C. The P-value for the regression coefficient is _____. The value of adjusted R-squared is _____.

D. According to states, about 60 percent of Colorado residents are prochoice. In Arkansas, by contrast, only about 40 percent of the public holds this view. Based on the regression equation (fill in the blanks),

You would estimate that Colorado would have about _____ abortion restrictions.

You would estimate that Arkansas would have about _____ abortion restrictions.

E. Adjusted R-squared is equal to _____. This means that _____

_____.

F. Run twoway to obtain a scatterplot with a linear prediction overlay. Suppress the legend. Add the following titles and notes: (i) y-axis title, "Number of abortion restrictions"; (ii) title, "Number of Abortion Restrictions, by Percent Public Prochoice "; (iii) note, "Source: States dataset." Also (iv) change the color and pattern of the linear prediction line. If you prefer, make other enhancements to the graph's appearance. Print the graphic.

5. Suppose that a critic, upon examining the variables in states.dta and viewing your results in Exercise 4, expresses skepticism about the relationship between mass-level abortion attitudes and the number of state-level restrictions on abortion:

"There is a key aspect of state governance that you have not taken into account: the percentage of state legislators who are women (womleg_2011). If you were to examine the correlation coefficients among abortlaw10, ProChoice, and womleg_2011, you will find two things. First, the womleg_2011-abortlaw10 correlation will be negative and pretty strong . . . say, at least -.50. Second, the womleg_2011-ProChoice correlation will be positive and fairly strong—at least +.50. Third, when you perform a multiple regression analysis of abortlaw10, using ProChoice and womleg_2011 as independent variables, you will find that womleg_2011 is statistically significant, while ProChoice will fade to statistical insignificance."

A. Obtain a correlation matrix for abortlaw10, ProChoice, and womleg_2011. Write the correlation coefficients next to the question marks in the following table.

		No. of abortion restrictions (abortlaw10)	Percent mass public prochoice (ProChoice)	Percent female legislators (womleg_2011)
No. of abortion restrictions (abortlaw10)	Pearson correlation	1		
Percent mass public prochoice (ProChoice)	Pearson correlation	?	1	
Percent female legislators (womleg_2011)	Pearson correlation	?	?	1

B. Consider the skeptical critic's first claim regarding the relationship between womleg_2011 and abortlaw10. According to the correlation coefficient, this claim is

Correct because _____

_____.

Incorrect because _____

_____.

C. Consider the skeptical critic's second claim regarding the relationship between womleg_2011 and ProChoice. According to the correlation coefficient, this claim is

Correct because _____

_____.

Incorrect because _____

_____.

D. Run the multiple regression suggested by the critic. Write the correct values next to the question marks in the following table:

abortlaw10	Coefficient	t-ratio	P-value
ProChoice	?	?	?
womleg_2011	?	?	?
constant	?		

E. Based on the evidence in Part D, is the critic's third claim regarding the multiple regression analysis correct? This claim is

❑ Correct because _____

_____

_____.

❑ Incorrect because _____

_____

_____.

F. Modify the twoway syntax from Exercise 4 to create a bubble plot that depicts the relationship between abortlaw10(y-axis) and ProChoice (x-axis), weighted by womleg_2011. Add a subtitle to the syntax: "Weighted by Percent Female State Legislators." Print the graph.

6. (Dataset: gss2012. Variables: tolerance, educ, age, polviews, [aw=gssw], [pw=gss].) What factors affect a person's level of tolerance of unpopular groups? Consider three hypotheses:

H1: In a comparison of individuals, older people will be less tolerant than younger people.

H2: In a comparison of individuals, those with higher levels of education will have higher levels of tolerance than those with lower levels of education.

H3: In a comparison of individuals, conservatives will be less tolerant than liberals.

Gss2012 includes the following variables, as described in this table:

Gss2012 variable	Label	Coding	Status in this exercise
tolerance	Tolerance	0 (low) to 15 (high)	dependent variable
age	R's Age (years)	18 to 89	independent variable
educ	Highest Year of School	2 to 22	independent variable
polviews	Ideological Self-Placement	1 (ExtrmLib) to 7 (ExtrmCons)	independent variable

A. Run correlate. (Don't forget to include "[aw=gssw].") Focus on the correlations between the dependent variable and each of the independent variables. Write the correlations in the following table.

	Tolerance
age	?
educ	?
polviews	?

B. Based on the *direction* of each correlation coefficient, does it appear that each hypothesis has merit? Answer yes or no, and explain:

_____

_____

_____

_____

_____

C. Run a multiple regression analysis. (Don't forget to include "[pw=gssw].") After you run the model, run the script to obtain adjusted R-squared. Fill in the following table.

tolerance	Coefficient	t-ratio	P-value
age	?	?	?
educ	?	?	?
polviews	?	?	?
constant	?		
Adjusted R-squared	?		

D. Based on the evidence in Part C, does it appear that each hypothesis has merit? Answer yes or no, and explain.

_____

_____

_____

_____

_____

_____

_____

E. Use the regression equation to estimate the tolerance score for the typical respondent, which we will define as a person having the median values of all the independent variables. Run summary with the detail option (and "[aw=gssw]") to obtain the median values for each independent variable. Write the medians in the table that follows (the median of polviews already appears in the table).

	age	educ	polviews
Median	?	?	4

F. When you use the median values to estimate the tolerance score for the typical person, you obtain an estimate equal to (fill in the blank) _____.

That concludes the exercises for this chapter.

NOTES

1. Regression analysis on variables measured by percentages can be confusing. Always stay focused on the exact units of measurement. One percentage point would be 1.00. So if Relig_high increases by 1.00, then womleg_2011 decreases, on average, by .47, or .47 of a percentage point.
2. The t-ratio for the y-intercept permits you to test the null hypothesis that, in the population, the y-intercept is 0. In this case we have no interest in testing the hypothesis that states having 0 highly religious residents have 0 percent women in their state legislatures.
3. Of course, the smallest value of BA_or_more in the actual data is substantially higher than 0. If you do a quick summarize run, you will find that the lowest value of BA_or_more is 17.3 percent.
4. Nick Winter's corr_svy (September 28, 2001) does allow probability weights and will return appropriately weighted tests of statistical significance. To download this package, run "ssc install corr_svy."
5. To see all stored results, type "ereturn list."
6. See Michael D. Martinez and Jeff Gill, "The Effects of Turnout on Partisan Outcomes in US Presidential Elections 1960–2000," _Journal of Politics_ 67, no. 4 (2005): 1248–1274. Martinez and Gill find that the Democratic advantage from higher turnouts has declined over time.

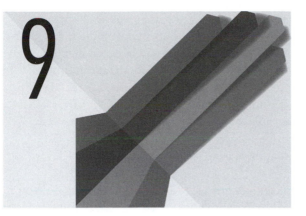

9

Dummy Variables and Interaction Effects

Commands Covered

xi: regression *dep_var* i.*indep_var*	Automatically creates dummy independent variable(s) and performs dummy variable regression
char *varname* [omit] #	Overrides Stata's default for defining the omitted category of a dummy variable
test *varname1* = *varname2*	Tests the null hypothesis that two regression coefficients are not significantly different from each other
predict *new_var*	Creates a new variable containing predicted values of the dependent variable for each value of the independent variable(s)

With Stata, you can easily adapt regression analysis to different research situations. In one situation you might have nominal or ordinal independent variables. Provided that these variables are dummy variables, you can run a regression analysis, using categorical variables to predict values of an interval-level dependent variable. In this chapter you will learn how to use dummy variables in regression analysis. In a second research situation, you might suspect that the effect of one independent variable on the dependent variable is not the same for all values of another independent variable—that is, that interaction is going on in the data. Provided that you have computed an interaction variable, Stata will run multiple regression to estimate the size and statistical significance of interaction effects. In this chapter you will learn how to perform and interpret multiple regression with interaction effects.

REGRESSION WITH DUMMY VARIABLES

A dummy variable can take on only two values, 1 or 0. Each case being analyzed either has the characteristic being measured (a code of 1) or does not have it (a code of 0). For example, a dummy variable for gender might code females as 1 and males as 0. Everybody who is coded 1 has the characteristic of being female, and everybody who is coded 0 does not have that characteristic. To appreciate why this 0 or 1 coding is the essential feature of dummy variables, consider the following regression model, which is designed to test the hypothesis that women will give Democratic presidential nominee Barack Obama higher feeling thermometer ratings than will men:

Obama feeling thermometer = a + b(female)

In this formulation, gender is measured by a dummy variable, female, which is coded 0 for males and coded 1 for females. Since males are scored 0 on the dummy, the constant or intercept, a, will tell us the average Obama rating among men. Why so? Substituting 0 for the dummy yields: a + b*0 = a. In the language of dummy variable regression, males are the "omitted" category, the category whose mean value on the dependent variable is captured by the intercept, a. The regression coefficient, b, will tell us how much to adjust the intercept for women—that is, when the dummy switches from 0 to 1. Thus, just as in any regression, b will estimate the average change in the dependent variable for a unit change in the independent variable. Since in this case a unit change in the independent variable is the difference between men (coded 0 on female) and women (coded 1 on female), then the regression coefficient will reflect the mean difference in Obama ratings between males and females. It is important to be clear on this point: The coefficient, b, does not communicate the mean Obama rating among females. Rather, it estimates the mean *difference* between males and females. (Of course, an estimated value of the dependent variable among females can be easily arrived at by summing a and b: a + b*1 = a + b.) As with any regression coefficient, we can rely on the coefficient's t-ratio and P-value to test the null hypothesis that there is no statistically meaningful gender difference in thermometer ratings of Obama.

Let's open nes2012 and figure out how to use gender as an independent variable in a regression analysis of Obama thermometer ratings. We'll use Obama_therm as the dependent variable. The independent variable, gender, is a nominal-level measure, coded 1 for males and 2 for females. Because of the way it is currently coded, gender could not be used in regression analysis. How can we create a variable coded 0 for males and 1 for females? One solution is to run tabulate and use the generate option to compute a set of indicator variables, one of which could become our 0-1 female dummy.[1]

Stata programmers, however, have come up with a better solution—the xi: prefix. As applied to regression analysis, the general syntax of the xi: prefix is as follows:

xi: regression *dep_var* i.*indep_var*

You type "xi:" followed by the regression command and the name of the dependent variable. You then type "i." followed immediately (without a space) by the name of the independent variable. The variable prefix "i." tells Stata to create a set of dummy variables from the independent variable. By default, the lowest-coded value of the independent variable is treated as the omitted category and assigned a value of 0 on the dummy. Because males have the lower numeric code on gender (code 1), the xi: prefix will create a dummy variable that codes males 0 and females 1.

The xi: prefix is best understood firsthand. The basic command is: "xi: reg Obama_therm i.gender."[2] Because we are analyzing nes2012, we must also include the weight, "[pw=nesw]":

```
xi:reg Obama_therm i.gender [pw=nesw]

i.gender            _Igender_1-2           (naturally coded; _Igender_1 omitted)
(sum of wgt is    5.4795e+03)

Linear regression                                      Number of obs =      5495
                                                       F(  1,  5493) =     21.88
                                                       Prob > F      =    0.0000
                                                       R-squared     =    0.0071
                                                       Root MSE      =    34.203
```

Stata automatically sets the lowest-coded value, code 1 on gender ("Male"), as the omitted category.

Obama_therm	Coef.	Robust Std. Err.	t	P>|t|	[95% Conf. Interval]
_Igender_2	5.776884	1.235066	4.68	0.000	3.355664 8.198103
_cons	53.44051	.8620204	61.99	0.000	51.75061 55.13041

Stata automatically created a dummy variable, _Igender_2, coded 0 for men and 1 for women. How can we be sure that women, not men, are coded 1 on _Igender_2? In the first line of output, Stata reports that it set the lowest-coded value on gender ("Male," coded 1) as the omitted category. Also, the numeric suffix "_2" on _Igender_2 tells us that cases coded 2 on the original variable, gender, are coded 1 on the new dummy. Stata plugged the dummy into the analysis and arrived at estimates for the constant and regression coefficient:

Obama feeling thermometer = 53.44 + 5.78 * _Igender_2.

How would we interpret these estimates? As always, the constant estimates the value of the dependent variable when the independent variable is 0. Because males have a value of 0 on _Igender_2, the mean thermometer rating of Barack Obama for males is 53.44, the intercept. The regression coefficient on _Igender_2 communicates the mean change in the dependent variable for each unit change in the independent variable. So when the dummy switches from 0 to 1, the Obama rating goes up, on average, about 5.8 degrees. We can use this value to estimate the mean rating for females: 53.44 + 5.78 = 59.22. So men rated Obama at about 53 and women rated him at about 59. Was this gender difference produced by random sampling error? Not according to the P-value, which equals 0.000. Do gender differences account for a big chunk of the variation in Barack Obama thermometer ratings? Not exactly. According to plain R-squared, gender alone accounts for about seven tenths of one percent of the variation in the dependent variable, a finding echoed by adjusted R-squared:

```
dis "Adjusted R2 = " e(r2_a)


.   dis "Adjusted R2 = " e(r2_a)
Adjusted R2 = .00689655
```

Clearly, there must be other variables "out there" that contribute to the explanation of Obama's ratings. Let's expand the model.

We would expect partisanship to have a big effect on the Obama thermometer scale. Democrats should score higher on the dependent variable than do Independents or Republicans. Plus, we know that women are more likely than men are to be Democrats, so the Obama_therm-_Igender_2 relationship might be the spurious result of partisan differences, not gender differences. Dataset nes2012 contains pid_3, which codes Democrats as 1, Independents as 2, and Republicans as 3. Pid_3 is a categorical variable, so we cannot use it in a regression—not in its present form, anyway. But we can use pid_3 to create a dummy variable for partisanship.

We actually need to create not one but two dummy variables from pid_3. Why two? Here is a general rule about dummy variables: If the variable you want to "dummify" has K categories, then you will need K – 1 dummies to measure the variable. Because pid_3 has three categories, we will need two dummy variables. We will ask Stata to create a Democrat dummy, which will be coded 1 for Democrats and 0 for Republicans and Independents. We will also create a Republican dummy, coded 1 for Republicans and 0 for Democrats and Independents. Independents, then, will be the omitted category—uniquely identified by their code of 0 on the Democrat dummy and their code of 0 on the Republican dummy.

By seeking to make Independents the omitted category, we find ourselves at odds with a Stata default. Because Democrats have the lowest numeric code on pid_3 (code 1), the xi: prefix will create dummies for Independents (coded 2 on pid_3) and Republicans (coded 3 on pid_3), and it will assign Democrats a code of 0 on both, making Democrats the omitted category. This default does not suit our purpose. Happily, we can use the char command to tell Stata how we want things done. The general format of the char command is as follows:

char *varname* [omit] #

We would replace "varname" with the variable name (pid_3) and replace "#" with the numeric code of the category we want Stata to treat as omitted (code 2). So the command would be "char pid_3 [omit] 2":

char pid_3 [omit] 2

Stata silently makes the requested change.[3] Now run the following command, which will produce a dummy variable regression that uses gender and partisanship to predict Obama thermometer ratings—"xi: reg Obama_therm i.gender i.pid_3 [pw=nesw]":

```
xi:reg Obama_therm i.gender i.pid_3 [pw=nesw]
```

```
i.gender            _Igender_1-2        (naturally coded; _Igender_1 omitted)
i.pid_3             _Ipid_3_1-3         (naturally coded; _Ipid_3_2 omitted)
(sum of wgt is   5.4626e+03)
```

Linear regression

Number of obs =	5474
F(3, 5470) =	962.64
Prob > F =	0.0000
R-squared =	0.4278
Root MSE =	25.983

Obama_therm	Coef.	Robust Std. Err.	t	P>|t|	[95% Conf. Interval]	
_Igender_2	2.897294	.9531334	3.04	0.002	1.028774	4.765815
_Ipid_3_1	29.48878	1.097208	26.88	0.000	27.33781	31.63974
_Ipid_3_3	-27.21512	1.277864	-21.30	0.000	-29.72024	-24.70999
_cons	52.02128	.9855884	52.78	0.000	50.08914	53.95343

```
. dis "Adjusted R2 = " e(r2_a)
Adjusted R2 = .42745567
```

Again Stata created a gender dummy, _Igender_2, coded 0 for males and 1 for females.[4] Stata also created two partisanship dummies, one having the numeric suffix "_1" and one having the suffix "_3". In the way that the xi: prefix names new variables, _Ipid_3_1 is the Democrat dummy (since Democrats are coded 1 on the original variable), and _Ipid_3_3 is the Republican dummy (coded 3 on the original variable). Let's write out the regression equation and have a closer look at the estimates. To enhance readability, we will substitute "Female" for _Igender_2, "Democrat" for _Ipid_3_1, and "Republican" for _Ipid_3_3:

Obama thermometer rating = 52.02 + 2.90*Female + 29.49*Democrat – 27.22*Republican

First, get oriented by using the constant, 52.02, as a point of reference. Again, because this value estimates the dependent variable when all the independent variables are 0, 52.02 is the mean Obama rating for males who are Independents. Why so? Because all the dummies are switched to 0: Female is 0 (that's the "male" part of the intercept), and both the Democrat dummy and the Republican dummy are 0 (that's the "Independent" part of the intercept). The regression coefficient on Female tells us how much to adjust the "male" part of the intercept, controlling for partisanship. The regression coefficients on the partisanship dummies tell us how much to adjust the "Independent" part of the intercept, controlling for gender. Thus, compared with Independents, Democrats average more than 29 degrees higher—and Republicans score 27 degrees lower—on the Obama thermometer. The partisan coefficients are large and statistically significant, with huge t-ratios and miniscule P-values. These results suggest that Democrats are significantly different from Independents—and that Republicans, too, are significantly different from Independents—on the Obama thermometer. And, because the coefficient on Democrat is so large and positive and the coefficient on Republican is so large and negative, in this case it would make little sense to ask whether the two effects, +29.49 and – 27.22, are significantly different from each other. Obviously they are. (Sometimes it makes a great deal of sense to ask whether two effects are significantly different from each other. The test command is designed for this purpose. See "A Closer Look" on pages 153–154 for a discussion of the test command.)

What about the effect of gender? The coefficient on Female, 2.90, tells us that women, on average, score only about 3 degrees higher on the Obama scale, controlling for partisanship. This effect trumps the null hypothesis (t = 3.04 with P-value = 0.002). In the earlier regression, using the female dummy alone, we found a gender difference of nearly 6 degrees. That regression, of course, didn't account for the fact that women are more likely than men are to be Democrats. After taking party differences into account, the gender difference fades from 6 degrees to 3 degrees—still statistically significant, but considerably weaker.

Overall, the model performs fairly well. The adjusted R-squared value of .4275 tells us that all of the independent variables, taken together, account for about 42.75 percent of the variation in the dependent variable. So the "glass is 43 percent full." A skeptic would point out, of course, that the "glass is still 57

A Closer Look   The test Command

In dummy variable regression, all of the effects are gauged relative to the constant or intercept–the mean value of the dependent variable for the omitted category. For any given regression coefficient, you can determine how much to adjust the intercept. And by enlisting the t-ratio and P-value you can tell if the adjusted mean is significantly different from the intercept. For dummified categorical variables having more than two values, you may also want to know whether two non-omitted categories have effects that are significantly different from each other. Consider the nes2012 variable, deathpen, a four-category ordinal measure of opinions about capital punishment. This variable is coded 1 ("Approve strongly"), 2 ("Approve"), 3 ("Oppose"), or 4 ("Oppose strongly"). The following xi: regression analyzes the effect of deathpen on Obama thermometer ratings:

```
xi: reg Obama_therm i.deathpen [pw=nesw]
```

Obama_therm	Coef.	Robust Std. Err.	t	P>|t|	[95% Conf. Interval]	
_Ideathpen_2	8.834735	1.610946	5.48	0.000	5.676624	11.99285
_Ideathpen_3	19.04017	1.846281	10.31	0.000	15.4207	22.65963
_Ideathpen_4	20.98009	1.722782	12.18	0.000	17.60273	24.35745
_cons	49.04045	.8761493	55.97	0.000	47.32284	50.75806

The constant records the mean value for the omitted category ("Approve strongly," coded 1 on deathpen), a chilly 49.0 degrees. The coefficient on _Ideathpen_2 makes the adjustment for respondents saying "Approve," telling us to adjust the constant upward by 8.83 degrees. The coefficient on_Ideathpen_3 shows the effect among those taking the "Oppose" position (add 19.04 to the constant), and _Ideathpen_4's coefficient estimates the relative effect for respondents holding the "Oppose strongly" opinion (add 20.98 to the constant). According to the t-ratios and P-values, each of these effects is significantly greater than 0. Thus, respondents coded 2, 3, or 4 on the deathpen gave Obama significantly higher ratings than did respondents who strongly approve of capital punishment. But are these effects significantly different from each other? For example, do respondents in code 3 ("Oppose") rate Obama significantly higher than do respondents in code 2 ("Approve")? The test command provides the answer.

The test command is one of many postestimation commands, procedures that use most-recently estimated parameters to adjust predictions, create new variables, or test hypotheses.[1] Applied to the problem of determining whether two regression coefficients are significantly different from each other, the test command syntax is as follows:

test *varname1 = varname2*

To test the difference between _Ideathpen_2 and _Ideathpen_3, we would type, "test _Ideathpen_2 = _Ideathpen_3":

```
test  _Ideathpen_2 = _Ideathpen_3

( 1)  _Ideathpen_2 - _Ideathpen_3 = 0

      F(  1,  5344) =   23.31
           Prob > F =   0.0000  ←
```

(continued)

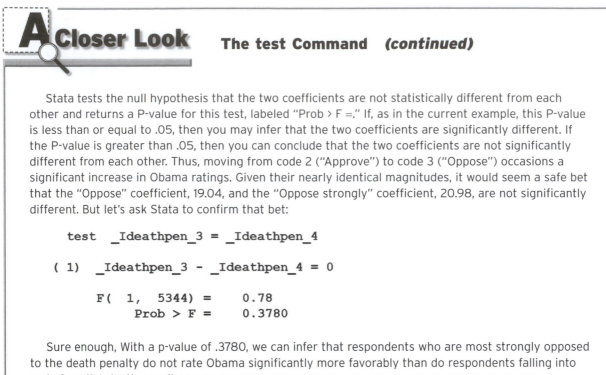

A Closer Look The test Command *(continued)*

Stata tests the null hypothesis that the two coefficients are not statistically different from each other and returns a P-value for this test, labeled "Prob > F =." If, as in the current example, this P-value is less than or equal to .05, then you may infer that the two coefficients are significantly different. If the P-value is greater than .05, then you can conclude that the two coefficients are not significantly different from each other. Thus, moving from code 2 ("Approve") to code 3 ("Oppose") occasions a significant increase in Obama ratings. Given their nearly identical magnitudes, it would seem a safe bet that the "Oppose" coefficient, 19.04, and the "Oppose strongly" coefficient, 20.98, are not significantly different. But let's ask Stata to confirm that bet:

```
test  _Ideathpen_3 = _Ideathpen_4

( 1)  _Ideathpen_3 - _Ideathpen_4 = 0

        F(  1,  5344) =      0.78
             Prob > F =      0.3780
```

Sure enough, With a p-value of .3780, we can infer that respondents who are most strongly opposed to the death penalty do not rate Obama significantly more favorably than do respondents falling into code 3 on the death penalty measure.

---

[1]As you know, Stata retains in memory the estimates from the most recently estimated model. However, by using the estimates command you can save the results for any model and replay them later. The test command has four different syntactical forms, only one of which is described here.

percent empty." Before going on to the next section, you may want to exercise your new skills by getting the xi: prefix to create new dummies and further expanding the model.

INTERACTION EFFECTS IN MULTIPLE REGRESSION

Multiple regression is a linear and additive technique. It assumes a linear relationship between the independent variables and the dependent variable. It also assumes that the effect of one independent variable on the dependent variable is the same for all values of the other independent variables in the model. In the regression we just estimated, for example, multiple regression assumed that the effect of being female is the same for all values of partisanship—that Democratic females are about 3 degrees warmer toward Barack Obama than are Democratic males and that Republican females and Independent females also are 3 degrees warmer than are their male counterparts. This assumption works fine for additive relationships. However, if interaction is taking place—if, for example, the gap between male and female ratings is significantly larger among Republicans than among Democrats or Independents—then multiple regression will not capture this effect. Before researchers model interaction effects by using multiple regression, they have usually performed preliminary analyses that suggest such effects are occurring in the data.

Consider an interesting theory in American public opinion. According to this perspective, which we will call the "polarization perspective," political disagreements are often more intense among people who are interested in and knowledgeable about public affairs than they are among people who are disengaged or who lack political knowledge.[5] For example, it seems reasonable to hypothesize that individuals who oppose the legalization of marijuana would rate conservatives more highly than those who support legalization. So if we were to compare ratings on a conservative feeling thermometer for anti-pot and pro-pot respondents, we should find a higher mean among the anti-pot group. According to the polarization perspective, however, this relationship will be weaker for people with low political knowledge than for people with higher political knowledge. Among people with lower political knowledge, the mean difference in conservative ratings may be more modest, with legalization opponents giving conservatives somewhat higher average ratings than do legalization supporters. As political knowledge increases, however, this mean difference should increase, reflecting greater polarization between the anti- and pro-pot camps. Thus, the strength of the relationship between marijuana opinions and evaluations of conservatives will depend on the level of political knowledge.

Dataset nes2012 contains ftgr_cons, which records respondents' feeling thermometer ratings of "conservatives." Another variable, pot_legal3, is a 3-point gauge of respondents' legalization attitudes, coded 0 ("Favor"), 1 ("Middle"), and 2 ("Oppose"). A third variable, preknow3, measures each respondent's political knowledge by three values: 0 ("Low"), 1 ("Mid"), or 2 ("High").

A preliminary analysis will reveal whether the polarization perspective has merit. The following command will produce a breakdown table reporting mean values of ftgr_cons for each combination of pot_legal3 and preknow3:

```
tab preknow3 pot_legal3 [aw=nesw], sum(ftgr_cons) nost noobs nofreq
```

Means of POST: Feeling thermometer: CONSERVATIVES

Pol Knowledge	Legalize Marijuana?			Total
	Favor	Middle	Oppose	
Low	49.28	50.69	58.82	53.01
Mid	47.91	55.27	63.96	55.57
High	44.42	51.83	67.88	54.56
Total	46.77	52.64	64.31	54.53

In the way that the table is set up, we would assess the effect of the legalization attitudes variable, at each level of political knowledge, by reading from left to right. Examine the low-knowledge row. As we move from "Favor" to "Oppose," do mean conservative ratings increase? Yes, they do. Conservatives are rated at 49.28 degrees among prolegalization respondents, 50.69 among those taking the middle position, and 58.82 among antilegalization respondents. End to end, this is a bit less than a 10-degree increase. The relationship is substantially stronger, however, at medium and high levels of political knowledge. For people with "Mid" knowledge, conservative ratings rise from 47.91 to 63.96, a 16-point increase. And the relationship is stronger still for individuals at the highest knowledge level, for whom the data show about a 23-point difference in ratings of conservatives, from 44.42 at the "Favor" end to 67.88 at the "Oppose" end. So, it looks like the ftgr_cons-pot_legal3 relationship does indeed strengthen as political knowledge increases. How would we use regression analysis to estimate the size and statistical significance of these relationships?

We would begin building the model in a familiar way, by estimating the effects of each independent variable, pot_legal3 and preknow3, on the dependent variable, ratings of conservatives (ftgr_cons):

conservative rating = a + b1*pot_legal3 + b2*preknow3

This is a simple additive model. The constant, a, estimates ftgr_cons for respondents who have a value of 0 on both independent variables—prolegalization respondents who have low political knowledge. The parameter, b1, estimates the effect of each unit increase in pot_legal3, from 0 to 2. The parameter, b2, tells us the effect of each unit increase in preknow3, from 0 to 2.

Think about why the simple additive model does not adequately represent the complex relationships we discovered in the mean comparison analysis. For low-knowledge respondents, for whom preknow3 is equal to 0, the b2*preknow3 term drops out, so the model reduces to

conservative rating = a + b1*pot_legal3

Our previous analysis revealed that, for low-knowledge people, conservative ratings increase from 49.28 (among prolegalization respondents) to 58.82 (among antilegalization respondents), about a 10-point effect. Based on those results, we know that the constant, a, will be equal to about 50 and that the coefficient, b1, will be about 5. (Regression will linearize the 10-point distance, dividing it in half for each increment of pot_legal3.) Now consider how the simple model would estimate the effect of pot_legal3 for medium-knowledge respondents, for whom preknow3 is equal to 1:

conservative rating = a + b1*pot_legal3 + b2*1

which is the same as

conservative rating = (a + b2) + b1*pot_legal3

The coefficient, b2, adjusts the constant. If b2 is positive, we can say that higher-knowledge people give conservatives higher ratings, on average, than do lower-knowledge people. A negative sign on b2 will mean that higher-knowledge people give conservatives lower average ratings than do lower-knowledge people. That's fine. But notice that, in the simple additive model, b1 remains unaffected as knowledge goes up. Yet the mean comparison analysis clearly showed that the effect of pot_legal3 on conservative ratings—estimated by b1—strengthens as knowledge increases. We need to add an adjustment to the regression, an adjustment that permits b1 to change as preknow3 increases.

In multiple regression, this adjustment is accomplished by including an interaction variable as an independent variable. To create an interaction variable, you multiply one independent variable by the other independent variable. Consider how we would create an interaction variable for the problem at hand: pot_legal3 * preknow3. All respondents who are coded 0 on preknow3 will, of course, have a value of 0 on the interaction variable. As political knowledge increases, however, so will the magnitude of the interaction variable. Let's include this term in the model just discussed and see what it looks like:

conservative rating = a + b1*pot_legal3 + b2*preknow3 + b3(pot_legal3*preknow3)

The simple additive model did not permit b1 to change as knowledge increased. Consider how the interaction term, "pot_legal3*preknow3," remedies this situation. Using medium-knowledge respondents (preknow3 equals 1) to illustrate, the interaction model would be

conservative rating = a + b1*pot_legal3 + b2(1) + b3(1*pot_legal3)

which is the same as

conservative rating = (a + b2) + (b1+b3)*pot_legal3

As in the simple model, b2 tells us by how much to adjust the constant as knowledge increases. The key difference is the role of b3, which tells us by how much to adjust the *effect* of pot_legal3 as knowledge increases. Because the positive relationship between conservative ratings and pot_legal3 gets stronger as preknow3 increases, we are expecting a positive sign on b3. The t-ratio and P-value on b3 will allow us to test the null hypothesis that the effect of pot_legal3 on the dependent variable is the same at all levels of political knowledge.

Let's work through the research problem and get Stata to estimate the model for us. Use generate to calculate the interaction variable. The expression for creating the variable, which we will name "interact," is "gen interact = pot_legal3 * preknow3":

```
gen interact = pot_legal3*preknow3
```

Now we're set to estimate our model. Type and run "reg ftgr_cons pot_legal3 preknow3 interact [pw=nesw]":

```
reg ftgr_cons pot_legal3 preknow3 interact [pw=nesw]
```

Linear regression

```
Number of obs  =     5369
F(  3,  5365) =   123.67
Prob > F      =   0.0000
R-squared     =   0.1088
Root MSE      =   22.752
```

ftgr_cons	Coef.	Robust Std. Err.	t	P>|t|	[95% Conf. Interval]	
pot_legal3	4.651002	.8876453	5.24	0.000	2.910856	6.391147
preknow3	-2.627738	.7806428	-3.37	0.001	-4.158115	-1.097361
interact	3.487866	.6263849	5.57	0.000	2.259897	4.715835
_cons	49.19874	1.079768	45.56	0.000	47.08195	51.31552

```
.  dis "Adjusted R2 = " e(r2_a)
Adjusted R2 = .10833932
```

The regression equation for estimating conservative thermometer ratings (ftgr_cons) is shown below. (To simplify the discussion, coefficients are rounded to one decimal. Also, the interaction term is represented by its computational expression, "pot_legal3 * preknow3.")

ftgr_cons = 49.2 + 4.7*pot_legal3 – 2.6*preknow3 + 3.5*(pot_legal3 * preknow3)

Consider how this model applies to low-knowledge respondents, that is, when preknow3 = 0. For all these individuals, the third term is equal to zero (that is, -2.6*0 = 0), and the last term is zero as well (pot_legal3 * 0 = 0). So, for low-knowledge types, the first two terms, "49.2 + 4.7*pot_legal3," do all the predictive work. The constant, 49.2, is the estimated mean of ftgr_cons for those who favor legalization (code 0 on pot_legal3): 49.2 + 4.7*0 = 49.2. What about low-knowledge individuals who take a middle position on the issue? The estimate is: 49.2 + 4.7*1 = 53.9. For those in the "Oppose" camp: 49.2 + 4.7*2 = 58.6. Thus, at low levels of political knowledge, predicted ratings increase by approximately 10 points, from 49 to about 59, just as the mean comparison analysis suggested.

Now consider how this model applies to high-knowledge respondents, that is, when preknow3 = 2. Things get more complicated, but we can still use the simple additive model as a starting point. For example, high-knowledge legalization supporters "start" with the same estimate as their like-minded, low-knowledge counterparts: 49.2 + 4.7 * 0 = 49.2. In what ways do we need to adjust this initial estimate? Because marijuana supporters ("Favor") are coded 0 on pot_legal3, the interaction term drops out: 3.5*(0 * 2) = 0. No adjustment is required there. But notice that the negative coefficient on preknow3, -2.6, comes into play: −2.6*2 = −5.2. Thus, compared to their low-knowledge counterparts, high-knowledge "Favor" respondents are 5.2 degrees chillier toward conservatives: 49.2 − 5.2 = 44.0.

Let's move to the other end of the marijuana issue—high-knowledge marijuana opponents, coded 2 on preknow3 and coded 2 on pot_legal3. To be sure, these respondents "start" where low-knowledge opponents ended: 49.2 + 4.7*2 = 58.6. However, two adjustments must be made. First, adjust the estimate downward to account for the effect of high knowledge: -2.6*2 = -5.2. Second, add the huge positive boost supplied by the interaction effect: 3.5*(2 * 2) = 14.0. Putting it all together: 58.6 − 5.2 + 14.0 = 67.4. Whereas, by our earlier estimate, the high-knowledge "Favor" group rated conservatives at 44.0, the high-knowledge "Oppose" group rated conservatives at 67.4. These estimates fit the results of the mean comparison analysis quite nicely.

GRAPHING LINEAR PREDICTION LINES FOR INTERACTION RELATIONSHIPS

A point emphasized throughout this book is that visual representations can often help to simplify and clarify complex relationships. This is again illustrated by Figure 9-1, which shows the relationship between marijuana opinions (x-axis) and predicted values of the conservative feeling thermometer (y-axis) for each value of preknow3. The visual signature of interaction is plainly evident here. The line depicting the relationship at the lowest level of knowledge slopes upward by about 10 points, from 49 at the "Favor" end to about 59 at the "Oppose" end. At medium levels of knowledge the line rakes upward more steeply, signaling the strengthening of the relationship as political knowledge moves up a notch. And the high-knowledge line is the steepest of the three, connecting endpoint 44.0 degrees for prolegalization respondents with endpoint 67.4 degrees for antilegalization respondents. It is quite clear from the graphic that, although the direction of the ftgr_cons-pot_legal3 relationship is the same at all three values of preknow3, the relationship gets stronger as political knowledge increases.

Figure 9-1 Linear Prediction Lines for Interaction Relationships

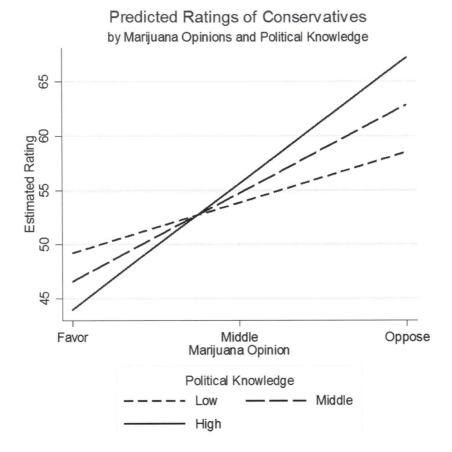

To create a linear prediction overlay, first use the regression model's estimates to generate a predicted value of the dependent variable, ftgr_cons, for each respondent. Second, run twoway to graph predicted values of ftgr_cons (y-axis) across values of pot_legal3 (x-axis), using the if qualifier to request a separate line for each level of preknow3. The first step is accomplished with the predict command, which works with the estimates of the most-recently run regression model. (Are the model's estimates still there? Type and run "estimates." Stata will return the results of the most recent model.) The syntax of the predict command follows:

predict *new_var*

Just as we did in our hand calculations, Stata will generate a new variable containing predicted conservative ratings for respondents having different values of pot_legal3 and preknow3. If we wanted to name the new variable ftgr_cons_pred, we would type and run, "predict ftgr_cons_pred":

```
            predict ftgr_cons_pred


     .  predict ftgr_cons_pred
    (option xb assumed; fitted values)
    (447 missing values generated)
```

The term "xb" means "linear prediction," which Stata has fitted using the model's coefficients.

Now for the linear prediction overlay. Like any Stata graph, a bare bones overlay is fairly easy to obtain. And, like any Stata graph, a nicely optioned, presentable result requires considerably more typing and attention to detail. If you are running interaction regressions and performing preliminary analyses of potentially interesting variables, a basic graph requires only a few lines of code. Using our current example,

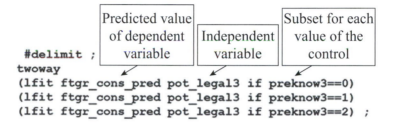

```
#delimit ;
twoway
(lfit ftgr_cons_pred pot_legal3 if preknow3==0)
(lfit ftgr_cons_pred pot_legal3 if preknow3==1)
(lfit ftgr_cons_pred pot_legal3 if preknow3==2) ;
```

Type "twoway" followed by the first parenthetical, which specifies the low-knowledge line ("if preknow3==0"). Copy/paste the first parenthetical onto the next Do-file line, changing "preknow3==0" to "preknow3==1". Copy/paste again, requesting the line for "preknow3==2". Run the code. In terms of unadorned graphics output, it's Stata déjà vu all over again (Figure 9-2). Figure 9-3's annotated syntax describes how to produce the linear prediction overlay in Figure 9-1.

Figure 9-2   Linear Prediction Lines for Interaction Relationships (basic graph)

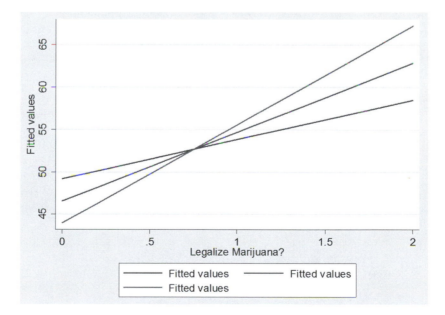

Figure 9-3 Creating a Linear Prediction Overlay

```
#delimit ;
twoway
(lfit ftgr_cons_pred pot_legal3 if preknow3==0,
  lcolor(black) lwidth(medthick) lpattern(dash))
(lfit ftgr_cons_pred pot_legal3 if preknow3==1,
  lcolor(black) lwidth(medthick) lpattern(longdash))
(lfit ftgr_cons_pred pot_legal3 if preknow3==2,
  lcolor(black) lwidth(medthick) lpattern(solid)),

aspect(.75)

legend(order(1 "Low" 2 "Middle" 3 "High") size(small))
legend(on region(lwidth(none)))
legend(title("Political Knowledge",  size(small)))
graphregion(fcolor(white) ifcolor(white))

ytitle("Estimated Rating", size(small))
ylabel( , labsize(small))
xtitle("Marijuana Opinion", size(small))
xlabel(#3, labsize(small)valuelabel)
title("Predicted Ratings of Conservatives", size(medsmall))
subtitle("by Marijuana Opinions and Political Knowledge",
    size(small));
```

> Make the lines fairly thick, so that they are prominent. The line patterns also become more pronounced, as the control variable increases in value: dash, longdash, solid.

> Stata graphs become shorter and wider as text elements are added. Control this tendency by fixing the aspect ratio at .75 (75 percent as tall as it is wide).

> All legend, title, and label options are aimed at shrinking labels and text, and washing out color, which visually competes with the pattern of the lines in the graphic space. Two points about Stata's default fonts: (1) They are gargantuan; (2) they appear even larger when graphs are copy/pasted into a Word document. Request "small" for everything, except for the main title, for which "medsmall" works well. Here are some specific points about the options shown here.
> The leading comma in ylabel means to accept the default y-axis labels.
> The xlabel options mean: provide three labels (one for each value of pot_legal3); make the labels small; and use value labels, not numeric codes.

EXERCISES

1. (Dataset: world. Variables: free_overall, gdp_cap3.) In this exercise, you will use xi: regression to analyze the relationship between economic development and economic freedom. Dataset world.dta contains free_overall, an interval-level measure of freedom that ranges from 0 (least free) to 100 (most free). The dataset also contains gdp_cap3, a three-category ordinal measure of per capita GDP, an indicator of economic development. Codes range from 1 (low-GDP countries), through 2 (middle-GDP countries), to 3 (high-GDP countries).

   A. Imagine running the following xi: regression command: "xi: reg free_overall i.gdp_cap3." Stata would create a set of dummies from gdp_cap3 and use them as variables in the following model:

   free_overall = a + b1* _Igdp_cap3_2 + b2* _Igdp_cap3_3.

   Complete the matching exercise below by drawing a line connecting the desired estimate on the left to the appropriate coefficient (or combination of coefficients) on the right.

Your estimate of the . . .	Would be provided by (the) . . .
mean difference between countries with the lowest GDP and the highest GDP . . .	constant
mean of the dependent variable for the highest-GDP countries. . .	b1
mean of the dependent variable for the lowest-GDP countries . . .	constant + b2
mean difference between the lowest-GDP and the middle-GDP countries . . .	b2

B. Run "xi: reg free_overall i.gdp_cap3." The regression equation for estimating free_overall is (fill in the blanks, putting the constant in the first blank):

free_overall = _____ + _____ * _Igdp_cap3_2 + _____ * _Igdp_cap3_3.

C. Use the regression coefficients to arrive at estimated mean values of free_overall for countries at each level of per capita GDP. Write the estimates in the following table.

GDP per capita	Estimated mean on free_overall scale
Low	?
Middle	?
High	?

D. Examine the t-ratio and P-value on _Igdp_cap3_2. Do the middle-GDP per capita countries score significantly higher on free_overall than do the lowest-GDP per capita countries? (circle one)

no   yes

Briefly explain:

_____

_____

E. Examine the t-ratio and P-value on _Igdp_cap3_3. Do the highest-GDP per capita countries score significantly higher on free_overall than do the lowest-GDP per capita countries? (circle one)

no   yes

Briefly explain:

_____

_____

F. Run the test command to determine whether the highest-GDP per capita countries score significantly higher on free_overall than do the middle-GDP per capita countries. Do the highest-GDP per capita countries score significantly higher on free_overall than do the middle-GDP per capita countries? (circle one)

no   yes

Briefly explain:

_____

_____

G. According to adjusted R-squared, GDP per capita accounts for _____ percent of the variation in free_ overall.

2. (Dataset: world. Variables: gini10, hi_gdp, democ_regime, rich_democ.) As a country becomes richer, do more of its citizens benefit economically? Or do economic resources become inequitably distributed across society? The answer may depend upon the type of regime in power. Democratic regimes, which need to appeal broadly for votes, may adopt policies that redistribute wealth. Dictatorships, by contrast, are less concerned with popular accountability, and so might hoard economic resources among the ruling elite, creating a less equitable distribution of wealth. This explanation suggests a set of interaction relationships. It suggests that, when we compare poorer democracies with richer democracies, richer democracies will have a *more equitable* distribution of wealth. However, it also suggests that, when we compare poorer dictatorships with richer dictatorships, richer dictatorships will have a *less equitable* distribution of wealth. In this exercise you will investigate this set of relationships.

The dataset world contains the variable gini10, which measures the extent to which wealth is inequitably distributed in society. Gini10 can take on any value between 0 (equal distribution of wealth) and 100 (unequal distribution of wealth). So, lower values of gini10 denote less economic inequality, and higher values of gini10 denote greater economic inequality. Gini10 is the dependent variable. The dataset also has a dummy variable, hi_gdp, that classifies each country as low GDP (coded 0) or high GDP (coded 1). Hi_gdp will serve as the measure of the independent variable, level of wealth. Another dummy, democ_regime, which categorizes each country as a dictatorship (coded 0 on democ_regime) or democracy (coded 1 on democ_regime), is the control variable.

A. Exercise a skill you learned in Chapter 5. To see whether interaction is occurring, obtain a breakdown table that shows the relationship between gini10 and hi_gdp, controlling for democ_regime. Write the mean values of gini10 next to the question marks (?) in the table that follows.

Is regime a democracy?	Low GDP	High GDP
No	?	?
Yes	?	?

B. Examine the table in Part A. It would appear that interaction (circle one)

is   is not

occurring in the data. Explain your reasoning.

_____

_____

_____

C. World contains rich_democ, an interaction variable computed by the expression hi_gdp*democ_regime. Rich_democ takes on the value of 1 for high-GDP democracies and the value of 0 for all other countries. Run regression, using gini10 as the dependent variable and hi_gdp, democ_regime, and rich_democ as independent variables. The regression equation for estimating gini10 is as follows (fill in the blanks, putting the constant in the first blank):

$$gini10 = \underline{\hspace{1.5em}} + \underline{\hspace{1.5em}} * hi\_gdp + \underline{\hspace{1.5em}} * democ\_regime + \underline{\hspace{1.5em}} * rich\_democ$$

D. Suppose someone claimed that, from the standpoint of statistical significance, low-GDP dictatorships have a significantly more equitable distribution of wealth than do low-GDP democracies.

This claim is (circle one)

correct   incorrect

because

_____

_____

_____.

E. Suppose someone claimed that, as GDP increases, wealth becomes significantly more equitably distributed in democracies but not in dictatorships.

This claim is (circle one)

correct   incorrect

because

_____

_____

_____.

F. Using the predict command, generate a new variable, gini10_pred, which contains predicted values of gini10. Use twoway to obtain a linear prediction overlay that shows the relationship between gini10_pred (y-axis) and hi_gdp (x-axis) separately for democracies and dictatorships. Refer to this chapter's examples (Figure 9-1 and Figure 9-3) to request appropriate options for titles, labels, and the legend. Print the graph.

3. (Dataset: nes2012 Variables: Prochoice_scale, relig_imp2, preknow3, [pw=nesw].) One of the examples in this chapter discussed the polarization perspective—the idea that political conflict is more pronounced among people who are more knowledgeable about politics than it is among less-knowledgeable people. Perhaps the same pattern applies to the relationship between strength of religious attachment and abortion opinions. That is, it could be that religious commitment has a strong effect on abortion attitudes among politically knowledgeable people but that this effect is weaker for people who have lower knowledge about politics.

The dataset nes2012 contains Prochoice_scale, which ranges from 1 to 65, with higher values denoting a stronger prochoice position. A dummy variable, relig_imp2, captures the importance of religion: less important (coded 0 and labeled "No") or more important (coded 1 and labeled "Yes"). Just as in this chapter's example, use preknow3, which measures political knowledge by three values: 0 ("Low"), 1 ("Mid"), and 2 ("High"). In this exercise you will compute an interaction variable. You will then run and interpret a multiple regression that includes the interaction variable you created.

A. Use generate to create an interaction variable, relig_inter, by multiplying relig_imp2 by preknow3. (The numeric expression will be relig_imp2*preknow3.) Think about relig_inter, the interaction variable you computed. A respondent with a weak religious affiliation (coded 0 on relig_imp2) has what value on relig_inter? (circle one)

  a value of 0   a value of 1   a value equal to his or her value on preknow3

A respondent with a strong religious affiliation (coded 1 on relig_imp2) has what value on the relig_inter? (circle one)

  a value of 0   a value of 1   a value equal to his or her value on preknow3

B. Run regression, using Prochoice_scale as the dependent variable and relig_imp2, preknow3, and relig_inter as the independent variables. (Remember to include [pw=nesw].) According to the results, the multiple regression equation for estimating scores on Prochoice_scale is as follows (fill in the blanks, putting the constant in the first blank):

_____ + _____* relig_imp2 + _____* preknow3 + _____* relig_inter

C. Use the regression coefficients to arrive at estimates of the dependent variable, Prochoice_scale, for each value of relig_imp2, by preknow3. Write the estimates in the following table.

Political knowledge	Is Religion Important to R?	
	No	Yes
Low	?	?
Mid	?	?
High	?	?

D. Using the predict command, generate a new variable, Prochoice_pred, which contains predicted values of Prochoice_scale. Run twoway to create a linear prediction overlay that graphs Prochoice_pred (y-axis) and relig_imp2 (x-axis) for each value of preknow3. (Hint: The twoway syntax for this exercise is very similar to the syntax you ran in replicating Figure 9-1. Copy/paste the Figure 9-1 syntax, and modify the variable names and, where necessary, the titles and labels.) Print the graph.

E. Consider all of the evidence you have developed in this exercise. Think about the polarization perspective. Does the analysis support the idea that, as political knowledge increases, religiosity plays a larger role in shaping abortion opinions? Answer yes or no, and explain your reasoning.

_____

_____

_____

_____

_____

_____

_____

4. (Dataset: gss2012. Variables: black, homosex2, partyid, [pw=gssw].) If one were trying to predict party identification on the basis of opinions on social issues, such as homosexuality, one would expect most blacks to be Republicans. Indeed, blacks are considerably more likely to oppose homosexuality than are whites. According to the gss2012 data, for example, over 70 percent of blacks say that homosexuality is "always wrong," compared with 50 percent of whites. Yet on the gss2012's party identification scale (which ranges from 1 to 7, with higher scores denoting stronger Republican identifications), blacks average around 2, compared with an average of 4 for whites. Why? A plausible idea is that social issues lack *salience* for blacks. Issues such as homosexuality may matter for whites—whites who think homosexuality is wrong are more likely to be Republicans than are whites who do not think it is wrong—but they have no effect for blacks. According to this argument, blacks who think homosexuality is wrong are no more likely to be Republican than are blacks who do not think homosexuality is wrong. Or so the argument goes. Is this idea correct? More research needs to be done on this question.[6]

You can model salience with interaction variables. Consider the 7-point party identification scale (partyid) as a dependent variable, ranging from "Strong Democrat" at 1 to "Strong Republican" at 7. Now bring in two independent variables: a dummy variable for race (black, with blacks scored 1 and whites scored 0) and a dummy variable gauging opposition to homosexuality (homosex2, scored 1 if the respondent said homosexuality is "always wrong" and 0 for "not always wrong"). Finally, think about (but don't generate yet) an interaction variable, black_wrong, created by multiplying black and homosex2. Examine the regression model that follows.

$$partyid = a + b1*black + b2*homosex2 + b3*black\_wrong$$

A. The interaction variable, black_wrong, will take on a value of 1 for (check one)

❑ blacks who think that homosexuality is "always wrong."

❑ blacks who think that homosexuality is "not always wrong."

❑ all respondents.

B. To gauge the effect of homosex2 among whites, you would need to compare values of partyid for "not always wrong" whites and "always wrong" whites. Which of the following will estimate partyid for "not always wrong" whites? (check one)

_____a   _____a + b1   _____a + b2

Which of the following will estimate partyid for "always wrong" whites? (check one)

_____a   _____a + b1   _____a + b2

C. Remember that higher scores on partyid denote stronger Republican identifications. If the salience argument is correct—the idea that heightened opposition to homosexuality leads to stronger Republican leanings among whites but not blacks—then the sign on the coefficient, b2, will be (circle one)

negative.   positive.   zero.

If the salience argument is correct, then the sign on the coefficient, b3, will be (circle one)

negative.   positive.   zero.

D. Use generate to create black_wrong. The multiplicative expression is homosex2*black. Run regression to obtain estimates for the model. (Remember to include [pw=gssw].) The regression equation for estimating partyid is as follows (fill in the blanks, putting the constant in the first blank):

partyid = _____ + _____*black + _____*homosex2 + _____*black_wrong

E. Which of the variables in the model have statistically significant effects on partyid? Check all that apply.

_____black   _____homosex2   _____black_wrong

F. Use the model to estimate partyid for "not always wrong" whites and "always wrong" whites. For "not always wrong" whites you obtain _____, and for "always wrong" whites you obtain _____.

G. Use the model to estimate partyid for "not always wrong" blacks and "always wrong" blacks. For "not always wrong" blacks you obtain _____, and for "always wrong" blacks you obtain _____.

H. Using the predict command, generate a new variable, partyid_pred, which contains predicted values of partyid. Use twoway to obtain a line graph that shows the relationship between partyid_pred (y-axis) and homosex2 (x-axis) separately for whites and blacks. Apply all the graphing skills you have learned in this chapter to create a nicely optioned, presentation quality graph. Print the graph.

I. Consider all the evidence you have adduced. Based on the evidence, the salience idea appears to be (circle one)

correct.   incorrect.

Explain your answer.

_____

_____

_____

_____

_____

_____

_____

NOTES

1. The following command would create two indicator variables, gendum1 and gendum2: "tab gender, gen(gendum)." Since females are coded 2 on gender, the second indicator variable, gendum2, would be coded 0 for males and 1 for females.
2. If you type the command without the xi: prefix ("regress Obama_therm i.gender"), Stata will create the requested dummy variable. However, Stata's "dummifying" capabilities are more limited without the xi: prefix. Thus, here we instruct in the use of xi:. See Mitch Abdon's Stata Daily blog, "i. without the prefix -xi-," March 1, 2011, http://statadaily.ikonomiya.com/tag/xi/.
3. The changes made with the char command (which stands for "Characteristics") remain in effect while the dataset is open and are preserved when the dataset is saved. The following command resets the default: "char *varname* [omit]."
4. Stata retains the most recently created xi: variables, but subsequent xi: runs automatically overwrite any previously created xi: variables. Run "drop _I*" to delete any existing xi: variables that you do not want to save.
5. See John R. Zaller's influential work, *The Nature and Origins of Mass Opinion* (New York: Cambridge University Press, 1992).
6. See Quentin Kidd, Herman Diggs, Mehreen Farooq, and Megan Murray, "Black Voters, Black Candidates, and Social Issues: Does Party Identification Matter?" *Social Science Quarterly* 88, no. 1 (2007): 165–176.

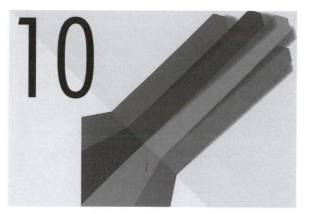

10

Logistic Regression

You now have an array of data analysis skills that give you the know-how to perform the appropriate analysis for just about any situation you will encounter. To analyze the relationship between two categorical variables—variables measured at the nominal or ordinal level—you would enlist the tabulate command. If the dependent variable is an interval-level scale and the independent variable is categorical, then tabulate with the summarize option would be one way to go. Alternatively, you might run xi: regression to estimate the effect of a dummy variable (or variables) on the dependent variable. Finally, if both the independent and dependent variables are interval-level, then the regress command would be the appropriate technique. There is, however, a common research situation you are not yet equipped to tackle.

In its most specialized application, logistic regression is designed to analyze the relationship between an interval-level independent variable and a *binary* dependent variable. A binary variable, as its name suggests, can assume only two values. Binary variables are just like the indicator variables or dummy variables you have created and analyzed in this book. A case either has the attribute or behavior being measured, or it does not. Voted/did not vote, married/not married, favor/oppose gay marriage, and South/non-South are all examples of binary variables.

Consider a binary dependent variable that is of keen interest to students of political behavior, whether people voted in an election. This variable, of course, has only two values: individuals either voted (coded 1 on the binary variable) or they did not vote (coded 0). Now think about an interval-level independent variable often linked to turnout, years of education. As measured by the General Social Survey, this variable ranges from 0 (no formal schooling) to 20 (20 years of education). One would expect a positive relationship between the independent and dependent variables. As years of education increase, the probability of voting should increase as well. So people with fewer years of schooling should have a relatively low probability of voting, and this probability should increase with each additional year of education. Now, we certainly can conceptualize this relationship as positive. However, for statistical and substantive reasons, we may not assume that it is linear—that is, we cannot assume that a 1-year change in education occasions a consistent increase in the probability of voting. Because ordinary least squares (OLS) regression assumes linearity between the independent and dependent variables, we may not use the regress command to analyze this relationship. But as luck and statistics would have it, the researcher may assume a linear relationship between education and the *logged odds* of voting. Let's put the relationship into logistic regression form and discuss its special properties:

logged odds (voting) = a + b(years of education).

This logistic regression model is quite OLS-like in appearance. Just as in OLS regression, the constant or intercept, a, estimates the dependent variable (in this case, the logged odds of voting) when the independent variable is equal to zero—that is, for people with no formal education. And the logistic regression coefficient, b, will estimate the change in the logged odds of voting for each 1-year increase in education. What is more, the analysis will produce a standard error for b, permitting us to test the null hypothesis that education has no effect on turnout. Finally, Stata output for logistic regression will provide an R-squared type of measure, giving us an idea of the strength of the relationship between education and the likelihood of voting. In all of these ways, logistic regression is comfortably akin to linear regression.

However, logistic regression can be more difficult to interpret than OLS. In ordinary regression, the coefficients of interest, the constant (a) and the slope (b), are expressed in actual units of the dependent variable. If one were to use OLS to investigate the relationship between years of education (X) and income in dollars (Y), the regression coefficient on education would communicate the dollar-change in income for each 1-year increase in education. With OLS, what you see is what you get. In the logistic regression model, by contrast, the coefficients of interest are expressed in terms of the logged odds of the dependent variable. The constant (a) will tell you the logged odds of voting when education is zero, and the regression coefficient (b) will estimate the change in the logged odds for each unit-change in education. Logged odds, truth be told, have no intuitive appeal. Thus, the researcher often must translate logistic regression results into language that makes better intuitive sense.

THE LOGIT COMMAND AND THE LOGISTIC COMMAND

There are two Stata commands that perform binary logistic regression, the logit command and the logistic command. The logit command provides estimates for the coefficients in the logistic regression model. Applied to the education-voting equation, the logit command would display estimates for the constant, a, and the coefficient, b—both of which are expressed in terms of the logged odds of the dependent variable. The logistic command runs the same analysis as the logit command. However, the logistic command will express the coefficients either as odds ratios or, by specifying the coef option, as logged odds. Odds ratios, as we will see, are easier to interpret than are logged odds coefficients.

Because the logistic command, at the user's discretion, will report odds ratios or logistic regression coefficients, this book mostly focuses on the logistic command. However, output from the logit command provides information that will help you to understand how logistic regression works. For our first analysis, then, we will illustrate the use of the logit command and the logistic command.

The syntax of the logit command is as follows:

logit *dep_var indep_var(s)* [pw = *probability_weightvar*]

The syntax of the logistic command is identical except, of course, for the command name:

logistic *dep_var indep_var(s)* [pw = *probability_weightvar*]

(Both commands permit probability weights.) Open gss2012. Open a new Do-file.

Let's run the voting-education analysis and learn how to interpret Stata's output. The dataset gss2012 contains voted081, coded 0 for respondents who did not vote in the 2008 election and coded 1 for those who did vote. The dataset also has educ_yrs, which records the number of years of schooling for each respondent. First run logit, and then run logistic. Type and run, "logit voted081 educ_yrs [pw = gssw]"; then type and run, "logistic voted04 educ_yrs [pw = gssw]":

```
logit voted081 educ_yrs  [pw=gssw]

logistic voted081 educ_yrs [pw=gssw]


.  logit voted081 educ_yrs  [pw=gssw]

Iteration 0:    log pseudolikelihood = -1032.7789
Iteration 1:    log pseudolikelihood =  -960.1459
Iteration 2:    log pseudolikelihood = -958.81824
Iteration 3:    log pseudolikelihood = -958.81643
Iteration 4:    log pseudolikelihood = -958.81643
```

```
Logistic regression                    Number of obs   =       1788
                                       Wald chi2(1)    =      55.48
                                       Prob > chi2     =     0.0000
Log pseudolikelihood = -958.81643      Pseudo R2       =     0.0716
```

voted081	Coef.	Robust Std. Err.	z	P>|z|	[95% Conf. Interval]	
educ_yrs	.226442	.0304005	7.45	0.000	.1668581	.286026
_cons	-2.06784	.4046636	-5.11	0.000	-2.860967	-1.274714

```
.  logistic voted081 educ_yrs [pw=gssw]
```

```
Logistic regression                    Number of obs   =       1788
                                       Wald chi2(1)    =      55.48
                                       Prob > chi2     =     0.0000
Log pseudolikelihood = -958.81643      Pseudo R2       =     0.0716
```

voted081	Odds Ratio	Robust Std. Err.	z	P>|z|	[95% Conf. Interval]	
educ_yrs	1.25413	.0381262	7.45	0.000	1.181587	1.331127
_cons	.1264586	.0511732	-5.11	0.000	.0572134	.2795108

First consider the output from the logit command. Just as in the output from Stata's regression command, the numbers in the column labeled "Coef." are the estimates for the constant and the regression coefficient. Plug these estimates into the model:

Logged odds (voted081) = -2.07 + .226(educ_yrs).

What do these coefficients tell us? Again, the constant says that, for people with no education, the estimated logged odds of voting is equal to -2.07. And the logistic regression coefficient on educ_yrs says that the logged odds of voting increases by .226 for each 1-year increase in education. So, as expected, as the independent variable increases, the likelihood of voting increases too. Does education have a statistically significant effect on the likelihood of voting? In OLS regression, Stata determines statistical significance by calculating a t-statistic and an accompanying P-value. In logistic regression, Stata calculates a z-statistic and reports a P-value. Interpretation of this P-value, displayed in the column labeled "P>|z|," is directly analogous to ordinary regression. If the P-value is greater than .05, do not reject the null hypothesis. Conclude that the independent variable does not have a significant effect on the dependent variable. If the P-value is less than or equal to .05, then reject the null hypothesis, and infer that the independent variable has a significant relationship with the dependent variable. In our output, the P-value for educ_yrs is 0.000, so we can conclude that, yes, education has a significant effect on voting turnout.

Now turn your attention to the output for the logistic command, and consider how Stata has made educ_yrs's regression coefficient more meaningful. Note the entry next to educ_yrs in the column labeled "Odds Ratio." Here Stata has reported the value 1.25413 (which rounds to 1.25) for the independent variable, educ_yrs. Where did this number originate? Stata obtained this number by raising the natural log base e (approximately equal to 2.72) to the power of the logistic regression coefficient, .226. This procedure translates the logged odds regression coefficient into an odds ratio. An odds ratio tells you by how much the odds of the dependent variable change for each unit change in the independent variable. An odds ratio of less than 1 says that the odds decrease as the independent variable increases (a negative relationship). An odds ratio equal to 1 says that the odds do not change as the independent variable increases (no relationship). And an odds ratio of greater than 1 says that the odds of the dependent variable increase as the independent variable increases (a positive relationship). An odds ratio of 1.25 means that respondents at a given level of education are 1.25 times more likely to have voted than are respondents at the next lower level of education. So people with, say, 10 years of education are 1.25 times more likely to have voted than are people with 9 years of education, people with 14 years are 1.25 times more likely to have voted than people with 13 years, and so on.

The value of the odds ratio can be used to obtain an even more understandable estimate, the *percentage change in the odds* for each unit change in the independent variable. Mercifully, simple arithmetic accomplishes this task. Subtract 1 from the odds ratio, and multiply by 100. In our current example: (1.25 – 1) * 100 = 25. So we can now say that each 1-year increment in education increases the odds of voting by 25 percent. As you can see, when the relationship is positive—that is, when the logistic regression coefficient is greater than 0 and the odds ratio is greater than 1—figuring out the percentage change in the odds requires almost no thought. Just subtract 1 from the odds ratio and move the decimal point two places to the right. But be alert for negative relationships, when the odds ratio is less than 1. (In the exercises at the end of this chapter, you will interpret negative relationships.) Suppose, for example, that the odds ratio were equal to .25, communicating a negative relationship between the independent variable and the probability of the dependent variable. The percentage change in the odds would be equal to (.25 – 1) * 100 = -75.0, indicating that a one unit change in the independent variable decreases the odds of the dependent variable by 75 percent.

How strong is the relationship between years of education and the likelihood of voting?

It is here that the "Iteration" lines of the logit results (reproduced below) become instructive:

```
Iteration 0:    log pseudolikelihood = -1032.7789
Iteration 1:    log pseudolikelihood =  -960.1459
Iteration 2:    log pseudolikelihood = -958.81824
Iteration 3:    log pseudolikelihood = -958.81643
Iteration 4:    log pseudolikelihood = -958.81643
```

In figuring out the most accurate estimates for the model's coefficients, logistic regression uses a technique called maximum likelihood estimation (MLE). When it begins the analysis, MLE finds out how well it can predict the observed values of the dependent variable *without* using the independent variable as a predictive tool. So MLE first determined how accurately it could predict whether individuals voted by not knowing how much education they have. The log likelihood in the "Iteration 0" line, equal to -1032.7789, summarizes this initial, "know-nothing" prediction. MLE then brings the independent variable into its calculations, running the analysis again—and again and again—in order to find the best possible predictive fit between years of education and the likelihood of voting. According to the logit output, MLE ran through five iterations, finally deciding that it had maximized its ability to predict voting by using education as a predictive instrument. The log likelihood in the "Iteration 4" line, equal to -958.81643, summarizes this final-step prediction. This final number represents the "know something" model—that is, it summarizes how well we can predict voting by knowing education.

In logistic regression, you can get an idea of how well a model performs by comparing the initial log likelihood (the know-nothing model) with the final log likelihood (the know-something model). Obviously, if using education to predict voting worked about as well as not using education to predict voting, then the final log likelihood would be about the same as the initial log likelihood. If, by contrast, education greatly improved the model's predictive power, then the two log likelihoods would be very different—the final log likelihood would be much closer to 0 than the initial log likelihood.[1]

Stata's logit and logistic commands report chi-square test statistics and accompanying P-values, which tell us whether the know-something model provides significantly better predictions than the know-nothing model. In probability-weighted logistic regression (like the current example), Stata returns the Wald chi-square statistic (labeled "Wald chi2"). In unweighted analyses, Stata reports a different chi-square statistic, the likelihood ratio ("LR chi2").[2] Directly beneath the chi-square test statistic, Stata reports its P-value ("Prob > chi2"), which in this case is equal to 0.0000. Conclusion: Compared to how well we can predict voting without knowing education, including education as a predictor significantly enhances the predictive performance of the model.

For all logistic regressions, weighted and unweighted, Stata returns pseudo R-squared ("Pseudo R2"). OLS researchers are quite fond of R-squared, the overall measure of strength that gauges the amount of variation in the dependent variable that is explained by the independent variable(s). Because of the statistical foundations of logistic regression, however, the notion of "explained variation" has no direct analog in logistic regression. Even so, methodologists have proposed various "pseudo R-squared" measures that seek to communicate the strength of association between the dependent and independent variables. Stata reports the measure suggested by McFadden:[3]

(initial log likelihood – final log likelihood) / (initial log likelihood)

For the voted081-educ_yrs model, we would have

dis (-1032.7789 - (-958.81643))/-1032.7789 = -73.96247/ -1032.7789 = .0716

Stata's logit and logistic results record this value next to "Pseudo R2." With a value of about .07, one would conclude that education, though related to voting, by itself provides a less-than-complete explanation of it.[4]

By now you are aware of the interpretive challenges presented by logistic regression analysis. In running good old OLS, you had a mere handful of statistics to report and discuss: the constant, the regression coefficient(s) and accompanying P-value(s), and R-squared. That's about it. With logistic regression, there are more statistics to record and make sense of. Below is a tabular summary of the results of the voted081-educ_yrs analysis. You could use this tabular format to report the results of any logistic regressions you perform:

Model Estimates and Model Summary: Logged Odds (voting) = a + b (education)				
Model estimates	Coefficient	P-value	Odds ratio	Percentage change in odds
Constant	−2.068			
Education	.226	0.0000	1.25	25.0
Model summary	Statistic	P-value		
Wald chi-square*	55.48	0.0000		
Pseudo R-squared	.072			
* For unweighted analyses: "LR chi2"				

LOGISTIC REGRESSION WITH MULTIPLE INDEPENDENT VARIABLES

The act of voting might seem simple, but we know that it isn't. Certainly, education is not the only characteristic that shapes the individual's decision on whether to vote or to stay home. Indeed, we have just seen that years of schooling, although clearly an important predictor of turnout, returned a so-so pseudo R-squared, indicating that other factors might also contribute to the explanation. Age, race, marital status, strength of partisanship, political efficacy—all of these variables are known predictors of turnout. What is more, education might itself be related to other independent variables of interest, such as age or race. Thus, one might reasonably want to know the partial effect of education on turnout, controlling for the effects of these other independent variables. When performing

OLS regression, the researcher can enter multiple independent variables into the model and estimate the partial effects of each one on the dependent variable. Logistic regression, like OLS regression, can accommodate multiple predictors of a binary dependent variable. Consider this logistic regression model:

$$\text{logged odds (voting)} = a + b_1 (\text{educ\_yrs}) + b_2 (\text{age})$$

Again we are in an OLS-like environment. As before, educ_yrs measures number of years of formal education. The variable, age, measures each respondent's age in years, from 18 to 89. From a substantive standpoint, we would again expect educ_yrs's coefficient, b_1, to be positive: As education increases, so too should the logged odds of voting. We also know that older people are more likely to vote than are younger people. Thus, we should find a positive sign on age's coefficient, b_2. Just as in OLS, b_1 will estimate the effect of education on voting, controlling for age, and b_2 will estimate the effect of age on the dependent variable, controlling for the effect of education. Finally, the chi-square statistics and pseudo R-squared will give us an idea of how well both independent variables explain turnout.

Let's see what happens when we add age to our model. Because we want coefficients and odds ratios for the independent variables, we will again enter two commands. This time we will run the logistic command with the coef option ("logistic voted081 educ_yrs age [pw=gssw], coef"), followed by the logistic command without the coef option ("logistic voted081 educ_yrs age [pw=gssw]"):

```
logistic voted081 educ_yrs age [pw=gssw] , coef
logistic voted081 educ_yrs age [pw=gssw]
```

```
. logistic voted081 educ_yrs age [pw=gssw] , coef
```

Logistic regression

			Number of obs	=	1784
			Wald chi2(2)	=	159.79
			Prob > chi2	=	0.0000
Log pseudolikelihood = -884.30831 | | | Pseudo R2 | = | 0.1408 |

voted081	Coef.	Robust Std. Err.	z	P>|z|	[95% Conf. Interval]	
educ_yrs	.2711818	.0309627	8.76	0.000	.210496	.3318675
age	.0432758	.0043782	9.88	0.000	.0346947	.051857
_cons	-4.627789	.4697783	-9.85	0.000	-5.548538	-3.707041

```
. logistic voted081 educ_yrs age [pw=gssw]
```

Logistic regression

			Number of obs	=	1784
			Wald chi2(2)	=	159.79
			Prob > chi2	=	0.0000
Log pseudolikelihood = -884.30831 | | | Pseudo R2 | = | 0.1408 |

voted081	Odds Ratio	Robust Std. Err.	z	P>|z|	[95% Conf. Interval]	
educ_yrs	1.311513	.040608	8.76	0.000	1.23429	1.393568
age	1.044226	.0045718	9.88	0.000	1.035304	1.053225
_cons	.0097763	.0045927	-9.85	0.000	.0038931	.0245501

Plug the coefficient estimates into the model:

$$\text{logged odds (voting)} = -4.628 + .271(\text{educ\_yrs}) + .043(\text{age})$$

Interpretation of these coefficients follows a straightforward multiple regression protocol. The coefficient on educ_yrs, .271, tells us that, controlling for age, each additional year of education increases the logged odds of voting by .271. And notice that, controlling for education, age is positively related to the likelihood of voting. Each 1-year increment in age produces an increase of .043 in the logged odds of voting. According to the z-statistics and accompanying P-values, each independent variable is significantly related to the dependent variable.

Now consider Stata's helpful translations of the coefficients, from logged odds to odds ratios, which are displayed in the "Odds Ratio" column of the second set of results. Interestingly, after controlling for age, the effect of education is stronger than its uncontrolled effect, which we analyzed earlier. Taking respondents' age differences into account, each additional year of schooling increases the odds ratio by 1.312 and boosts the odds of voting by about 31 percent: (1.312 – 1) * 100 = 31.2. For age, too, the odds ratio, 1.044, is greater than 1, again communicating the positive relationship between age and the likelihood of voting. If one were to compare two individuals having the same number of years of education but who differed by 1 year in age, the older person would be 1.044 times more likely to vote than the younger person. Translating 1.044 into a percentage change in the odds: (1.044 – 1) * 100 = 4.4. Conclusion: Each additional year in age increases the odds of voting by about 4 percent.[5]

Overall, how does the voted081-educ_yrs-age model perform? According to the pseudo R-squared (.141), adding age to the model increased its explanatory power, at least when compared with the simple analysis using education as the sole predictor, which returned a pseudo R-squared of .072. And the Wald statistic, 159.79, defeats the null hypothesis (P-value = 0.0000) and suggests that, compared to the know-nothing model, both independent variables significantly improve our ability to predict the likelihood of voting. Clearly, the voted081-educ_yrs model and the voted081-educ_yrs-age model both outperform the know-nothing model, in which neither independent variable is used to predict the likelihood of voting. But is the voted081-educ_yrs-age model significantly better than the more parsimonious voted081-educ_yrs model? Yes, it is. (To find out how to compare the performance of different logistic regression models, see "A Closer Look.")

A Closer Look

The estimates Command and the lrtest Command

Does knowing the independent variables offer significant predictive leverage—compared, that is, with not knowing the independent variables? For any logistic regression model, as we have seen, this question is answered by the chi-square statistic (Wald chi-square or LR chi-square), a test statistic that compares the model's final log likelihood with its initial log likelihood. However, you may wish to compare two models, one of which (the "full" model) uses more independent variables than does a more austere counterpart (the "reduced" model). Two commands, the estimates command and the lrtest command, will help you make these model-to-model comparisons.

Suppose we want to compare the full voted081-educ_yrs-age model with the reduced voted081-educ_yrs model. After running the logit command or the logistic command to obtain estimates for the reduced model ("logistic voted081 educ_yrs"), we would store the model's estimates using the estimates command. The relevant syntax of the estimates command is as follows:

estimates store *name*

In this command syntax, *name* is a user-supplied name for the model. Applied to our example, we would type, "estimates store educ_model." Next we would run the full-model logistic regression, including age as a predictor: "logistic voted081 educ_yrs age." (We could store the full model's estimates, too, but we really don't need to, because Stata retains in memory the estimates from the most recently fitted model.) We then would enter the lrtest command, which will return an LR chi-square test statistic comparing the full model's likelihood with the reduced model's likelihood. The syntax of the lrtest command is this:

lrtest *name*, force

(continued)

A Closer Look

The estimates Command and the lrtest Command *(continued)*

In this command, *name* is the model name used in the estimates command. The force option directs Stata to perform the command, even if it doesn't want to.[1] Thus we would type, "lrtest educ_model, force." Stata will assume (correctly) that we wish to compare the most recently estimated model, the full model, with the model named "educ_model," the reduced model. Here are the results from all the commands:

```
Logistic regression                           Number of obs   =       1788
                                              Wald chi2(1)    =      55.48
                                              Prob > chi2     =     0.0000
Log pseudolikelihood = -958.81643             Pseudo R2       =     0.0716
```

voted081	Odds Ratio	Robust Std. Err.	z	P>|z|	[95% Conf. Interval]	
educ_yrs	1.25413	.0381262	7.45	0.000	1.181587	1.331127
_cons	.1264586	.0511732	-5.11	0.000	.0572134	.2795108

```
.  estimates store educ_model

.  logistic voted081 educ_yrs age [pw=gssw]

Logistic regression                           Number of obs   =       1784
                                              Wald chi2(2)    =     159.79
                                              Prob > chi2     =     0.0000
Log pseudolikelihood = -884.30831             Pseudo R2       =     0.1408
```

voted081	Odds Ratio	Robust Std. Err.	z	P>|z|	[95% Conf. Interval]	
educ_yrs	1.311513	.040608	8.76	0.000	1.23429	1.393568
age	1.044226	.0045718	9.88	0.000	1.035304	1.053225
_cons	.0097763	.0045927	-9.85	0.000	.0038931	.0245501

```
.  lrtest educ_model, force

Likelihood-ratio test                         LR chi2(1)   =     149.02
(Assumption: educ_model nested in .)          Prob > chi2  =     0.0000
```

In the lrtest results, Stata reports a LR chi-square of 149.02. Stata arrived at this number by starting with the log likelihood of the reduced model (-968.81643), subtracting the log likelihood of the full model (-884.30831), and then multiplying the result by -2: -2*(-958.81643 – (-884.30831)) = 149.02. Just as with any likelihood ratio, this number is a chi-square test statistic.[2] With a P-value of 0.0000, we can conclude that, compared with using education alone, adding age as an independent variable significantly improves the predictive power of the model.

---

[1] Why might Stata refuse to run lrtest? If the two models are estimated using different numbers of cases (Ns), Stata will not run lrtest. In analyzing survey data, we almost always reduce the valid N when we add predictors–any cases included in the reduced-model analysis that have missing values on the added variable(s) will be dropped from the full-model analysis. For the voted081-educ_yrs model, N = 1,788. For the voted081-educ_yrs-age model, N = 1,784.

[2] Degrees of freedom is equal to the number of predictors in the full model minus the number of predictors in the reduced model.

WORKING WITH PREDICTED PROBABILITIES

You now know how to perform basic logistic regression analysis, and you know how to interpret the logistic regression coefficient in terms of an odds ratio and in terms of a percentage change in the odds. No doubt, odds ratios are easier to comprehend than are logged odds. And percentage change in the odds seems more understandable still. Having said this, most investigators prefer to think in terms of probabilities. One might reasonably ask, "Controlling for age, what is the effect of a 1-year increase in education on the probability of voting?" Inconveniently, with logistic regression the answer is always, "It depends."

In the first analysis we ran, which examined the education-voting relationship, logistic regression assumed that there is a linear relationship between years of education and the logged odds of voting. This linearity assumption permitted us to arrive at an estimated effect that best fits the data. However, the technique also assumed a nonlinear relationship between years of education and the probability of voting. That is, it assumed that for people who lie near the extremes of the independent variable—respondents with either low or high levels of education—a 1-year increase in education will have a weaker effect on the probability of voting than will a 1-year increase for respondents in the middle range of the independent variable. People with low education are unlikely to vote, so a 1-year change should not have a huge effect on this likelihood. The same holds for people with many years of schooling. They are already quite likely to vote, and a 1-unit increase should not greatly enhance this probability. It is in the middle range of the independent variable that education should have its most potent marginal impact, pushing individuals over the decision threshold from "do not vote" to "vote." So the effect of a 1-year marginal change in education is either weaker or stronger, depending upon where respondents "are" on the education variable.

In logistic regression models having more than one independent variable, such as the voted081-educ_yrs-age analysis, working with probabilities becomes even more problematic. The technique assumes that the independent variables have additive effects on the logged odds of the dependent variable. Thus for any combination of values of the independent variables, one obtains an estimated value of the logged odds of the dependent variable by adding up the partial effects the predictor variables. However, logistic regression also assumes that the independent variables have interactive effects on the probability of the dependent variable. For example, in the case of younger respondents (who have a lower probability of voting), the technique might estimate a large effect of education on the probability of voting. For older respondents (who have a higher probability of voting), logistic regression may find a weaker effect of education on the probability of voting. So the effect of each independent variable on the probability of the dependent variable will depend on the values of the other predictors in the model.

These challenges notwithstanding, researchers have proposed several intuitively accessible ways to represent probabilities.[6] One approach is to report changes in the probability of the dependent variable across the values of a particularly interesting independent variable, while holding all other independent variables constant at their sample-wide means. Thus, one retrieves "marginal effects at the means," or MEMs. In the current example, we might estimate the probability of voting at each value of educ_yrs, from 0 to 20, while holding age constant at its mean. This would allow us to answer the question, "For the 'average' respondent (in terms of age), how does the probability of voting change as education increases?"

A second, more nuanced approach is to report changes in the probability of the dependent variable across the range of an interesting independent variable—and to do so separately, for discrete categories of a another independent variable. Thus, one presents "marginal effects at representative values," or MERs. In the current example, we might estimate the probability of voting at each value of educ_yrs, from 0 to 20, for two different age groups: a younger group (18–30 years old) and an older group (60 and above). This would enable us to answer these questions: "In what ways does education affect the probability of voting for younger people? How do these effects differ from education's effect for older people?"

A powerful postestimation command, margins, will provide tabular output for MEMs or MERs, depending on the requested options. The probabilities that are calculated using margins can then be graphed with the marginsplot command. So, first you run logistic regression, then you run margins—after which you run marginsplot. The margins and marginsplot commands allow many options, some of which are highly specialized. In this book, we will consider straightforward illustrations that address common research situations.

The margins Command with the atmeans Option

How would we get Stata to return the marginal effect of each year of education, holding age constant at its mean? Assuming a from-scratch start (no estimates in memory), we first would obtain the model estimates:

```
logistic voted081 educ_yrs age [pw=gssw]
```

[output not shown]

Now consider the following margins command:

```
margins, at(educ_yrs=(0(1)20)) atmeans vsquish
```

This is basic MEMs syntax. The argument, "at (educ_yrs=(0 (1) 20))," instructs Stata to calculate a probability of voting for people with 0 years of schooling (the first-named value) through 20 years of schooling (the last-named value), in increments of 1 year (the middle, parenthesized value): 0 years, 1 year, 2 years, 3 years, . . . , 20 years. Alternatively, if we typed, "at (educ_yrs=(0 (2) 20))," Stata would return probabilities at 0 years, 2 years, 4 years, . . . , 20 years. The "atmeans" options tells Stata to calculate requested probabilities while holding all other independent variables constant at their means. Finally, "vsquish" requests that the output be displayed in compact format. Go ahead and type and run the margins command. Stata reports margins output in two parts, as shown in Figure 10-1.

The first part of margins output displays the indexing that Stata uses to associate predicted probabilities (the "_at" values) with reported values of the predicted probabilities. This is important information because, in reading the second part of the output, you do not want to confuse the indexed row numbers with values of the independent variable. Predicted probabilities are reported in the "Margin" column.

What happens to the predicted probability of voting as education increases? Notice that, in the lower range of the independent variable, between 0 (Row 1) years and about 5 years (Row 6), the predicted probabilities are quite low (between .07 and about .23), and these probabilities increase on the order of .02 to .04 for each increment in education. Now shift your focus to the upper reaches of education, and note much the same thing. Beginning at about 16 years of schooling (row 17), the estimated probability of voting is at or above about .86—a high likelihood of turning out—and so increments in this range have weaker effects on the probability of voting. In education's middle range, the probabilities increase at a "faster" marginal rate.

Suppose that you had to pick a 1-year increment in education that has the largest impact on the probability of voting. What would that increment be? Study the results, and think about the phenomenon you are analyzing. Remember that voting is an up or down decision. A person either decides to vote or she decides not to vote. But between which two values of education does a "vote" decision become more likely than a "do not vote" decision? You may have noticed that, between 9 years and 10 years (between rows 10 and 11), the predicted probabilities increase from .471 to .539, a difference of .068 and the largest marginal increase in the data. And it is between these two values of education that, according to the analysis, the binary decision shifts in favor of voting—from a probability of less than .50 to a probability of greater than .50. The interval between 9 years and 10 years is the "sweet spot"—the interval with the largest impact on the probability of voting, and the interval in which the predicted probability switches from less than .50 to more than .50. [7]

As we have seen throughout this book, Stata's graphics can add visual clarity and elegance to the description of relationships. Figure 10-2 was obtained by running the single-word command, marginsplot, after the margins command. By default, marginsplot will graph predicted probabilities at each value of the independent variable (as specified in the margins command that precedes it), plus the 95 percent confidence interval of each prediction. (Why are the confidence intervals so wide at lower levels of education? Because Stata calculated predicted probabilities on so few cases. In gss2012, only 16 percent of respondents have 11 or fewer years of education.) Given its option-less simplicity, Figure 10-2

Figure 10-1   Margins Output (atmeans option)

```
Expression   : Pr(voted081), predict()
1._at        : educ_yrs    =           0
               age         =    47.88448 (mean)
2._at        : educ_yrs    =           1
               age         =    47.88448 (mean)
3._at        : educ_yrs    =           2
               age         =    47.88448 (mean)
4._at        : educ_yrs    =           3
               age         =    47.88448 (mean)
5._at        : educ_yrs    =           4
               age         =    47.88448 (mean)
6._at        : educ_yrs    =           5
               age         =    47.88448 (mean)
7._at        : educ_yrs    =           6
               age         =    47.88448 (mean)
8._at        : educ_yrs    =           7
               age         =    47.88448 (mean)
9._at        : educ_yrs    =           8
               age         =    47.88448 (mean)
10._at       : educ_yrs    =           9
               age         =    47.88448 (mean)
11._at       : educ_yrs    =          10
               age         =    47.88448 (mean)
12._at       : educ_yrs    =          11
               age         =    47.88448 (mean)
13._at       : educ_yrs    =          12
               age         =    47.88448 (mean)
14._at       : educ_yrs    =          13
               age         =    47.88448 (mean)
15._at       : educ_yrs    =          14
```

> The numbered "_at" rows are paired with values of the independent variable, educ_yrs. For example, "4._at" corresponds to 3 years of education.

> Stata calculates each probability while holding age constant at 47.88448 years, its mean.

[Some output omitted...]

> Stata uses "_at" row numbers, not values of the independent variable, to present the data. Row 1 is 0 years of education; row 7 is 6 years of education, and so on.

	Margin	Delta-method Std. Err.	z	P>|z|	[95% Conf. Interval]	
_at						
1	.0720546	.0273169	2.64	0.008	.0185144	.1255948
2	.092426	.0317168	2.91	0.004	.0302622	.1545897
3	.1178255	.0361461	3.26	0.001	.0469805	.1886704
4	.1490586	.0402732	3.70	0.000	.0701245	.2279927
5	.1868177	.0436651	4.28	0.000	.1012356	.2723998
6	.2315393	.045826	5.05	0.000	.141722	.3213565
7	.2832376	.0462805	6.12	0.000	.1925295	.3739457
8	.3413517	.0446967	7.64	0.000	.2537477	.4289556
9	.4046578	.0410203	9.86	0.000	.3242595	.485056
10	.4713033	.0355725	13.25	0.000	.4015824	.5410242
11	.5389879	.0290688	18.54	0.000	.4820141	.5959617
12	.6052647	.0225504	26.84	0.000	.5610668	.6494626
13	.6678845	.0172511	38.72	0.000	.634073	.7016959
14	.7250824	.0142439	50.90	0.000	.6971649	.7529999
15	.7757373	.013566	57.18	0.000	.7491485	.8023261
16	.8193837	.0140188	58.45	0.000	.7919073	.8468601
17	.8561112	.0144618	59.20	0.000	.8277667	.8844557
18	.8864057	.01442	61.47	0.000	.8581429	.9146684
19	.9109851	.0138459	65.79	0.000	.8838476	.9381226
20	.9306621	.01286	72.37	0.000	.9054569	.9558673
21	.9462461	.0116205	81.43	0.000	.9234702	.9690219

nonetheless communicates the essence of the nonlinear relationship between education and the probability of voting. A more finely honed version appears in Figure 10-3. (For Figure 10-3's annotated syntax, see Figure 10-4.)

Figure 10-2 Predicted Probabilities with Marginsplot (command only)

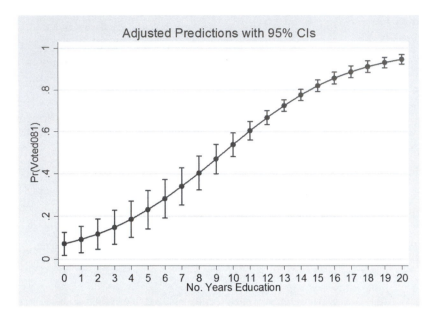

Figure 10-3 Predicted Probabilities with Marginsplot (command plus options)

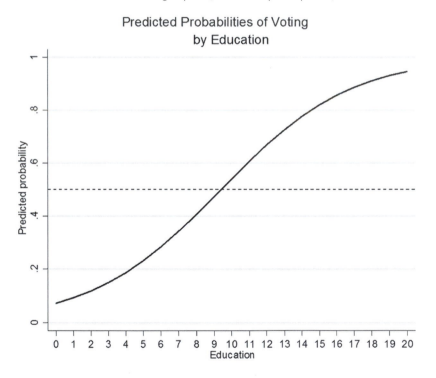

Margins, with the atmeans option, easily accommodates additional independent variables. For example, suppose you wished to add income (gss2012 variable, rincom06) to the model. Run the new model, and then request margins with the atmeans option:

```
logistic voted081 educ_yrs age rincom06 [pw=gssw]

margins, at(educ_yrs=(0 (1) 20)) atmeans
```

Stata would report the predicted probability of voting at each value of educ_yrs, holding age and rincom06 constant at their sample means.

Figure 10-4   Creating a Marginsplot Graph

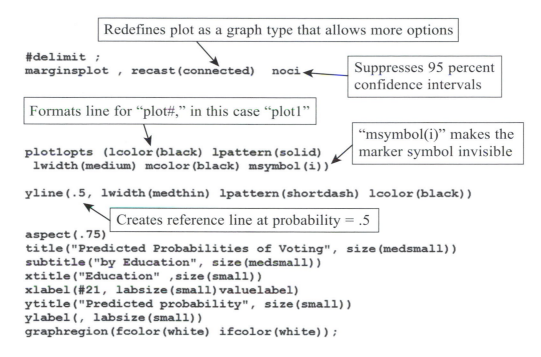

```
#delimit ;
marginsplot , recast(connected)  noci

plot1opts (lcolor(black) lpattern(solid)
  lwidth(medium) mcolor(black) msymbol(i))

yline(.5, lwidth(medthin) lpattern(shortdash) lcolor(black))

aspect(.75)
title("Predicted Probabilities of Voting", size(medsmall))
subtitle("by Education", size(medsmall))
xtitle("Education" ,size(small))
xlabel(#21, labsize(small)valuelabel)
ytitle("Predicted probability", size(small))
ylabel(, labsize(small))
graphregion(fcolor(white) ifcolor(white));
```

Callout labels:
- Redefines plot as a graph type that allows more options
- Suppresses 95 percent confidence intervals
- Formats line for "plot#," in this case "plot1"
- "msymbol(i)" makes the marker symbol invisible
- Creates reference line at probability = .5

The MEMs approach is perhaps the most prevalent methodology for describing predicted probabilities. However, for some research questions, MEMs may prove inadequate. Suppose that, based on a controlled cross-tab, we have reason to think that education works differently for younger people than for older people. If one were to estimate and compare the effects of education among two groups of respondents—those who are, say, 30 years of age or younger, and those who are 60 or older—what would the comparison reveal? What margins option would show us the relationship between education and the predicted probability of voting separately for these two age groups? Such questions require estimates of marginal effects at representative values, or MREs. Margins with the over option will give us the results we want.

The margins Command with the over Option

The over option, as its name implies, runs the margins command separately, once for each value of a categorical variable (called a *factor*) specified in the option. What if the model you have estimated does not contain the factor you want to use? No matter: The variable specified in the over option does not need to be in the model. Consider this set of commands:

```
logistic voted081 educ_yrs age [pw=gssw]

gen     agevar = 1 if age<=30 & age !=.
replace agevar = 2 if age>=60 & age !=.

#delimit ;

margins if agevar!=.;

over(agevar)

at(educ_yrs=(0(1)20)) vsquish ;
```

Callout labels:
- Gererates a factor that measures two age groups
- If qualifier; now Stata will ignore missing data
- Runs margins for each value of agevar

Stata's indexing is more complicated than with the atmeans option, but we can still sort it out (Figure 10-5). Consider the dramatically different effects of education for the two age groups. To be sure, the relationship is positive for both groups, but the patterns of marginal effects are not the same at all. For younger people with low levels of education (between 0 and 8 years of schooling) the probability of voting is extraordinarily low, in

Figure 10-5 Margins Output (over option)

```
over          : agevar
1._at         : 1.agevar
                     educ_yrs        =          0
                2.agevar
                     educ_yrs        =          0
2._at         : 1.agevar
                     educ_yrs        =          1
                2.agevar
                     educ_yrs        =          1
3._at         : 1.agevar
                     educ_yrs        =          2
                2.agevar
                     educ_yrs        =          2
4._at         : 1.agevar
                     educ_yrs        =          3
                2.agevar
                     educ_yrs        =          3
5._at         : 1.agevar
                     educ_yrs        =          4
                2.agevar
                     educ_yrs        =          4
```

> Stata's indexing refers to values of age and education. For example, "4._at" has predicted probabilities for each age group at 3 years of education.

[Some output omitted...]

> Scan the Margin column. The younger group crosses .5 between 12 and 13 years of education. The older group crosses .5 between 5 and 6 years of education.

_at#agevar						
1 1	.0293893	.0121077	2.43	0.015	.0056586	.05312
1 2	.1735489	.0585345	2.96	0.003	.0588235	.2882744
2 1	.0381903	.0144919	2.64	0.008	.0097867	.066594
2 2	.2150206	.0638405	3.37	0.001	.0898954	.3401457
3 1	.0494909	.0171604	2.88	0.004	.0158571	.0831247
3 2	.2631052	.0676307	3.89	0.000	.1305515	.3956589
4 1	.0639105	.0200584	3.19	0.001	.0245967	.1032242
4 2	.3174564	.0693384	4.58	0.000	.1815556	.4533572
5 1	.0821642	.0230811	3.56	0.000	.0369261	.1274022
5 2	.3771774	.068569	5.50	0.000	.2427847	.51157
6 1	.1050403	.0260619	4.03	0.000	.0539598	.1561208
6 2	.4408144	.0652191	6.76	0.000	.3129873	.5686414
7 1	.1333514	.0287696	4.64	0.000	.0769641	.1897387
7 2	.5064558	.0595456	8.51	0.000	.3897486	.6231631
8 1	.1678499	.0309215	5.43	0.000	.1072449	.228455
8 2	.5719342	.0521469	10.97	0.000	.4697281	.6741402
9 1	.2091043	.0322275	6.49	0.000	.1459394	.2722691
9 2	.6350921	.0438532	14.48	0.000	.5491414	.7210428
10 1	.2573437	.0324703	7.93	0.000	.193703	.3209843
10 2	.6940504	.0355579	19.52	0.000	.6243582	.7637425
11 1	.3122971	.0316208	9.88	0.000	.2503214	.3742728
11 2	.7474096	.0280448	26.65	0.000	.6924428	.8023764
12 1	.3730712	.0299592	12.45	0.000	.3143523	.4317902
12 2	.7943459	.021858	36.34	0.000	.7515051	.8371867
13 1	.4381227	.0281213	15.58	0.000	.383006	.4932394
13 2	.8345944	.0172271	48.45	0.000	.80083	.8683588
14 1	.5053659	.026922	18.77	0.000	.4525998	.558132
14 2	.868351	.0140502	61.80	0.000	.8408131	.8958889
15 1	.5724163	.0268722	21.30	0.000	.5197477	.6250849
15 2	.8961333	.0119655	74.89	0.000	.8726813	.9195853
16 1	.6369161	.0277641	22.94	0.000	.5824995	.6913328
16 2	.9186416	.0105307	87.23	0.000	.8980017	.9392814
17 1	.6968528	.0288733	24.13	0.000	.6402622	.7534434
17 2	.9366433	.0094013	99.63	0.000	.918217	.9550696
18 1	.7507827	.0295006	25.45	0.000	.6929625	.8086028
18 2	.9508918	.0083886	113.36	0.000	.9344505	.9673331
19 1	.7979161	.0292698	27.26	0.000	.7405484	.8552839
19 2	.9620763	.0074212	129.64	0.000	.947531	.9766216
20 1	.8380713	.0281278	29.80	0.000	.7829419	.8932007
20 2	.9707984	.0064896	149.59	0.000	.958079	.9835177
21 1	.8715425	.0262293	33.23	0.000	.8201339	.9229511
21 2	.9775652	.0056071	174.34	0.000	.9665755	.9885549

the .03 to .21 range. Indeed, the educational increment with the largest marginal effect—the increment in which the probability of voting switches from less than .5 to more than .5—occurs beyond high school, between 12 and 13 years of schooling. Compare the probability profile of younger respondents—sluggish marginal effects in the lower range of education, a high "switchover" threshold—with the profile of older respondents. Does education work the same way as we read down the column and focus on agevar equal to 2? Here the probabilities start at a higher level (about .17) and build quite rapidly, crossing the .5 threshold at a fairly low level of education, between 5 and 6 years of schooling.[8]

Figure 10-6 Predicted Probabilities with Marginsplot (over option)

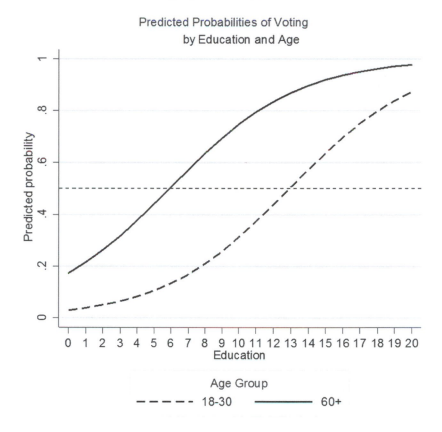

When you use the MERs method to explore complex relationships, you will want to complement your analyses with appropriate graphic support (Figure 10-6). With two exceptions—the addition of a second plot line, and the inclusion of a legend—the marginsplot syntax for Figure 10-6's graph is quite similar to the syntax described in Figure 10-4:

```
#delimit ;
marginsplot , recast(connected)
plot1opts (lcolor(black) lpattern(dash) lwidth(medium)
 mcolor(black) msymbol(i) )
plot2opts (lcolor(black) lpattern(solid) lwidth(medium)
 mcolor(black) msymbol(i) )
aspect (.75)
yline(.5, lwidth(medthin) lpattern(shortdash) lcolor(black)) noci
title("Predicted Probabilities of Voting", size(small))
subtitle("by Education and Age", size(small))
xtitle("Education" ,size(small))
xlabel(#21, labsize(small)valuelabel)
ytitle("Predicted probability", size(small))
ylabel(, labsize(small))
legend(order(1 "18-30" 2 "60+") size(small))
legend(title("Age Group",size(small)))
legend(on region(lcolor(none)))
graphregion(fcolor(white) ifcolor(white));
```

MERS-MEMS HYBRIDS

This chapter has introduced two basic approaches to analyzing predicted probabilities in logistic regression relationships. Margins with the atmeans option, the MEMs approach, is quite straightforward: Specify the range of an interesting independent variable (the "let vary" variable), and then use atmeans to set all other independent variables at their sample means (the "held constant" variables). Margins with the over option, the MERs approach, adds complexity: Generate a factor (or use a factor variable that already exists in the dataset), specify the factor in the over option, and then specify the range of an interesting independent variable.

Of course, MERs-MEMs hybrids are eminently doable with the margins command. For example, let's first expand the preceding logistic regression model to include two other predictors of turnout: income (gss2012 variable, rincom06) and strength of partisanship (gss2012 variable, partisan). Partisan is a dummy, coded 1 for strong Democrats or strong Republicans and coded 0 for all nonstrong partisans and independents. Following is the logistic regression command for the expanded model:

```
logistic voted081 educ_yrs age rincom06 partisan [pw=gssw]
```

[Output omitted]

Now, consider this MERs-MEMs idea. Just as in the preceding example, we will use agevar in the over option and retrieve predicted probabilities at each value of educ_yrs. However, this time we want to hold rincom06 and partisan at their sample means. Experience teaches that there is one correct way (and myriad incorrect ways) to accomplish this. First, run summary to obtain the means of the held-constant variables, rincom06 and partisan:

```
. sum rincom06 partisan [aw=gssw]
```

Variable	Obs	Weight	Mean	Std. Dev.	Min	Max
rincom06	1142	1201.43036	14.35584	6.087912	1	25
partisan	1974	1975.00052	.2628774	.4403079	0	1

Then, copy/paste the rincom06 mean (14.35584) and the partisan mean (.2628774) into the same parenthesized "at" argument that contains the let-vary variable, educ_yrs:

```
#delimit;
margins if agevar!=., over(agevar) vsquish
at(educ_yrs=(0(1)20)
  rincom06= 14.35584  ◄──  Set the mean values of the held-constant variables in
  partisan= .2628774)  ;    the same "at" expression as the let-vary variable.
```

Stata will calculate predicted probabilities for each agevar-educ_yrs combination and hold rincom06 and partisan at the specified values for each combination.

EXERCISES

1. (Dataset: states. Variables: Obama_win12, Gun_scale11, Relig_high.) As you know, presidential elections in the United States take place within an unusual institutional context. Naturally, candidates seek as many votes as they can get, but the real electoral prizes come in winner-take-all, state-sized chunks: The plurality-vote winner in each state receives all the electoral college votes from that state. Cast in logistic regression terms, each state represents a binary outcome—it either goes Democratic or Republican. What variables shape this outcome? As a candidate for the Democratic nomination in 2008, Barack Obama pointed toward several plausible variables. During a campaign appearance, Obama suggested that many voters, frustrated by the disappearance of economic opportunities, "cling to guns or religion or antipathy to people who aren't like them or anti-immigrant sentiment or antitrade sentiment as a way to explain their frustrations." Obama said that these factors helped explain why his electoral support was weaker in certain geographical areas of the country.[9]

    Obama's remarks suggest the following hypothesis: In comparing states, those with higher percentages of highly religious residents were less likely to have been won by Obama than were states having lower percentages of highly religious residents.

Dataset states contains Obama_win12, a binary variable coded 1 if the state's electoral vote went to Democratic candidate Barack Obama in 2012 and coded 0 if the state went to Republican Mitt Romney. This is the dependent variable. The dataset also has Relig_high, the percentage of state residents who are highly religious. Relig_high is the independent variable.

A. Run "logistic Obama_win12 Relig_high, coef." Run "logistic Obama_win12 Relig_high." The following table contains seven question marks. Write the correct value next to each question mark.

Model estimates	Coefficient	Odds ratio	P-value
Constant	?		
Relig_high	?	?	?
Model summary	Statistic		P-value
LR chi-square	?		?
Pseudo R-squared	?		

Before proceeding to Part B, review the procedure for converting an odds ratio into a percentage change in the odds for negative relationships.

B. After converting the odds ratio to a percentage change in the odds of an Obama win, you can say that a 1-point increase in Relig_high decreases the odds of an Obama win by _____ percent.

C. The lowest value on Relig_high is approximately 20 percent. The highest value is approximately 60 percent. The median state has a value of 38 percent. Run margins, requesting predicted probabilities of Obama_win12 from 20 to 60, in increments of 1. In interpreting the results, be sure to match the indexed value with the value of Relig_high. (Hint: Stata associates a Relig_high value of 20 with _at value 1.)

For a state in which 20 percent of its residents are highly religious, the predicted probability of an Obama win is equal to _____. For a state in which 60 percent of its residents are highly religious, the predicted probability of an Obama win is equal to _____. The probability of an Obama win in the median state is equal to _____.

D. A Democratic strategist must decide in which states to concentrate her limited campaign resources. To achieve maximum effect, this strategist should concentrate her campaign on (check one)

❏ A state in which 30 percent of its residents are highly religious.

❏ A state in which 40 percent of its residents are highly religious.

❏ A state in which 50 percent of its residents are highly religious.

E. Briefly explain your reasoning in Part D:

_____

_____

_____

_____

F. Suppose you want to improve the predictive performance of the Obama_win12-Relig_high model by adding a second independent variable, the Brady campaign's rating of states' gun laws (Gun_scale11). Higher scores on Gun_scale11 denote more restrictions on firearms ownership. You reason that the full Obama_win12-Relig_high-Gun_scale11 model will produce significantly better predictions than the simple Obama_win12-Relig_high model. However, a critic plausibly suggests that the two independent variables, Relig_high and Gun_scale11, are themselves related—less religious states will have more gun restrictions than will more religious states. This critic argues that adding Gun_scale11 to the model will not significantly enhance your ability to predict electoral outcomes.

Run estimates store to save the estimates from the Obama_win12-Relig_high model. (Choose a descriptive name for the model, such as "relig_model.") Now run the logistic command for the full model. Obtain odds ratios, not coefficients.

Refer to the odds ratios for the Obama_win12-Relig_high-Gun_scale11 model. Controlling for Relig_high, a 1-point increase in Gun_scale11 increases the odds of an Obama win by about (circle one)

22 percent. 44 percent. 144 percent.

G. Run lrtest to find out whether adding Gun_scale11 to the model provides significantly improved predictions of Obama_win12. The lrtest has an LR chi-square equal to _____ and a P-value equal to _____. Based on this information, may you infer that using two independent variables, Relig_high and Gun_scale11, yields significantly better predictions of an Obama win than does using Relig_high by itself? (check one)

❑ No, adding Gun_scale11 to the model does not provide significantly better predictions.

❑ Yes, adding Gun_scale11 to the model does provide significantly better predictions.

2. (Dataset: world. Variables: democ_regime, frac_eth, gdp_10_thou.) In Chapter 5, you tested this hypothesis: In comparing countries, those having lower levels of ethnic heterogeneity are more likely to be democracies than are those having higher levels of ethnic heterogeneity. This hypothesis says that, as heterogeneity goes up, the probability of democracy goes down. You then reran the analysis, controlling for a measure of countries' economic development, gross domestic product per capita. For this independent variable, the relationship is thought to be positive: As economic development increases, so does the likelihood that a country will be democratic. In the current exercise, you will reexamine this set of relationships, using a more powerful method of analysis, logistic regression.

World contains democ_regime, frac_eth, and gdp_10_thou. The variable, democ_regime, is coded 1 if the country is a democracy and coded 0 if it is not a democracy. This is the dependent variable. One of the independent variables, frac_eth, can vary between 0 (denoting low heterogeneity) and 1 (high heterogeneity). The other independent variable, gdp_10_thou, measures gross domestic product per capita in units of $10,000.

A. Run "logistic democ_regime frac_eth gdp_10_thou, coef." Run "logistic democ_regime frac_eth gdp_10_thou." The following table contains nine question marks. Write the correct value next to each question mark.

Model estimates	Coefficient	Odds ratio	P-value
Constant	.842		
frac_eth	?	?	?
gdp_10_thou	?	?	?
Model summary	Statistic		P-value
LR chi-square	?		?
Pseudo R-squared	?		

B. Use the odds ratios to calculate a percentage change in the odds. Controlling for gdp_10_thou, a 1-unit change in frac_eth, from low heterogeneity to high heterogeneity (check one)

❏ increases the odds of democracy by about 20 percent.

❏ decreases the odds of democracy by about 20 percent.

❏ decreases the odds of democracy by about 80 percent.

Controlling for frac_eth, each $10,000 increase in per capita gross domestic product (check one)

❏ increases the odds of democracy by about 104 percent.

❏ increases the odds of democracy by about 204 percent.

❏ increases the odds of democracy by about 40 percent.

C. Run the margins command to calculate the estimated probability of democracy at each value of frac_eth, between 0 and 1, in increments of .1. Hold gdp_10_thou constant at its mean. As an empirical matter, the most homogeneous country in world has a value of 0 on frac_eth, and the most heterogeneous country has a value of approximately .9 on frac_eth. The predicted probability of democracy for a highly homogeneous country (frac_eth = 0) with an average level of gdp_10_thou is equal to _____. The predicted probability of democracy for a highly heterogeneous country (frac_eth = .9) with an average level of gdp_10_thou is equal to _____.

D. Run marginsplot to graphically display the results of the margins. Using this chapter's examples as guides, request all appropriate options. (Hint: The marginsplot syntax for graphing the effect of education on the probability of voting, holding age constant, has most of the options you need. Be sure to change the titles and labels as necessary.) Print the graph.

3. (Dataset: nes2012. Variables: Obama_vote, pid_x, pres_econ, [pw=nesw].) When it comes to shaping vote choice in US elections, party identification is preeminent—a powerful heuristic for deciding which candidate to support. Yet one can imagine circumstances in which the pull of party might be weaker. Retrospective evaluations, the approval or disapproval of an incumbent's performance, might work to alter the effect of partisanship. Consider two Democrats, one who thinks President Obama has done a good job of handling the economy, and another who thinks he's done a poor job. Would the poor-job Democrat be less likely than the good-job Democrat to vote for Obama? If so, how much less likely? And what about Independents, voters who lack partisan identifications? Do retrospective assessments have the largest impact among these voters? More generally, is the relationship between party identification and vote choice different for those with negative retrospective opinions than for those with positive retrospective opinions? The following nes2012 variables will help you answer these questions.

Variable	Definition	Coding
Obama_vote	Vote choice in 2012	0 = Romney vote; 1 = Obama vote
pid_x	Party identification	1 = Strong Democrat
		2 = Weak Democrat
		3 = Independent Democrat
		4 = Independent
		5 = Independent Republican
		6 = Weak Republican
		7 = Strong Republican
pres_econ	Approval of Obama's handling of economy	0 = Disapprove
		1 = Approve

Run the appropriate logistic regression model to estimate the effects of pid_x and pres_econ on Obama_vote. (Remember to include "[pw=nesw].") Obtain odds ratios.

A. Consider the odds ratio on pres_econ. Controlling for party identification, when you compare an approver with a disapprover, the approver was about how many times more likely to have voted for Obama than the disapprover?

about _____ times more likely

B. Run margins with the over option to obtain the probability of an Obama vote at each value of party identification, separately for disapprovers and approvers. Among which party identification group—Strong Democrats, Weak Democrats, Independent Democrats, Independents, Independent Republicans, Weak Republicans, or Strong Republicans—does presidential approval have its largest impact on the probability of an Obama vote?

The largest impact is among (fill in the blank) _____. Explain how you know.

_____

_____

_____

C. In which party identification group does presidential approval have its smallest impact on the probability of an Obama vote?

The smallest impact is among (fill in the blank) _____. Explain how you know.

_____

_____

_____

D. Run marginsplot to graphically display the results of the margins. Using this chapter's examples as guides, request all appropriate options. (Hint: The marginsplot syntax for graphing the effect of education on the probability of voting, separately for two age groups, has most of the options you need. Be sure to change the titles and labels as necessary.) Print the graph.

E. Examine the graph you produced in Part D. Consider this statement: "The effect of party identification on vote choice is stronger among disapprovers than among approvers." Does this statement appear to be correct or incorrect? (circle one)

incorrect   correct

Explain your answer.

_____

_____

_____

_____

_____

NOTES

1. Because likelihoods can vary between 0 and 1, the logs of likelihoods can vary between large negative numbers (any likelihood of less than 1 has a negatively signed log) and 0 (the log of 1 is equal to 0). As a model's predictive power improves, therefore, log likelihoods approach 0.

2. Stata reports degrees of freedom in bold typeface within the parentheses next to "Wald chi2." Degrees of freedom is equal to the number of independent variables in the model. Because the model in our current example has one independent variable, the likelihood ratio is labeled "Wald chi2(1)."

3. Daniel McFadden, "Conditional Logit Analysis of Qualitative Choice Behavior," *Frontiers in Econometrics,* ed. Paul Zarembka (New York: Academic Press, 1974), 105–142. See especially pp. 120–121.

4. For additional pseudo R-square measures, download Ben Jann's module, estout (version 3.17 02 June 2014). For example, estout's estadd command returns the Cox-Snell and Nagelkerke's R-squared measures, which are familiar to SPSS researchers. To download estout, type "ssc install estout."

5. When using interval-level independent variables with many values, you will often obtain logistic regression coefficients and odds ratios that appear to be quite close to null hypothesis territory (coefficients close to 0 and odds ratios close to 1) but that nonetheless trump the null hypothesis. Remember that logistic regression, like OLS, estimates the marginal effect of a one-unit increment on the logged odds of the dependent variable. In the current example, logistic regression estimated the effect of a 1-year change in age (from, say, an age of 20 years to 21 years) on the logged odds of voting. The investigator may describe the relationship in terms of larger increments. Thus, if a 1-year increase in age (from 20 years to 21 years) increases the odds of voting by an estimated 4 percent, then a 10-year increase in age (from 20 years to 30 years) would produce a 40 percent increase in the odds of voting.

6. The discussion and terminology here draw on the insights of Richard Williams, "Using the Margins Command to Estimate and Interpret Adjusted Predictions and Marginal Effects," *The Stata Journal* 12, no. 2 (2012): 308–331.

7. The largest marginal effect of the independent variable on the probability of the dependent variable is sometimes called the *instantaneous effect*. In our example, the instantaneous effect is equal to .068, and this effect occurs between 9 years and 10 years of education. The effect of a 1-unit change in the independent variable on the probability of the dependent variable is always greatest for the interval containing a probability equal to .5. The instantaneous effect, calculated by hand, is equal to b * .5 * (1-.5), in which b is the value of the logistic regression coefficient. For a discussion of the instantaneous effect, see Fred C. Pampel, *Logistic Regression: A Primer*, Sage University Papers Series on Quantitative Applications in the Social Sciences, series no. 07-132 (Thousand Oaks, CA: SAGE, 2000), 24–26.

8. See Raymond E. Wolfinger and Steven J. Rosenstone's classic study of turnout, *Who Votes?* (New Haven: Yale University Press, 1980). Using probit analysis, a technique that is very similar to logistic regression, Wolfinger and Rosenstone explore the effects of a range of demographic characteristics on the likelihood of voting.

9. Obama reportedly made this remark at a fundraising event in San Francisco on April 6, 2008. See http://thepage.time.com/transcript-of-obamas-remarks-at-san-francisco-fundraiser-sunday/.

Doing Your Own Political Analysis

In working through the guided examples in this book, and in performing the exercises, you have developed some solid analytic skills. The datasets that you have analyzed throughout this book could, of course, become the raw material for your own research. You would not be disappointed, however, if you were to look elsewhere for excellent data. High-quality social science data on a wide variety of phenomena and units of analysis—individuals, census tracts, states, countries—are increasingly accessible via the Internet and might serve as the centerpiece for your own research. Your school, for example, may be a member of the Inter-university Consortium for Political and Social Research (ICPSR), the premier organizational clearinghouse for datasets of all kinds.[1] In this chapter, we will take a look at various sources of available data and provide practical guidance for inputting it into Stata. In the process, we will also cover situations in which you are confronted with raw, uncoded data—perhaps from an original questionnaire you developed and administered—that you need to code and analyze.

To get you thinking about doing your own research, we begin by laying out the stages of the research process and by offering some manageable ideas for original analysis. We then consider different data sources and procedures for inputting the data into Stata's Data Editor. Finally, we will describe a serviceable format for an organized and presentable research paper.

FIVE DOABLE IDEAS

Let's begin by describing an ideal research procedure and then discuss some practical considerations and constraints. In an ideal world you would

1. Observe an interesting behavior or relationship and frame a research question about it

2. Develop a causal explanation for what you have observed and construct a hypothesis

3. Read and learn from the work of other researchers who have tackled similar questions

4. Collect and analyze the data that will address the hypothesis

5. Write a research paper or article in which you present and interpret your findings

In this scenario, the phenomenon that you observe in Stage 1 drives the whole process. First, think up a question; then research it and obtain the data that will address it. As a practical matter, the process is almost never this clear-cut.[2] Often someone else's idea or assertion may pique your interest. For example, you might read articles or attend lectures on a variety of topics—democratization in developing countries, global environmental issues, ideological change in the Democratic or Republican Party, the effect of election laws on turnout and party competition, and so on—that suggest hypotheses you would like to examine. So you may begin the process at Stage 3, then return to Stage 1 and refine your own ideas. Furthermore, the availability of relevant data, considered in Stage 4, almost always plays a role in the sorts of questions we address. Suppose, for example, that you want to assess organizational efforts to mobilize black voters in your state in the last presidential election. You want precinct-level registration data, and you need to compare these numbers with the figures from previous elections. You would soon become an expert in the bureaucratic hassles and expense involved in dealing with county governments, and you might have to revise your research agenda. Indeed, for professional researchers and academics, data collection in itself can be a full-time job. For students who wish to produce a competent and manageable project, the so-called law of available data can be a source of frustration and discouragement.

A doable project often requires a compromise between Stage 1 and Stage 4. What interesting question can you ask, given the available data? Fortunately, this compromise need not be as restrictive as it sounds. Consider five possibilities: political knowledge, economic performance and election outcomes, state courts and criminal procedure, electoral turnout in comparative perspective, and Congress.

Political Knowledge

As you may have learned in other political science courses, scholars continue to debate the levels of knowledge and political awareness among ordinary citizens. Do citizens know the length of a US senator's term of office? Do they know what constitutional protections are guaranteed by the First Amendment? Do people tend to know more about some things—Internet privacy or abortion policy, for example—and less about other things, such as foreign policy or international politics? Political knowledge is a promising variable, because the researcher is likely to find some people who know a lot about politics, some who know a fair amount, and others who know very little. One could ask, "What causes this variation?" Imagine constructing a brief questionnaire that asks eight or ten multiple-choice questions about basic facts and is tailored to the aspects of political knowledge you find most thought provoking.[3] After including questions that gauge some potentially important independent variables (partisanship, gender, liberalism/conservatism, college major, class standing), you could conduct an exploratory survey among perhaps fifty or one hundred of your fellow students.

Economic Performance and Election Outcomes

Here is one of the most widely discussed ideas in political science: The state of the economy before an election has a big effect on the election result. If the economy is strong, the candidate of the incumbent party does well, probably winning. If the economy is performing poorly, the incumbent party's nominee pays the price, probably losing. There are a couple of intriguing aspects to this idea. For one thing, it works well—but not perfectly. Moreover, the economy-election relationship has several researchable layers. Focusing on presidential elections, you can imagine a simple two-category measure of the dependent variable—the incumbent party wins, or the incumbent party loses. Now consider several stints in the reference section of the library, collecting information on some potential independent variables for each presidential election year: inflation rates, unemployment, economic growth, and so on. Alternatively, you could look at congressional or state-level elections or elections in several different countries. Or you could modify and refine the basic idea, as many scholars have done, by adding additional noneconomic variables you believe to be important. Scandal? Foreign policy crises? With some hands-on data collection and guidance from your instructor, you can produce a well-crafted project.

State Courts and Criminal Procedure

To what extent does a justice's partisanship (or political ideology) affect his or her ruling in a case? This is a perennial question in the annals of judicial research. The 2000 election comes to mind. The US Supreme Court based its pivotal decision on judicial principles, but it split along partisan lines. And, given the level of partisan acrimony that accompanies the nominations of would-be federal judges, members of the US Senate behave as if political ideology plays a role in judicial decision making. Original research on judicial proceedings, particularly at the federal level, is among the most difficult to conduct, even for seasoned scholars. But consider state judicial systems. Using an online resource available through most university servers, you could collect information about a large number of, say, criminal cases heard on appeal by the highest court in your state.[4] You could record whether the criminal defendant won or lost, then determine the party affiliations of the justices. Additionally, you might compare judicial decision making in two states—one in which judges are appointed and one in which they are elected. You could make this comparison at the individual justice level at one point in time. Or you could look at the same set of courts over time, using aggregate units of analysis.

Electoral Turnout in Comparative Perspective

The record of voter turnout in American presidential elections, while showing encouraging reversals in recent elections, is relatively low. The situation in other democratic countries is strikingly different. Turnouts in some Western European countries average well above 70 percent. Why? More generally, what causes turnout to vary between countries? Some scholars have focused on legal factors. Unlike the United States, some countries may not require their citizens to register beforehand, or they may penalize citizens for not voting. Other scholars look at institutional differences in electoral systems. Many countries, for example, have systems of proportional representation in which narrowly focused parties with relatively few supporters nonetheless can gain representation in the legislature. Are citizens more likely to be mobilized to vote under such institutional arrangements? Using data sources available on the Internet,[5] you could gather information on a number of democratic countries. You could then look to see if different legal requirements and institutional arrangements are associated with differences in turnout. This area of research might also open the door for some informed speculation on your part. What sort of electoral reforms, if instituted in the United States, might enhance electoral turnout? What other (perhaps unintended) consequences might such reforms have?

Congress

Political scholars have long taken considerable interest in questions about the US Congress. Some researchers focus on internal dynamics: the role of leadership, the power of party ties versus the pull of constituency. Others pay attention to demographics: Has the number of women and minorities who serve in Congress increased in the recent past? Still others look at ideology: Are Republicans, on average, becoming more conservative and Democrats more liberal in their congressional voting? The great thing about Congress is the rich data that are available. The US House and the US Senate are among the most-studied institutions in the world. Several annual or biannual publications chronicle and report a large number of attributes of members of the House and Senate.[6] And the Internet is rife with information about current and past Congresses. Liberal groups, such as Americans for Democratic Action, conservative groups, such as the American Conservative Union, and nonpartisan publications, such as the *National Journal,* regularly rate the voting records of elected officials and post these ratings on their Internet sites.[7]

INPUTTING DATA

Each of these five possibilities represents a practical compromise among posing an interesting question, obtaining available data, and using Stata to perform the analysis. However, as you will no doubt discover, data sources vary in their "input friendliness"—some data are easy to input into Stata, and other data require more typing. This section reviews different data sources and input procedures.

Stata Formatted Datasets

The least labor-intensive sources provide Stata datasets that are ready to download and analyze. One such source, the ICPSR's data clearinghouse at the University of Michigan, was mentioned at the beginning of this chapter: http://www.icpsr.umich.edu. But many other sites exist, often maintained by scholars, academic departments, and private foundations. For example, if you are interested in comparative politics or international relations, visit Pippa Norris's website at Harvard's John F. Kennedy School of Government: http://www.pippanorris.com/. Planning a project on the US Supreme Court? You will want to download Lee Epstein's (Northwestern University) Stata dataset, which contains information on every Supreme Court nominee since John Jay: http://scdb.wustl.edu/data.php. For links to a number of Stata datasets having a particular emphasis on Latino politics, see Professor Matt A. Barreto's site at the University of Washington: http://faculty.washington.edu/mbarreto/data/index.html. Are you interested in the political beliefs and civic behavior of young people? The Center for Information and Research on Civic Learning and Engagement

(CIRCLE) provides excellent data in Stata format: http://www.civicyouth.org/ResearchTopics/research-products-cat/data-sets/. More generally, the University of California–Berkeley's Survey Documentation and Analysis (SDA) website—a clearinghouse for the General Social Surveys, the American National Election Studies, and census microdata—allows you to download customized datasets and codebooks in a variety of formats, including Stata: http://sda.berkeley.edu/archive.htm.

Microsoft Excel Datasets

Much Internet data is not Stata-ready but, rather, is available in spreadsheet form, predominately in Microsoft Excel format. In these situations, you can copy/paste the data from Excel into the Stata Data Editor. There are a few caveats to keep in mind, however. To illustrate, consider a typical US Census site, http://www.census.gov/compendia/statab/cats/elections/presidential.html, which links an Excel dataset that records presidential election outcomes by state (Figure 11-1). This set provides an instructive example of a common "gotcha" in transferring data from Excel to Stata.

Stata recognizes two basic forms of data, numeric and string. Numeric data contain only numbers, including numbers with decimals. String data contain letters, words, symbols, or commas. Although some string data are essential—case identifiers, such as state or country names, are obvious examples—Stata much prefers to analyze numerics, not strings. In the current example, the data in the percent columns, which contain only numbers and decimal points, will be read as numeric. However, the data in the vote total columns ("Total Vote," "Democratic Party," "Republican Party") contain commas, which Stata will read as string data. Stata would be happy to let you paste these values into the Data Editor, but it would not be at all happy to analyze them for you. To remove the commas, and thereby convert the data from string to numeric, follow these steps, which are illustrated in Figure 11-2.

1. Select the columns you wish to edit by clicking the column header. To select multiple nonadjacent columns, select the first column, press and hold the Control key, and then select the second and other columns.

2. On Excel's main menu bar, click Format→Format Cells.

3. In the Category pane of the Format Cells window, select the Number tab.

4. In the Number tab, you will always want to uncheck the Use 1000 Separator box.

Depending on the exact character of the data, you may want to modify the value in the Decimal places box. If the data contain decimals, then specify the number of decimal places. In the current example, the numbers in the edited columns do not contain decimals, so we would type "0" in the Decimal places box.

To copy/paste the edited Excel data into the Stata Data Editor, follow these steps, which are described in Figure 11-3.

1. Select the Excel data rows that you want to paste into Stata. Make sure that the selection is square— that is, ensure that each row contains the same number of columns. Avoid selecting column headers and labels. Also, do not use Excel's row-number markers to make the selection. (This copies the desired columns, plus a number of empty columns.) Rather, select the data by clicking inside the matrix. After completing the selection, click the Copy icon on the Excel menu bar.

2. On the Stata menu bar, click the Data Editor (Edit) icon.

3. In the Data Editor, click the Paste icon. Stata pastes the data into the Data Editor, giving each variable a generic name: "var1," "var2," "var3," and so on.

4. Change the variable names by clicking Tools→Variables Manager on the main menu bar.

5. In the Variables Manager window, highlight the current variable name in the left-hand panel, and make changes in the Name box in the right-hand panel. By Stata's rules, a variable name may be from 1 to 32 characters in length, although 8–12 characters are usually adequate. Characters may be letters, numbers, and underscores. You may begin a name with an underscore, although Stata recommends that you not do this, because many of Stata's reserved names begin with underscores. As you have probably figured out by this point, Stata is case sensitive, so "Demvote" is different from "demvote."

Figure 11-1 Opening an Excel Dataset and Evaluating Its Stata-Friendliness

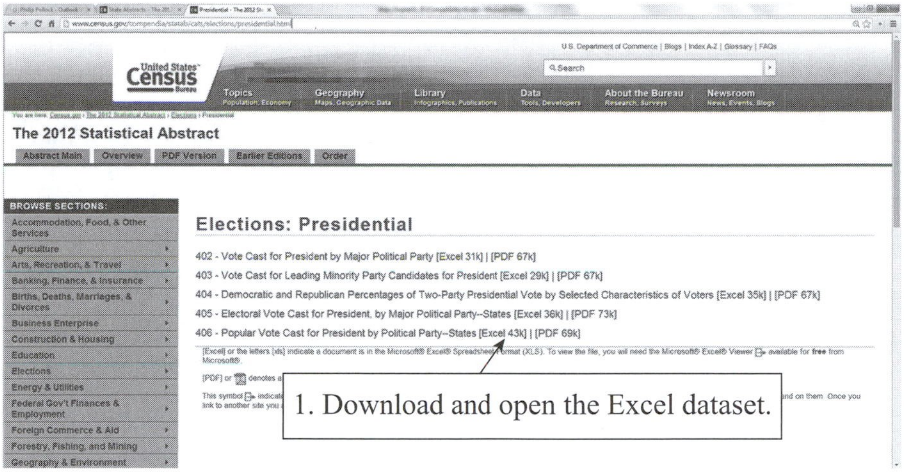

1. Download and open the Excel dataset.

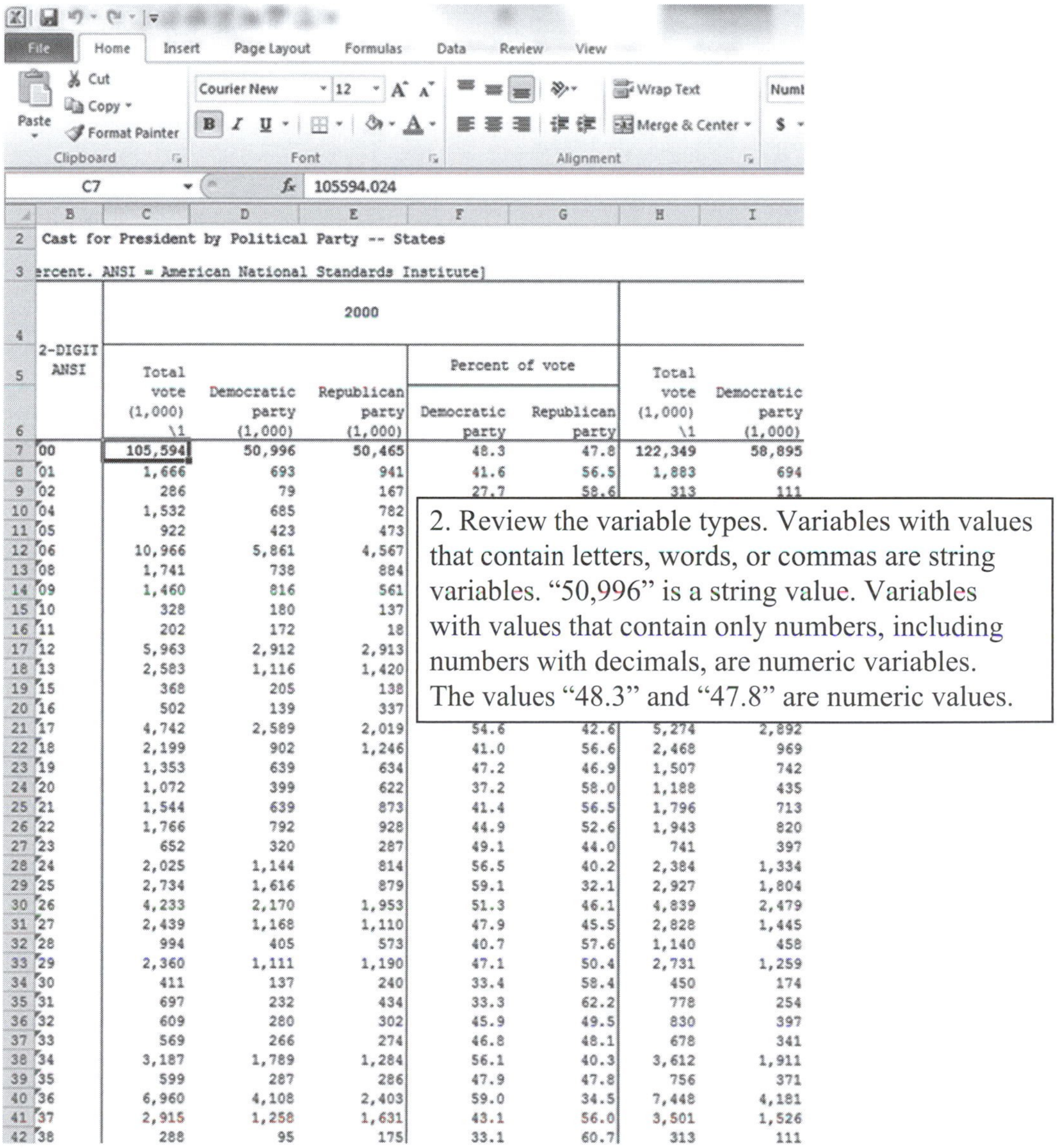

2. Review the variable types. Variables with values that contain letters, words, or commas are string variables. "50,996" is a string value. Variables with values that contain only numbers, including numbers with decimals, are numeric variables. The values "48.3" and "47.8" are numeric values.

Figure 11-2 Removing Commas from Data Values Using Excel

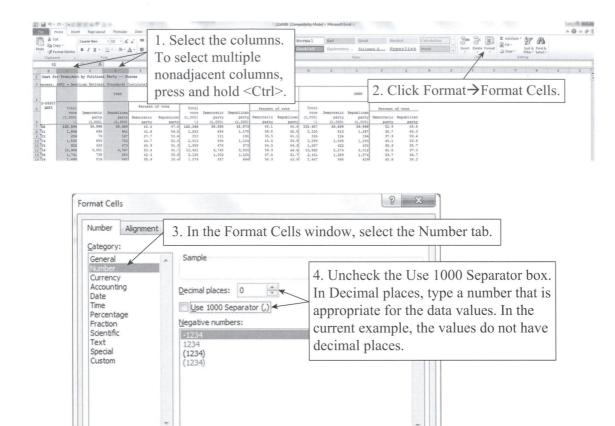

As we have just seen, if the data are available in Excel format, it is a relatively simple matter to copy/paste into Stata. The next remove is this: If the data are in html format, it is a relatively simple matter to copy/paste into Excel—or directly into Stata, if all the data are already Stata-friendly. Often a side trip through Excel is necessary. By way of illustration, consider the Americans for Democratic Action data on members of the US House, http://www.adaction.org/pages/publications/voting-records/2013vrgraphics.php (Figure 11-4). Every data element is a string—state and name (naturally), but also party designation ("D" or "R") and each rated vote (+, −, or ?). We would copy/paste the data into Excel (as shown in Figure 11-4) and find/replace unwanted strings with numbers. Once you are satisfied that things look okay, select the dataset, copy it to the clipboard, and dump it into Stata's Data Editor. (Refer to Figure 11-5.) Again, we would want to use the Variables Manager to supply useful names for the variables.

WRITING IT UP

Several of the datasets described thus far would provide great raw material for analysis. After inputting your data, you can let the creative juices flow—describing the variables, performing cross-tabulation and mean comparison analyses, running linear regression and logit models. Rewarding findings are guaranteed. Yet at some point the analysis ends, and the writing must begin. It is at this point, as well, that two contradictory considerations often collide. On one hand, you have an embarrassment of riches. You have worked on your research for several weeks, and you know the topic well—better, perhaps, than does anyone who will read the paper. There may be a large

Figure 11-3 Copy/Pasting from Excel into Stata's Data Editor

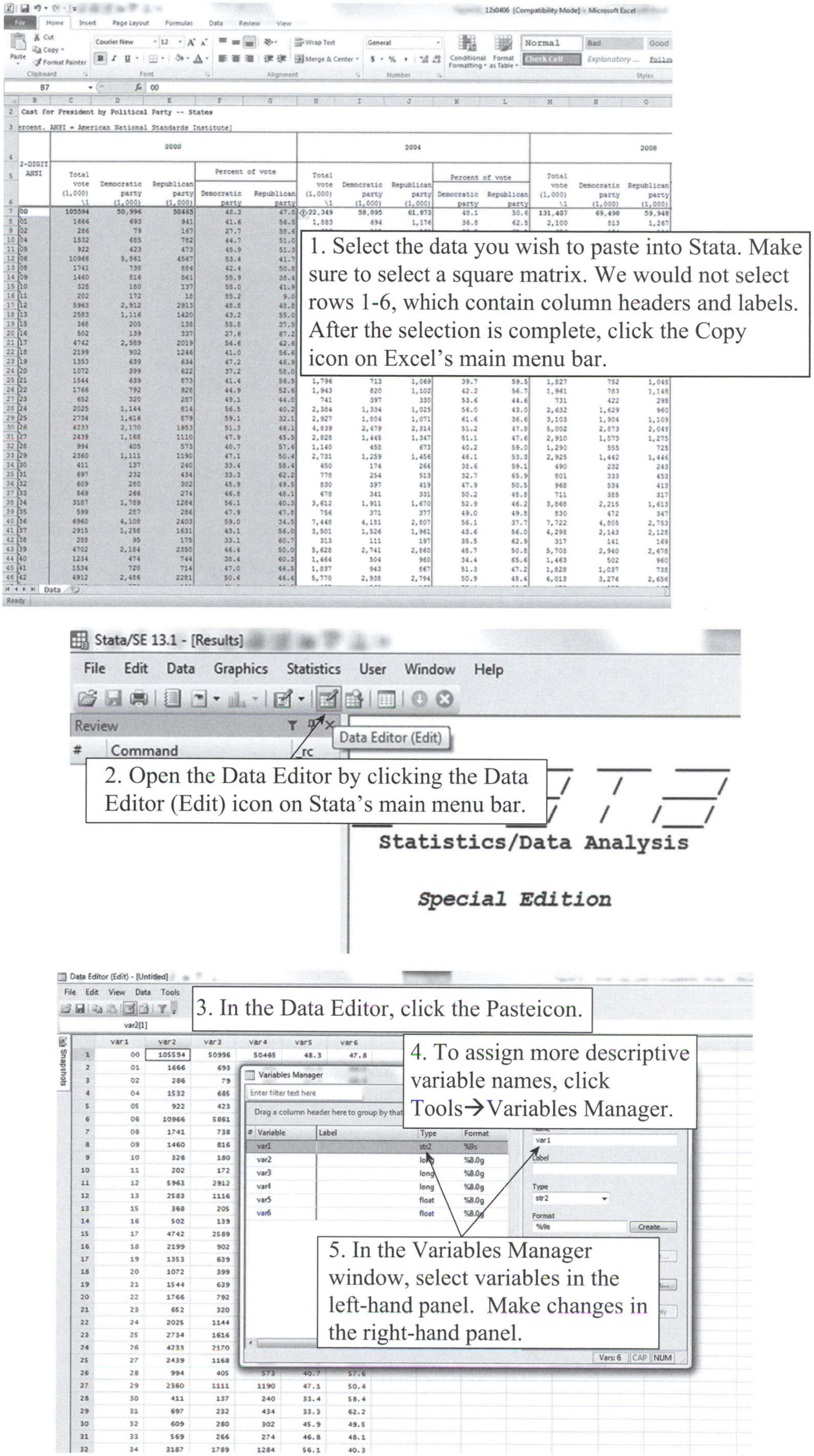
1. Select the data you wish to paste into Stata. Make sure to select a square matrix. We would not select rows 1-6, which contain column headers and labels. After the selection is complete, click the Copy icon on Excel's main menu bar.
Stata/SE 13.1 - [Results]
File Edit Data Graphics Statistics User Window Help
Data Editor (Edit)
2. Open the Data Editor by clicking the Data Editor (Edit) icon on Stata's main menu bar.
Statistics/Data Analysis
Special Edition
3. In the Data Editor, click the Pasteicon.
4. To assign more descriptive variable names, click Tools→Variables Manager.
5. In the Variables Manager window, select variables in the left-hand panel. Make changes in the right-hand panel.

Figure 11-4 Data in HTML Format

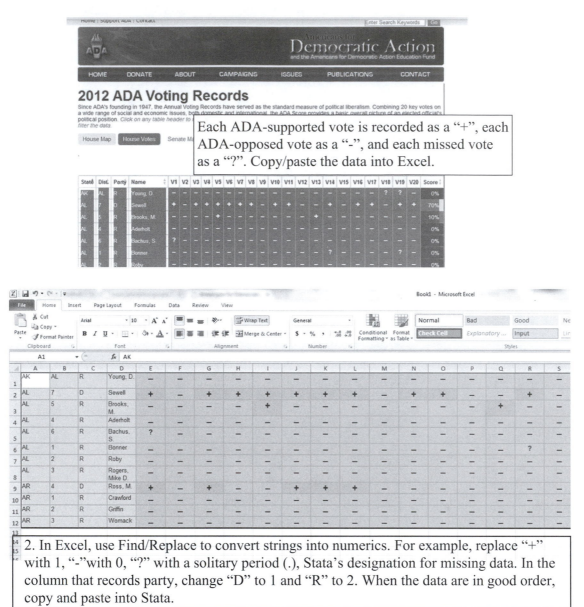

2. In Excel, use Find/Replace to convert strings into numerics. For example, replace "+" with 1, "-"with 0, "?" with a solitary period (.), Stata's designation for missing data. In the column that records party, change "D" to 1 and "R" to 2. When the data are in good order, copy and paste into Stata.

amount of material that you want to include in your paper. On the other hand, you want to get it written, and you do not want to write a book. Viewed from an instructor's perspective, the two questions most frequently asked by students are, "How should my paper be organized?" and "How long should it be?" (The questions are not necessarily asked in this order.)

Of course, different projects and instructors might call for different requirements.[8] But here is a rough outline for a well-organized paper of sixteen to twenty-four double-spaced pages (in twelve-point font).

I. The Research Question (3-4 pages)

    A. Introduction to the problem (1 page)

    B. Theory and process (1-2 pages)

    C. Propositions (1 page)

Figure 11-5   Copying HTML Data from Excel to Stata

	var1	var2	var3	var4	var5	var6	var7	var8	var9	var10	var11	var12
1	AK	AL	2	Young, D.	0	0	0	0	0	0	0	0
2	AL	7	1	Sewell	1	0	1	1	1	1	1	1
3	AL	5	2	Brooks, M.	0	0	0	0	1	0	0	0
4	AL	4	2	Aderholt	0	0	0	0	0	0	0	0
5	AL	6	2	Bachus, S.	.	0	0	0	0	0	0	0
6	AL	1	2	Bonner	0	0	0	0	0	0	0	0
7	AL	2	2	Roby	0	0	0	0	0	0	0	0
8	AL	3	2	Rogers, Mike D.	0	0	0	0	0	0	0	0
9	AR	4	1	Ross, M.	1	0	1	0	0	1	1	1
10	AR	1	2	Crawford	0	0	0	0	0	0	0	0
11	AR	2	2	Griffin	0	0	0	0	0	0	0	0
12	AR	3	2	Womack	0	0	0	0	0	0	0	0

Open the Data Editor (edit mode). Paste the data into the Data Editor. Numerics appear in black and strings in red. Use Tools→Variables Manager to supply descriptive variable names.

II. Previous Research (2-4 pages)

    A. Descriptive review (1-2 pages)

    B. Critical review (1-2 pages)

III. Data and Hypotheses (3-4 pages)

    A. Data and variables (1-2 pages)

    B. Measurement (1 page)

    C. Hypotheses (1 page)

IV. Analysis (5-8 pages, including tables)

    A. Descriptive statistics (1-2 pages)

    B. Bivariate comparisons (2-3 pages)

    C. Controlled comparisons (2-3 pages)

V. Conclusions and Implications (3-4 pages)

    A. Summary of findings (1 page)

    B. Implications for theory (1-2 pages)

    C. New issues or questions (1 page)

The Research Question

Because of its rhetorical challenges, the opening section of a paper is often the most difficult to write. In this section the writer must both engage the reader's interest and describe the purpose of the research. Here is a heuristic device that may be useful: In the first page of the write-up, place the specific research problem in the context of larger, clearly important issues or questions. For example, suppose your research is centered on the landmark healthcare legislation passed by Congress in 2010. A narrowly focused topic? Yes. A dry topic? Not at all. The opening page of this paper could frame larger questions about the sometimes conflicting roles of congressional party leadership and constituency interests in shaping the behavior of representatives and senators. Thus your analysis will advance our knowledge by illuminating one facet of a larger, more complex question.

Following the introduction, begin to zero in on the problem at hand. The "Theory and Process" section describes the logic of the relationships you are studying. Many political phenomena, as you have learned, have competing or alternative explanations. You should describe these alternatives, and the tension between them, in this section. Although a complete description of previous research does not appear in this section, you should give appropriate attribution to the most prominent work. These references tie your work to the scholarly community, and they raise the points you will cover in a more detailed review.

You should round out the introductory section of your paper with a brief statement of purpose or intent. Think about it from the reader's perspective. Thus far you have made the reader aware of the larger context of the analysis, and you have described the process that may explain the relationships of interest. If this process has merit, then it should submit to an empirical test of some kind. What test do you propose? The "Propositions" page serves this role. Here you set the parameters of the research— informing the reader about the units of analysis, the concepts to be measured, and the type of analysis to be performed.

Previous Research

Here you provide an intellectual history of the research problem, a description and critique of the published research on which the analysis is based. You first describe these previous analyses in some detail. What data and variables were used? What were the main findings? Did different researchers arrive at different conclusions? Political scientists who share a research interest often agree on many things. Yet knowledge is nourished through criticism, and in reviewing previous work you will notice key points of disagreement— about how concepts should be measured, what are the best data to use, or which variables need to be controlled. In the latter part of this section of the paper, review these points, and perhaps contribute to the debate. A practical point: The frequently asked question, "How many articles and books should be reviewed?" has no set answer. It depends on the project. However, here is an estimate: A well-grounded yet manageable review should discuss at least four references.

Data, Hypotheses, and Analysis

Together, the sections "Data and Hypotheses" and "Analysis" form the heart of the project, and they have been the primary concerns of this book. By now you are well versed in how to describe your data and variables and how to frame hypotheses. You also know how to set up a cross-tabulation or mean comparison table, and you can make controlled comparisons and interpret your findings.

In writing these sections, however, you should bear in mind a few reader-centered considerations. First, assume that the reader might want to replicate your study—collect the data you gathered, define and measure the concepts as you have defined and measured them, manipulate the variables just as you have computed and recoded them, and produce the tables you have reported. By explaining precisely what you did, your write-up should provide a clear guide for such a replication. Second, devote some space to a statistical description of the variables. Often you can add depth and interest to your analysis by briefly presenting the frequency distributions of the variables, particularly the dependent variable. Finally, exercise care in constructing readable tables. You can select, copy, and paste the tables generated by Stata directly into a word processor, but they always require further editing for readability.

Conclusions and Implications

No section of a research paper can write itself. But the final section comes closest to realizing this optimistic hope. Here you discuss the analysis on three levels. First, you provide a condensed recapitulation. What are the main findings? Are the hypotheses borne out? Were there any unexpected findings? Second, you describe where the results fit in the larger fabric of scholarly research on the topic. In what ways are the findings consistent with the work of previous researchers? Does your analysis lend support to one scholarly perspective as opposed to another? Third, research papers often include obligatory "suggestions for further research." Indeed, you may have encountered some methodological problems that still must be worked out, or you might have unearthed a noteworthy substantive relationship that could bear future scrutiny. You should describe these new issues or questions. Here, too, you are allowed some room to speculate—to venture beyond the edge of the data and engage in a little "what if?" thinking. After all, the truth is still out there.

NOTES

1. You can browse ICPSR's holdings at http://www.icpsr.umich.edu.
2. See L. J. Zigerell, "Of Publishable Quality: Ideas for Political Science Seminar Papers," *PS: Political Science & Politics,* 44, no. 03 (2011): 629–633.
3. For excellent guidance on the meaning and measurement of political knowledge, see Michael X. Delli Carpini and Scott Keeter, "Measuring Political Knowledge: Putting First Things First," *American Journal of Political Science,* 37, no. 4 (1993): 1179–1206.
4. The cases are available from LexisNexis at http://www.lexis-nexis.com/academic/universe/Academic/. See also the National Center for State Courts, Court Statistics Project at http://www.courtstatistics.org/.
5. Pippa Norris of Harvard's John F. Kennedy School of Government has compiled excellent comparative and international data that are available to the general public. These datasets are available in several formats, including that of Stata. See http://www.pippanorris.com/.
6. Examples include three books published by CQ Press: *Who's Who in Congress,* offered twice a year through 2001; *CQ's Politics in America,* edited by Brian Nutting and H. Amy Stern, published every 2 years; and *Vital Statistics on American Politics,* by Harold W. Stanley and Richard G. Niemi, which also appears every 2 years. *Vital Statistics* is an excellent single-volume general reference on American politics.
7. See http://www.adaction.org/, http://www.conservative.org/, and http://www.nationaljournal.com/njonline/.
8. For a comprehensive discussion of research writing, see Lisa A. Baglione, *Writing a Research Paper in Political Science: A Practical Guide to Inquiry, Structure, and Methods,* 2nd ed. (Thousand Oaks, CA: CQ Press, 2012).